POVERTY AND INEQUALITY

POVERTY AND INEQUALITY

Edited by David B. Grusky and Ravi Kanbur

*Essays by Amartya Sen, Martha C. Nussbaum,
François Bourguignon, William J. Wilson,
Douglas S. Massey, and Martha A. Fineman*

STANFORD UNIVERSITY PRESS

STANFORD, CALIFORNIA

2006

Stanford University Press
Stanford, California
©2006 by the Board of Trustees of the Leland Stanford
Junior University. All rights reserved.

Printed in the United States of America on acid-free,
archival-quality paper

Library of Congress Cataloging-in-Publication Data

Poverty and inequality / edited by David B. Grusky and
Ravi Kanbur ; essays by Amartya Sen . . . [et al.].
    p. cm.
  Includes bibliographical references and index.
  ISBN 0-8047-4842-X (cloth : alk. paper) —
ISBN 0-8047-4843-8 (pbk. : alk. paper)
    1. Poverty. 2. Equality. 3. Marginality, Social.
4. Social classes. 5. Social policy. I. Grusky,
David B. II. Kanbur, S. M. Ravi. III. Sen, Amartya
Kumar.

HV13.P68   2006
339.4'6—dc22
                           2005022563

Original Printing 2006

Last figure below indicates year of this printing:
15   14   13   12   11   10   09   08   07   06

Typeset by G&S Book Services in 10/14 Sabon

CONTENTS

François Bourguignon is the Chief Economist and Senior Vice-President of the World Bank. Since 1985 he has been Professor of Economics at the Ecole des Hautes Etudes en Sciences Sociales in Paris, where he founded and directed the Département et laboratoire d'Economie Théorique et Appliquée (DELTA), a research unit in theoretical and applied economics. He has held academic positions with the University of Chile, Santiago, and the University of Toronto. His recent publications include *The Impact of Economic Policies on Poverty and Income Distribution: Evaluation Techniques and Tools* (2004, edited with Luiz Pereira da Silva) and *The Microeconomics of Income Distribution Dynamics* (2005, edited with Francisco Ferreira and Nora Lustig).

Martha Albertson Fineman is the Robert W. Woodruff Professor of Law at Emory University and the Director of the Feminism and Legal Theory Project. Prior to coming to Emory she was the Dorthea S. Clarke Professor of Feminist Jurisprudence at Cornell Law School. She also held a Chair at Columbia University (1990–1999) and was on the faculty at the University of Wisconsin (1976–1990). Professor Fineman is the author of *The Illusion of Equality: The Rhetoric and Reality of Divorce Reform* (1991), *The Neutered Mother, the Sexual Family, and Other Twentieth Century Tragedies* (1995) and, most recently, *The Autonomy Myth: A Theory of Dependency* (2004).

David B. Grusky is Professor of Sociology at Stanford University and incoming Director of the new Program on Inequality at Stanford University. Before joining Stanford University, he taught at the University of Chicago and at Cornell University. His recent books include *Social Stratification* (2001), *Occupational Ghettos: The Worldwide Segregation of Women and Men* (2004, with Maria Charles), *Inequality: Classic Readings in Race, Class, and Gender* (with Szonja Szelényi, forthcoming), and *Mobility and Inequality* (forthcoming from Stanford University Press, with Stephen Morgan and Gary Fields).

Ravi Kanbur is T.H. Lee Professor of World Affairs, International Professor of Applied Economics and Management, and Professor of Economics at Cornell University. He studied at Cambridge and at Oxford, and has taught at the universities of Cambridge, Essex, Warwick, Princeton, and Columbia. He has also served on the senior staff of the World Bank, as Chief Economist for Africa, among other positions. He has published in the leading refereed economics journals including *American Economic Review* and *Journal of Political Economy*. His published volumes include *Q-Squared: Qualitative and Quantitative Methods of Poverty Appraisal* (editor, 2003) and *Spatial Inequality and Development* (co-editor with Anthony J. Venables, 2005).

Douglas S. Massey is Professor of Sociology at Princeton University and of Public Affairs in Princeton University's Woodrow Wilson School of Public and International Affairs. Prior to coming to Princeton in 2003, he taught at the University of Pennsylvania and the University of Chicago. His latest books are *Return of the L-Word: A Liberal Vision for the New Century* (Princeton University Press) and *Strangers in a Strange Land: Humans in an Urbanizing World* (Norton), both published in 2005.

Martha Nussbaum is Ernst Freund Distinguished Service Professor of Law and Ethics at The University of Chicago, appointed in Philosophy, Law, and Divinity. Among her books are *Sex and Social Justice* (1999), *Women and Human Development* (2000), *Upheavals of Thought: The Intelligence of Emotions* (2001), and *Hiding from Humanity: Disgust, Shame, and the Law* (2004). Her newest book, *Frontiers of Justice: Disability, Nationality, Species Membership*, will appear in the fall of 2005. She is currently writing a book on religious tensions in India, entitled *Democracy in the Balance*.

Amartya Sen is Lamont University Professor at Harvard University and was until recently the Master of Trinity College, Cambridge. His books include *Collective Choice and Social Welfare* (1970), *On Economic Inequality* (1973, 1997), *Poverty and Famines* (1981), *Choice, Welfare and Measurement* (1982), *Resources, Values and Development* (1984), *On Ethics and Economics* (1987), *The Standard of Living* (1987), *Inequality Reexamined* (1992), and *Development as Freedom* (1999), among others. His most recent book, *Rationality and Freedom* (2002), published by Harvard University Press, will be followed by a companion volume, *Freedom and Justice*.

William Julius Wilson is the Lewis P. and Linda L. Geyser University Professor at Harvard University. He is a MacArthur Prize Fellow and was awarded the National Medal of Science in 1998. His books include *Power, Racism and Privilege* (1973), *The Declining Significance of Race* (1978), *The Truly Disadvantaged* (1987), *When Work Disappears* (1996), and *The Bridge over the Racial Divide* (1999).

This book is dedicated to the simple premise that distributional issues of inequality and poverty must be approached with the same seriousness of purpose that is currently accorded the analysis of economic activity and output. Given this premise, an important goal is to develop a comprehensive framework for measuring poverty and inequality, ideally a framework truly the equal of our comparatively well-developed system for monitoring economic output. We have approached this formidable task by assembling an all-star cast of economists, sociologists, and philosophers and asking them to weigh in on the conceptual challenges that must be met in devising new approaches to measuring and understanding inequality and poverty.

The result, we think, is an extraordinary document that breaks new conceptual ground and provides the beginnings of a road map for measuring contemporary poverty and inequality. In some respects, it is fortunate that a comprehensive monitoring system has yet to be institutionalized, as it makes it possible to more readily build a new approach that is unencumbered by the narrow income-based formulations of the past. Although our contributors harbor no illusions about the difficulty of developing a true multidimensional monitoring system, there is much consensus that such a system should be our objective and that the conceptual and methodological obstacles, while daunting, can ultimately be overcome.

We well appreciate that some readers may approach a book on the conceptual foundations of poverty and inequality measurement with healthy skepticism. After all, haven't academics been discussing, debating, and documenting poverty and inequality endlessly, and isn't it high time to turn now to action rather than yet more debate? In the United States especially, the long-standing tendency has been to regard all academic study quite cynically, as a ritualized prelude to action that is as functionless as throat clearing is to speech. We can surely understand the frustration and indeed share it insofar as we too would have hoped that by now a consensual system for measuring poverty and inequality would be in place. However, the unfortunate fact of the matter is that such a system is not in place, and we can at least exploit this current deficit by taking into account emerging conceptual developments and thereby fashioning a system far superior to what was earlier imaginable.

This project grew out of an interdisciplinary conference on poverty and inequality that was jointly funded by the Poverty, Inequality, and Development Initiative of Cornell University and the Center for the Study of Inequality of Cornell University. The costs of producing this book were also subsidized by Stanford University. We are especially grateful to the members of the 2002–03 Cornell University Social Science seminar for participating in this conference and for providing comments on our introductory chapter.

We are likewise grateful to the editorial staff at Stanford University Press (SUP) for so patiently tolerating our long delays in delivering the book. We especially thank Patricia Katayama for her early support for this project, Judith Hibbard for unusually skilled production editing, and Carmen Borbon-Wu for her expert editorial assistance throughout. The very important task of editing the submitted materials and converting them into a coherent whole was completed most successfully by Frank Samson. Finally, we should note that Kate Wahl, our current SUP editor, seems constitutionally incapable of providing anything but sage advice, a rare and happy character trait that has served us extremely well. We are most grateful for her help.

David B. Grusky and Ravi Kanbur
February 2005

POVERTY AND INEQUALITY

CHAPTER ONE

Introduction

The Conceptual Foundations of Poverty and Inequality Measurement

David B. Grusky and Ravi Kanbur

There is a growing consensus among academics, policy makers, and even politicians that poverty and inequality should no longer be treated as soft social issues that can safely be subordinated to more important and fundamental interests in maximizing total economic output. This newfound concern with poverty and inequality, which dates back to at least the early 1990s (see Atkinson 1997), may be attributed to such factors as (1) the dramatic increase in economic inequality in many countries over the last quarter century, (2) the rise of a "global village" in which spectacular regional disparities in the standard of living have become more widely visible and hence increasingly difficult to ignore, (3) a growing commitment to a conception of human entitlements that includes the right to seek or secure employment and thereby be spared extreme deprivation, (4) an emerging concern that poverty and inequality may have negative macro-level effects on terrorism (cf. Krueger and Malecková 2003), total economic production (e.g., Bertola 2000), and ethnic unrest (e.g., Olzak forthcoming), and (5) a growing awareness of the negative individual-level effects of poverty on health, political participation, and a host of other life conditions. Although the growth of anti-inequality sentiment thus rests in part on an increased awareness of just how unequal and poverty-stricken the world is, it may also be attributed to an ever-evolving and accreting list of human rights (i.e., the "normative" account) as well as a growing appreciation of the negative externalities of inequality and poverty (i.e., a "consequentialist" account).

In what ways has the newfound concern with poverty and inequality manifested itself? This concern is, we would argue, principally revealed in the form of grassroots political mobilization on various anti-poverty platforms

1

as well as a growing acceptance of and commitment to anti-poverty and anti-inequality initiatives among elite opinion leaders and their organizations (e.g., Millenium Development Goals). By contrast, academic research on issues of inequality and poverty has not flourished to quite the same extent, and the modest takeoff in such scholarship that is under way has focused disproportionately on matters of description and the methodological intricacies of measurement rather than more fundamental conceptual issues that, as we see it, must now be taken on (see Srinivasan 2004). The present book therefore provides an unabashedly academic approach to poverty and inequality reduction that proceeds from the radical assumption that more in the way of careful reflection and conceptual ground clearing might serve us well.

We emphasize conceptual issues not out of some intrinsic fascination with theory (although we confess to that as well) but because we think that pressing problems of policy cannot be adequately addressed without first making conceptual advances. The need for new conceptual work is especially apparent, we think, on three distinct but related fronts (see Kakwani 2004; Reddy 2004):

> *Defining the dimensions*: Simple though it may seem, an important starting point is to develop and justify a list of valued resources that define the "inequality space," a list that presumably goes well beyond income (or wealth) alone. As many of our contributors note, there is a growing consensus that the income distribution cannot by itself satisfactorily capture the structure of poverty and inequality, yet much work remains in developing an elaborated list of endowments (e.g., schooling), investments (e.g., work experience), and living conditions (e.g., neighborhood attributes) that does suffice to describe this structure.
>
> *Characterizing multidimensional space*: Secondarily, new methods must be developed to measure inequality and poverty within the context of this multidimensional space, a task that is complicated because a great many parameters may be required to adequately characterize such a space. Moreover, given that various social groups (e.g., classes, ethnic groups, genders) exist within this space and constrain patterns of interaction, researchers must develop models that recognize that these groups can give rise to distinctive preferences (e.g., a "culture of poverty") that in turn affect how individuals react to poverty and inequality.
>
> *Remediation in a multidimensional world*: The third and final conceptual challenge is that of devising new approaches to remediation that remain viable under this more expansive definition of poverty and inequality. This task, which is arguably even more daunting than the foregoing two, requires targeting those

aspects of inequality and poverty (e.g., residential segregation) that are causal with respect to many outcomes and hence likely to bring about cascades of change.

On each of these three fronts, important advances have recently been made, and obviously we do not intend to minimize such advances. We wish merely to identify these three research fronts as especially deserving of continuing attention. In hopes of spurring such a commitment, we have invited six leading scholars of inequality and poverty to lay out these three conceptual challenges in more detail, to identify other challenges that should be the focus of future scholarship, and to outline possible solutions to them.

The chapters of our book address to varying degrees the three themes identified above. The first contribution, authored by Amartya Sen, lays out the case for a multidimensionalist understanding of inequality and poverty, while the following chapter by Martha Nussbaum renders the multidimensionalist approach more concrete by developing an explicit list of "fundamental entitlements." In the next chapter, François Bourguignon likewise argues that the old income paradigm is unduly limiting, but he goes on to emphasize that a new multidimensionalist approach must solve major problems in measurement and modeling to achieve a "level of operationality" comparable to that currently enjoyed by the old paradigm. The final three chapters all attend to the rise of social groups within multidimensionalist space and the importance of developing a measurement approach that captures this social lumpiness. The contributions of William Wilson and Douglas Massey address, in particular, the spatial concentration of poverty and the associated rise of an "underclass" and racially segregated neighborhoods, while the final contribution by Martha Fineman examines the peculiar institution of gender in which males and females are assembled together into families on spectacularly unequal terms.

As the foregoing makes evident, we have developed a book that is unapologetically conceptual in its approach, but hopefully not one that, by virtue of this emphasis, appeals only to ivory-tower types. We devote the rest of this introductory chapter to an intellectual history of inequality and poverty scholarship that situates our contributors in their disciplinary context and thus prepares the uninitiated to nonetheless profit from these contributions. We concentrate on the disciplines of economics and sociology because of our own backgrounds and because the most sustained commitment to understanding poverty and inequality is perhaps found within these disciplines.

This intellectual history reveals rather stark disciplinary differences in how the study of inequality and poverty have been pursued. These differences emerge, in part, because both disciplines have long-standing research traditions on poverty and inequality, traditions that are so well developed that their distinctive approaches have crystallized and differences have become magnified. This is not to suggest that the disciplines have developed independently of one another. Indeed, each discipline has worked with stylized and outdated understandings of the orientation of the other discipline, a state of affairs that this book seeks to begin to rectify. The purpose, then, of our introductory chapter is to rehearse the main conceptual tools with which the disciplines of economics and sociology have historically sought to organize and make sense of inequality and poverty. We do so separately for each of the two disciplines and then, at the close of the chapter, outline the conceptual issues that both disciplines should begin to address in analyzing poverty, inequality, and distributional questions more generally. This exercise will, we think, set an agenda in this area for the social sciences and cognate disciplines, an agenda to which the disciplines could contribute in their own particular way, singly or in concert.

THE VIEW FROM ECONOMICS

We begin with a characterization, perhaps controversial, of the last thirty years of research on distributional questions in economics, especially development economics. Somewhat arbitrarily, consider the period beginning with Atkinson's classic 1970 paper "On the Measurement of Inequality" (Atkinson 1970), and ending with Atkinson and Bourguignon's state-of-the-art edited volume, *Handbook of Income Distribution* (2000). These thirty years may be divided, very roughly, into a first phase stretching from the 1970s to the mid-1980s and a second phase stretching from the mid-1980s to the end of last century. The first phase was one of great conceptual ferment and was exciting for that reason, whereas the second phase was focused on consolidation, application, and fierce policy debates, especially on the distributional consequences of macroeconomic policies in developing and transitional economies. We review each of these two phases below.

The First Phase: Conceptual Ferment

The first phase, covering the 1970s and early 1980s, was one of conceptual ferment around four broad questions:

- How should inequality and poverty be measured?
- Should policy recommendations on issues of poverty reduction and equalization rest on simple utilitarian premises?
- Are households best treated as unitary entities?
- Can the complicating effects of social interaction be readily incorporated into analyses of poverty and inequality?

We consider in turn each of these conceptual questions and the conceptual ferment that they engendered.

The debate over how inequality and poverty are best measured has a long and distinguished history. In the 1970s, three key contributions defined this ongoing debate: Atkinson's 1970 paper "On the Measurement of Inequality" (Atkinson 1970), Sen's 1973 book *On Economic Inequality* (Sen 1973), and Sen's 1976 paper "Poverty: An Ordinal Approach to Measurement" (Sen 1976). These contributions provided a way into conceptualizing and operationalizing value judgments on distributional issues, serving as an antidote to a natural instinct among economists to avoid distributional questions, an instinct that goes back to debates in the 1930s launched by Robbins' *The Nature and Significance of Economic Science* (Robbins 1932). The appearance of these papers in the 1970s sparked a prolonged discussion of how to incorporate distributional value judgments. In the literature on poverty measurement, the culmination of this process was undoubtedly the famous 1984 paper by Foster, Greer, and Thorbecke, "A Class of Decomposable Poverty Measures" (Foster, Greer, and Thorbecke 1984). The poverty measure developed in that paper has now become the workhorse of applied work on poverty the world over.

The debate on utilitarianism and its usefulness in policy prescription also emerged in the 1970s as philosophical discourse began to enter and enrich economic work on distributional issues. The influential paper by Mirrlees, "An Exploration in the Theory of Optimal Income Taxation" (Mirrlees 1971), is famous for many reasons (including winning a Nobel Prize), but perhaps especially for its application of thoroughgoing utilitarianism to the policy question of how progressive income taxation should be. The shortcomings of such utilitarian fundamentalism were, by contrast, highlighted by Sen in a number of well-known works, including his 1987 book, *The Standard of Living* (Sen 1987). In a related line of analysis, Arrow (1973) introduced Rawls (1971) to mainstream economists in terms they would understand, namely maxi-min strategies in the face of uncertainty (also Nozick 1974). As Rawls argued, when people are placed under a "veil of ignorance," they should rationally support a constitution that aims for the greatest good of the worst off because, "but for the grace of God," any one of them could be the worst off. As a sign of this new intercourse between economics and philosophy, such journals as *Economics and Philosophy* and *Philosophy and Public Affairs* were filled with contributions from both disciplines.

At the same time, economists were also completing the conceptual work necessary to represent processes of social interaction in a wide range of economic models, including those pertaining to poverty and inequality. Within the rational choice framework, Akerlof, Spence, and Stiglitz sought to incorporate issues of imperfect and asymmetric information into economic models, thereby launching a body of work that won them the Nobel Prize in 2001. This framework was used by Akerlof (1970) and Stiglitz (1973) to analyze the underclass in developed economies and to explain why the very poor in developing countries failed to invest much in education. It was argued that, in the presence of imperfect and asymmetric information, the market economy can produce multiple equilibria, some more efficient and more equitable than others, and that public action and intervention was necessary to move away from the "bad" equilibria.

As a final example, we move to debates about the proper unit of analysis for poverty research, debates that flourished during this period because of concerns that the usual household-based analyses ignored intra-household exchange and thus glossed over inequalities prevailing *within* households. The obvious starting point here is again the work of Sen. In the 1970s and early 1980s, a series of publications (some of which are reprinted in Sen 1984) brought home to economists that "unitary" models of the household, models that ignore intra-household inequalities, simply could not capture or explain the evidence on deprivation among females in developing countries. Although slow to develop, this line of inquiry ultimately blossomed, leading to much important applied and policy analysis.

The Second Phase: Consolidation, Application, and Policy Debate

In the mid-1980s, the foregoing conceptual ferment on distributional issues gradually died down, and the field moved into a new phase of consolidation, application, and policy debate. This second phase was neither less useful or less exciting, just conceptually less innovative. How did this second phase play out? We answer this question by returning to each of the four arenas discussed in the prior section and considering how the literature in those arenas developed.

With respect to matters of measurement, the various "index wars" of the 1970s gradually waned, and attention turned to applying existing indices to data sets in rich and poor countries alike. This second phase was characterized, in particular, by increased availability of household survey data sets for developing countries. In Africa, for example, Cote d'Ivoire fielded the first high-quality nationally representative household survey in 1985, and presently more than a dozen countries have at least one such survey. Indeed, half a dozen African countries now have panel studies (in which the same households are surveyed two years in a row), as do many other countries throughout the less developed world. This increase in data availability means that the measures developed in the 1970s and 1980s will have many applications in the years to come.

The literature on intra-household bargaining and gender issues has also progressed to consolidation and application. When a group of economists (Alderman et al. 1995) wrote a paper entitled "Unitary versus Collective Models of the Household: Is It Time to Shift the Burden of Proof?" they provided a strongly affirmative answer to their rhetorical question, an answer that would once have been controversial but is no longer. There is of course still resistance from adherents of the "unitary" model, but the debate is more on the details of particular empirical tests, not on whether factors such as intra-household bargaining between the genders in principle have a role to play.

The asymmetric information literature that Akerlof, Spence, and Stiglitz spawned is now part of standard graduate courses. Indeed, basic textbooks in development economics, such as that of Basu (1997), apply this perspective to frame much of the discussion of underdevelopment. Also, other social structures, such as the caste system, are increasingly modeled and incorporated into standard economic discourses.

Finally, the interaction between economic and philosophical discourses has also "normalized," in the sense that much Kuhnian normal science appears in the new journals that were founded two decades or so ago. However, even though virtually all economists now know what is meant by the term "Rawlsian objective function," philosophical issues no longer animate them or their graduate students to the same extent that they did twenty or thirty years ago.

Has all ferment disappeared in the field? Surely not, but such ferment as can be found centers on issues of policy, not conceptual issues. In the wake of the oil price shocks of the 1970s, many developing countries in the 1980s adopted (or, depending on your point of view, were forced to adopt) programs of "structural adjustment." These programs, primarily introduced in Latin America and in Africa, contained the key elements of the "Washington Consensus," such as opening up economies to trade and capital flows and reducing the role of the state in the economy. With the fall of the Berlin Wall in 1989, countries of Central and Eastern Europe and the former Soviet Union also adopted, or were forced to adopt, similar policy packages. In the late 1990s, the world experienced a series of financial crises, which many attributed to these same policies, especially deregulation of financial markets and flows. The foregoing issues have now been subsumed under a general (and generally unhelpful) catchall heading of the debate on "globalization."

The debates of the last fifteen years in development economics have crystallized around the consequences of these policies and these developments, particularly for poverty and inequality (see Kanbur 1987; 2001). The conceptual advances of the first fifteen years, especially in the measurement of poverty and inequality, have of course been put to good use as new data sets have become available. The resulting debate has been fierce, with the term "Washington Consensus" acquiring the status of a term of abuse in some quarters. However, none of this debate has led to new conceptual questions, and indeed old and vague "market versus state" formulations continue to loom large in many of the exchanges. This conclusion is evident from the types of economic questions that abound in these debates: Is economic growth good for the poor? Is trade openness equitable and efficient? What exchange rate regime leads to least unemployment? Is international capital cartelized around the leadership of the Bretton Woods Institutions? Important as they are, these questions do not call forth major conceptual advances in the core of economics, at least not to the extent evident in the first phase. Fiercely debated? Yes. Conceptual ferment? No.

The Third Phase: Renewed Conceptual Ferment?

It is high time, then, to begin the task of rethinking the economic analysis of poverty and inequality. As Sen (Chapter 2, p. 30) notes, "there is room for more conceptual questioning and greater foundational scrutiny at this time, both for reexamining old problems (they rarely go away) and for addressing new questions that have emerged in the contemporary world." We identify below several conceptual problems that contemporary economists seem poised to take on.

Fixed and Rational Preferences?   We note, first, that economic analysis of poverty and inequality remains based on rational choice models. In empirical work, individual consumption is taken to be the indicator of individual well-being, meaning that an increase, for example, in cigarette or alcohol consumption is logged as an improvement (in well-being). This practice is of course justified on the grounds that the individual has (nominally) chosen those activities. Although recently developed theories of addiction and new "behavioral economic" models have permitted economists to relax conventional rational choice assumptions, these developments have to date scarcely made a dent in the empirical literature on the measurement of poverty and inequality. By way of illustration, note that the World Bank recently issued two reports that are difficult to reconcile, one on the individual and social costs of smoking in developing countries (World Bank 1999), and another on poverty in developing countries in which an increase in expenditure on cigarettes is recorded as a decrease in individual poverty (World Bank 2001). The seeming contradiction between these reports has simply not registered. Across a wide range of fields, behavioral economics has revolutionized economic analysis by marrying economics and psychology (see Thaler 1991; Rabin 1998; Camerer, Loewenstein, and Rabin 2003), a development that will continue to spread and enrich many fields. Eventually, economic analyses of poverty and inequality will no doubt reflect this development, although much is to be said, we think, for spurring such development along.

Whether or not individual preferences are rational, another long-standing assumption of economic analysis is that such preferences are fixed and "given," meaning that they are unaffected by changes in personal circumstances or in the cultural or institutional context. Despite widespread dissatisfaction with this assumption (how else could we explain advertising?) and past attempts to move beyond it, it still dominates theoretical and empirical economic analysis today. It is nonetheless clear that this assumption is no longer tenable. As Nussbaum (Chapter 3, p. 48) notes, "the utilitarian framework, which asks people what they currently prefer and how satisfied they are, proves inadequate to confront some pressing issues of justice." Likewise, economists interested in issues of race are beginning to allow for adaptive preferences in their positive and normative analysis (e.g., Austen-Smith and Fryer 2003), thereby bringing their approach into closer alignment with that of some sociologists featured in the volume (e.g., Wilson Chapter 5). This conceptual development is again one that could usefully be spurred along.

Individualism in Poverty and Inequality Measurement   The measurement of inequality and poverty, starting from Atkinson (1970), has long been individualistic in the sense that the object is to measure difference between individuals and to aggregate these differences in a single index. Within this formulation, the technical literature has developed the theory of "decomposable" measures, and the empirical literature uses these measures extensively (e.g., Foster, Greer, and Thorbecke 1984). However, when decomposability is insisted on for all possible subgroupings, Sen (Chapter 2, p. 44) points out that a basic conceptual problem emerges: "[M]athematically the demand that the breakdown works for every logically possible classification has the effect that the only measures of inequality or poverty that survive treat every individual as an island. . . . The mathematical form of decomposability has had the odd result of ruling out any comparative perspective (and the corresponding sociological insights), which is, in fact, fatal for both inequality and poverty measurement." Because of this mathematical implication, Sen (Chapter 2, p. 44) goes on to call for measures that are sensitive to group partitionings, an approach that recent research on "polarization" has indeed adopted (Zhang and Kanbur 2001; Duclos, Esteban, and Ray 2004).

The need to represent individuals in relation to each other, and in relation to groups, goes beyond such technical considerations of measurement. The policy recommendations coming out of the economics literature have been fundamentally individualistic in nature and have failed, therefore, to appreciate that inequality is institutionalized in ways that give rise to socially meaningful groups that take on a life of their own. It is well understood, for example, that gender inequality is a central dimension of inequality, but the precise nature of gender inequality as a social construct is something that economists, using conventional analytic and measurement tools, have not yet successfully modeled. As discussed above, this is partly because adaptive preferences are still to be fully incorporated into economic analysis, thus ruling out a discussion of "preferences that have adjusted to their second-class status" (Nussbaum, Chapter 3, p. 48; also see Fineman, Chapter 7). The more general problem within the economics literature is that concepts of human beings in constructed social contexts need to be developed further, a problem to which we return in our discussion of sociological accounts of inequality and poverty.

Income and Multidimensionalism   It is perhaps unsurprising that economics has seized on income as a major indicator of well-being and has accordingly treated income-enhancing policies as the centerpiece of any strategy to reduce poverty and inequality. As Bourguignon (Chapter 4, p. 76) notes "[M]uch of the economic literature on poverty relies on what may be referred to as the 'income poverty paradigm,'" a paradigm that is "technically close to achievement, [although] scholars as well as policymakers acknowledge that it does not permit a satisfactory analysis of all relevant issues related to poverty and inequality." The latter point is reiterated by Nussbaum (Chapter 3, p. 47): "the GNP [Gross National Product] approach . . . failed to take cognizance of other aspects of the quality of life that are not well correlated with economic advantage, even when distribution is factored in: aspects such as health, education, gender, and racial justice." Most obviously, the importance of mortality measurement in revising the "income poverty" paradigm is illustrated very simply and starkly by noting that whenever a poor person dies because of poverty (e.g., starvation, inadequate treatment for AIDS) *all* standard measures of income poverty will *fall*, including the well-known Foster, Greer, and Thorbecke (1984) family of measures. In a related illustration of the shortcomings of the income poverty paradigm, Bourguignon (Chapter 4, p. 77) also points out that income transfers to the poor typically fail to eliminate feelings of social exclusion (and may even exacerbate them), thus suggesting that income deprivation should not be regarded as the sole and defining feature of poverty.

The Human Development Index (HDI), which is a weighted sum of three components (income, literacy, and life expectancy), assesses the standard of living of individuals and populations in an explicitly multidimensional way and hence addresses some of the foregoing concerns (see UNDP 2001). The annual publication of the HDI is now an eagerly awaited event that inevitably leads to much debate and hand-wringing within nations that fare poorly on the index relative to their competitor nations (e.g., United States versus Canada, India versus Pakistan, Ghana versus Cote d'Ivoire). The benefits of HDI in terms of raising awareness of the multidimensionality of poverty have been incalculable, and it has been an integral part of the policy debates discussed in the previous section. But the conceptual foundations of HDI are clearly underdeveloped. If each component of income, literacy, and health improves, then we could perhaps declare an overall improvement in well-being. But what if the components move in opposite directions? How are they to be aggregated to arrive at an acceptable answer? And what is this overarching quantity to which aggregation leads? Or should we instead start from the meta-level and define an overarching concept (e.g., utility) into which each of the various dimensions feeds as a component?

Once again, Sen (Chapter 2) has provided a lead here with his ideas on "capabilities," and so too have Bourguignon (Chapter 4) and Nussbaum (Chapter 3). Much interesting and important work is under way. It would be fair to conclude, however, that concerns with multidimensionality have not to date penetrated into the mainstream of poverty analysis among economists, as simple estimation of the Foster, Greer, and Thorbecke (1984) income poverty measure is still very much the rule. Increasingly, education, health, and risk are treated as key ingredients of well-being, but such practice is diffusing only slowly, and typically each dimension is treated separately or as a subsidiary supplement to the income-based measure. For example, some scholars have sought to bring in "voice" as a supplementary dimension, but doing so in any integral way seems a long way off. Moreover, economists have not reached consensus on the dimensions that matter, nor even on how they might decide what matters (see Nussbaum, Chapter 3). Even in their rational choice frame, perhaps especially in this frame, economists have not yet succeeded in conceptualizing and then operationalizing the simultaneous evaluation of different dimensions of well-being, despite the remarkable efforts of some scholars. We suspect that releasing ourselves from the straitjacket of rational choice assumptions and moving to a more behavioral frame might well help in this endeavor.

THE VIEW FROM SOCIOLOGY

This ferment within economics partly arises from a renewed engagement with issues that were once regarded as the exclusive province of sociology. In this context, it is useful to next consider how the discipline of sociology has approached issues of poverty and inequality measurement, again proceeding with a brief historical review of the dominant measurement approaches. As we have just argued, "third-phase" economics has been partly animated by concerns fundamentally sociological in nature, yet we show below that economists have addressed these concerns in ways that are quite different from characteristic reactions within sociology. With respect to issues of measurement and operationalization, there appears to be rather little in the way of disciplinary cross-fertilization, despite the evidence of convergence in the conceptual challenges and problems that have been identified in each discipline.

This disjuncture in approaches is usefully exposed by rehearsing the history of poverty and inequality measurement within sociology over the last half century. As with economics, we proceed by identifying three phases within the field, thus again generating a highly stylized history. The debates in all three phases center around the question of how and whether inequality may be understood with models of social class that divide the population into mutually exclusive categories defined by employment status, occupation, and other job characteristics. As laid out below, the particular types of class models that are featured serve to distinguish the first two phases, while the third phase involves debates about whether class models of any kind suffice in representing contemporary poverty or inequality.

We choose to focus here on class-based approaches because they remain one of the few distinctively sociological approaches to poverty and inequality measurement. To be sure, many sociologists (e.g., Morris et al. 2001) carry out empirical research on income-based poverty and inequality, much like economists do. However, because sociological research on income draws directly on economic approaches and is accordingly derivative, nothing warrants a special review of that research here. It is perhaps more difficult to justify our decision to likewise omit from this review any detailed discussion of socioeconomic and prestige scales (e.g., Hauser and Warren 1997). After all, socioeconomic and prestige scales do have a distinctly sociological pedigree, and many sociologists have regarded them as an important alternative to income or class measures of inequality. We will nonetheless ignore such scales in the following review because they have largely fallen out of fashion and cannot, in any event, be readily applied to the study of poverty (as distinct from inequality). The three phases discussed below pertain, then, to class-based approaches exclusively.

The distinctive feature of class-based measurement is the presumption that the social location of individuals is determined principally by their employment status and job characteristics (especially occupation), the former determining the strength of their commitment to the formal labor force, and the latter revealing the market power and life chances of those with substantial commitment to the labor force. Under this formulation, the "underclass" includes those individuals (or families) with only a weak commitment to the labor market, while all other class categories serve to differentiate those who are strongly committed to the labor market but bring different skills, training, and abilities to it and are remunerated accordingly. Insofar as a distinctively sociological measure of poverty may be identified, it is accordingly the concept of an underclass (e.g., Wilson, Chapter 5; Massey, Chapter 6), a concept that serves within sociology much the same functions as that of "poverty" does within economics. Although sociologists are less concerned than economists with deriving exact head counts, these could readily be generated within the social class framework by simply operationalizing the concept of weak attachment and calculating the number of individuals (or households) falling into the weakly attached category. The remaining categories within a conventional social class scheme are typically defined in terms of occupational distinctions (e.g., professional, clerical, craft, laborer) or other job characteristics (e.g., amount of authority, type of employment contract).

The main advantage of class-based measurement, as argued by sociologists, is that class categories are institutionalized within the labor market and are accordingly more than purely nominal or statistical constructions. That is, just as social measurement within earlier historical periods (e.g., feudalism) is best carried out in terms of deeply institutionalized categories (e.g., serf, lord), so too there is much advantage in relying on such categories in the present day. The labor market, far from being a seamless and continuous distribution of incomes, is instead a deeply lumpy entity, with such lumpiness mainly taking the form of institutionalized groups (i.e., classes) that constitute "prepackaged" combinations of valued goods. These prepackaged combinations are

partly closed to (interclass) exchange, develop their own distinctive preferences and cultures, and define the boundaries of social isolation and participation. Within sociology, the implicit critique, then, of income-based approaches rests not so much on the argument that the income distribution is
just one of many distributions of interest (i.e., multidimensionalism), but
rather on the argument that measurement strategies based on the income
distribution alone impose an excessively abstract, analytic, and statistical lens
on a social world that has much institutionalized structure to it, a structure
that mainly takes the form of "occupation groups." The rise of class models
should therefore be understood as a distinctively sociological reaction to the
individualism of both the "income paradigm" as well as other unidimensional
approaches to measuring inequality (e.g., socioeconomic scales).

The foregoing account, which is a largely consensual rendition of the rationale for social class measurement, nonetheless conceals much internal debate within the field on how best to identify and characterize the boundaries
dividing the population into such classes. These debates can be conveyed by
rehearsing how the field has developed in three (somewhat) distinct phases
over the last fifty years. The social class models emerging in the first phase
provide sociological solutions, albeit very primitive ones, to the conceptual
problems that emerge when one attempts (1) to develop multidimensional
measurements, (2) to distinguish capabilities from outcomes, and (3) to understand the sources of social isolation. The social class models developed
in the second phase are oriented, by contrast, to the problems of adaptive
preferences and needs. Although such terms as "adaptive preferences," "capabilities," and even "social isolation" are not well diffused within sociology (at least not until recently), it is nonetheless useful to understand conventional class models as engaging with the ideas and concepts behind these
terms, however indirectly and unsatisfactorily. Finally, the third phase of
analysis within sociology is more self-critical, a phase marked by a growing
(if still minority) sentiment that class models are diminishingly useful in understanding new patterns of inequality and poverty. We discuss these three
phases in more detail below.

The First Phase: The Structuralist Rationale for Class Models

In the decades following World War II, there was of course much debate
about the usefulness of the class concept, with some sociologists (e.g.,
Nisbet 1959) arguing that the concept was a nonempirical, metaphysical

commitment that sociologists would do well to shed. Throughout this period, a large band of sociologists nonetheless continued to advocate for and apply class models (e.g., Wright 1979; Goldthorpe 1982), especially in the 1970s and 1980s as neo-Marxian formulations came into ascendancy.

Obviously, a wide variety of class formulations were on offer during this period, yet most of them shared the assumption that classes are prepackaged "bundles" of structural conditions (e.g., levels of education, income, health) that tend to cohere. The class of "craft workers," for example, historically comprised individuals with moderate educational investments (i.e., secondary school credentials), considerable occupation-specific investments in human capital (i.e., on-the-job training), average income coupled with substantial job security (at least until deindustrialization), middling social honor and prestige, quite limited authority and autonomy on the job, and comparatively good health outcomes (by virtue of union-sponsored health benefits and regulation of working conditions). By contrast, the underclass may be understood as comprising a rather different package of endowments and outcomes, a package that combines minimal educational investments (i.e., secondary school dropouts), limited opportunities for on-the-job training, intermittent labor force participation and low income, virtually no opportunities for authority or autonomy on the job (during those brief bouts of employment), relatively poor health (by virtue of lifestyle choices and inadequate health care), and much social denigration and exclusion. The other classes appearing in conventional class schemes (e.g., professional, managerial, routine nonmanual) may likewise be understood as particular combinations of "scores" on the fundamental endowments and outcomes of interest.[1] The long-standing presumption, of course, is that social classes cannot be reduced to a unidimensional scale because such endowments and outcomes do not necessarily vary together, an inconvenience that makes it inadvisable to resort to conventional socioeconomic scales or income-based measures of "social standing" (e.g., Jencks, Perman, and Rainwater 1988). The routine nonmanual class, for example, is characterized by superior educational endowments but relatively poor income and opportunities for promotion.

This formulation bears inadvertently on many of the concerns about poverty and inequality measurement that development economists have raised in recent years. Most notably, consider the affinity between (1) Sen's long-standing argument that capabilities (rather than outcomes) should be the object of measurement and (2) the class analytic presumption that classes are indicators of "life chances," where this concept refers to the *"typical chance* for a supply of goods, external living conditions, and personal life experiences" (Weber 1946 [2001]:133; italics added). In both cases, emphasis is placed on the opportunities that a given set of endowments afford, thus leaving open the possibility that such opportunities may be exercised or realized in different ways (depending on preferences or "luck"). This affinity in approaches is a striking example of how two disciplines can reach similar methodological conclusions through very different and quite independent pathways.

Although class membership has therefore been construed by Weberian class analysts as an indicator of capabilities (rather than outcomes), the question at hand is whether this interpretation is at all warranted. Is there any reason to believe that a contemporaneous measure of occupation better reveals capabilities than a contemporaneous measure of income? Surely, occupational outcomes are, no less than income, a reflection of past investments and other individual decisions, meaning that the preferences evinced in the past affect them. If there is any basis, then, for arguing that sociological approaches provide a better measure of endowments, it is merely in a forward-looking sense that takes for granted that past preferences have affected current situations but then asks how current situations constitute a fresh set of endowments that affect subsequent life chances. Under this formulation, a class analyst would no doubt argue (albeit with little in the way of evidence) that social classes outperform "income classes" in signaling such variables as schooling, on-the-job training, and working conditions (e.g., authority, autonomy), all of which may be understood as contemporaneous endowments that have implications for capabilities or life chances.

This interpretation leads us quite directly to the sociological approach to the problem of multidimensionality. For a class analyst, the space of outcomes and capabilities is presumed to have a relatively low dimensionality, indeed a dimensionality no more nor less than the number of postulated classes. That is, the social classes institutionalized in the labor market represent only a delimited range of "packages" of endowments and outcomes, meaning that only a small subset of the logically possibly combinations is empirically realized. It follows that the task of reducing a potentially complicated multidimensional space to some manageable number of dimensions is solved institutionally and does not require any complex statistical machinations (cf. Bourguignon, Chapter 4).[2] There are, to be sure, ongoing debates within the discipline about the number of social classes and where the dividing lines between them are best drawn, but the shared class analytic presumption is that some (reasonably parsimonious) class scheme exists that can adequately characterize this multidimensional space. The individuals falling within the classes comprising this scheme will accordingly have endowments (e.g., education) and outcomes (e.g., income) that are close to the averages prevailing for their classes. Moreover, even when individual scores deviate from class averages, the conventional class analytic assumption is that the contextual effect of the class is dominant and overcomes any individual-level effects. This type of contextual effect would appear to be ubiquitous; for example, the full professor who lacks a Ph.D. is typically just as marketable as a fully credentialed (but otherwise comparable) full professor, precisely because membership in the professorial class is a "master status" that tends to dominate all other individual-level ones.

The variant of multidimensionalism implicitly adopted by class analysts differs, then, from the variant advanced by Sen (Chapter 2) or Bourguignon (Chapter 4) because it recasts multidimensional space in terms of social classes that may be understood as institutionalized combinations of endowments and outcomes. As noted above, this approach to multidimensionality is distinctive in implying that (1) the multidimensional space of endowments and outcomes is reducible to a small number of classes, and (2) the class locations of individuals become "master statuses" that can dominate the effects of the constituent individual-level endowments and outcomes. In this sense, the sociological approach is profligate with assumptions that purchase a parsimonious representation of inequality, yet the empirical foundation for these assumptions remains largely unsubstantiated. The stereotypical distinction between the disciplines is accordingly reversed; that is, development economists seem rather willing to let the data speak for themselves, whereas sociologists operate under the spell of a class-analytic model that embraces a largely untested set of assumptions about the structure of the social world.

How, finally, might we understand the concept of social exclusion through class-analytic lens? The multidimensional space in which sociologists are interested includes, of course, the crucial dimension of social standing or prestige, conceived as the probability of receiving deference in social interactions with others. In a market economy, a main determinant of social standing is participation in the labor market and the associated willingness to "self-commodify" (e.g., Esping-Andersen 1999), the latter term nicely emphasizing how market economies render all forms of worth, even self-worth, a function of market valuation. When individuals fail to self-commodify, they fall outside the most fundamental institutions of the society, thereby reducing them to nonentities and social ciphers. This is why a mere transfer of income to the underclass (see Bourguignon, Chapter 4) is inconsequential in relieving feelings of social exclusion. If anything, such a transfer only draws attention to the initial failure to self-commodify. Although a class map also embodies distinctions of social standing among those who have an enduring commitment to the labor market, the social divide between the underclass and all other classes looms especially large because it captures this fundamental insider-outsider distinction.

The Second Phase: The Culturalist Rationale for Class Models

In the mid-1980s, Bourdieu (1984) and other sociologists (especially Wilson 1987) sought to develop a culturalist rationale for class models, a rationale that rested on the claim that classes are not merely constellations of structural conditions (e.g., endowments, outcomes) but are also socially closed groupings in which distinctive cultures emerge and come to influence attitudes, behaviors, or even preferences of class members.[3] To be sure, many sociologists continued throughout this period to work with more narrowly structuralist definitions of class (especially, Wright 1997; Goldthorpe and Erikson 1992), but Bourdieu (1984) and Wilson (1987) were instrumental in legitimating the idea that class-specific cultures are a defining feature of class systems.

What types of closure generate such class-specific cultures? Although workplace segregation (e.g., occupational associations) and residential segregation (e.g., urban ghettos) are the two main forms of closure, the underclass is of course mainly generated by residential segregation (not workplace segregation). As both Wilson (Chapter 5) and Massey (Chapter 6) emphasize, members of the underclass live in urban ghettos that are spatially isolated from mainstream culture, thus allowing a distinctively oppositional culture to emerge and reproduce itself. The effects of residential segregation operate, by contrast, in more attenuated form for other social classes; after all, residential communities map only imperfectly onto class categories (i.e., the demise of the "company town"), and social interaction within contemporary residential communities is in any event quite superficial and cannot be counted on to generate much in the way of meaningful culture.

If distinctive cultures emerge outside the underclass, they do so principally through the tendency for members of the same occupation to interact
disproportionately with one another in the workplace and in leisure activities.
In accounting, for example, for the humanist, antimaterialist, and otherwise
left-leaning culture and lifestyle of sociologists, class analysts would stress the
forces of social closure within the workplace, especially the liberalizing effects
of (1) lengthy professional training and socialization into the "sociological
worldview," and (2) subsequent interaction in the workplace with predominantly liberal colleagues (see Grusky and Sørensen 1998).

When classes are allowed to have cultures in this fashion, one naturally
wishes to better understand the content of those cultures and, in particular,
the relationship between such content and the structural conditions (i.e.,
endowments, outcomes, institutional setting) that a class situation implies.
The sociological literature encompasses three positions on this relationship,
as described in the following sections.

Culturally prescribed means: At one extreme, class cultures may be
understood as nothing more than "rules of thumb" that encode optimizing
behavioral responses to prevailing institutional conditions, rules that allow
class members to forego optimizing calculations themselves and rely instead
on cultural prescriptions that provide reliable and economical shortcuts
to the right decision. For example, Goldthorpe (2000) argues that working
class culture is disparaging of educational investments not because of some
maladaptive oppositional culture, but because such investments expose the
working class (more so than other classes) to a real risk of downward mobility. In most cases, working class children lack insurance in the form of
substantial family income or wealth, meaning that they cannot easily recover
from an educational investment gone awry (e.g., dropping out); and those
who nonetheless undertake such an investment therefore face the real possibility of substantial downward mobility. The emergence, then, of a working class culture that regards educational investments as frivolous may be
understood as encoding that conclusion and thus allowing working class
children to undertake optimizing behaviors without explicitly engaging in
decision tree calculations. The behaviors that a "rule of thumb" culture en-
courages are, then, deeply adaptive because they take into account the endowments and institutional realities that class situations encompass.

Culturally prescribed ends: The foregoing example may be understood
as one in which a class-specific culture instructs recipients about appropriate (i.e., optimizing) means for achieving ends that are widely pursued by *all*

classes. Indeed, the prior rule-of-thumb account assumes that members of the working-class share the conventional interest in maximizing labor market outcomes, with their class-specific culture merely instructing them about the approach that is best pursued in achieving that conventional objective. At the other extreme, one finds class-analytic formulations that represent class cultures as more overarching worldviews, ones that instruct not merely about the proper means to achieve ends but additionally about the proper valuation of the ends themselves. For example, some class cultures (e.g., aristocratic ones) place an especially high valuation on leisure, with market work disparaged as "common" or "polluting." This orientation presumably translates into a high reservation wage within the aristocratic class. Similarly, "oppositional cultures" within the underclass may be understood as worldviews that place an especially high valuation on preserving respect and dignity for class members, with of course the further prescription that these ends are best achieved by (1) withdrawing from and opposing conventional mainstream pursuits, (2) representing conventional mobility mechanisms (e.g., higher education) as tailor-made for the middle class and, by contrast, unworkable for the underclass, and (3) pursuing dignity and respect through other means, most notably total withdrawal from and disparagement of mainstream pursuits. This is a culture, then, that advocates that respect and dignity deserve an especially prominent place in the utility function and that further specifies how those ends might be achieved.

The preceding account may well make too much of the distinction between means and ends. After all, an oppositional culture may evolve merely because the underclass cannot easily achieve other, more widely diffused ends (e.g., securing high-status jobs), meaning that this class maximizes its utility by reorienting members toward the alternative objectives of respect and dignity. The latter ends are more readily achievable given the institutional constraints that the underclass faces and the constellation of endowments that they control. By this reformulation, underclass culture is again merely prescribing particular means (i.e., the pursuit of respect and dignity) that will best realize a widely diffused end, that of maximizing total utility (see Weber 1947:115–117, for a relevant discussion). Although some insights into the sources of an oppositional culture may be secured through this reformulation, most sociologists would nonetheless regard it as largely semantic and maintain that much is gained by understanding how certain middle-range "ends," such as the pursuit of respect and dignity, may be more important for some classes than others (thus leaving aside the largely metaphysical question of whether any particular constellation of ends maximizes total utility).

Maladaptive culture: The foregoing examples involve "adaptations" of two kinds: (1) the class culture that emerges may be understood as an adaptation to the institutional constraints within which class members operate, an adaptation that may take the form of prescribing means that are well suited to widely shared ends (e.g., labor market success) or prescribing ends that are readily achievable (e.g., respect, dignity), and (2) the class members are presumed to internalize or otherwise adapt themselves to a class culture that provides instructions, in either of these two ways, about how best to maximize their overall utility. These forms of adaptation assume, then, that class cultures serve class incumbents well. Are there class cultures that, by contrast, are quite fundamentally maladaptive, that do not serve the ends of class members? In the contribution by Wilson (Chapter 5), it is hinted that perhaps there are such cultures, with the main mechanism of such maladaptation being the propagation, through structural forces, of personality types that are counterproductive or dysfunctional. As Wilson argues, some members of the underclass may well doubt that they can succeed in the labor market, either because they suspect that they lack the ability to succeed, or because they believe that the labor market is punitive, unresponsive, or discriminatory and will not fairly reward their ability. This personality type is maladaptive insofar as it prevents individuals from undertaking behaviors that in the end would meet with more success than they anticipate. In effect, the underclass culture is a maladaptive lens that filters information in misleading and unduly cynical ways, engendering an excessive and unwarranted sense of futility and despondency, however understandable such a response may be.

As always, one could salvage an efficiency account by noting that, once one conditions on the presence of a "low-efficacy" personality, it is indeed psychically optimizing to yield to the sense of futility and forego conventional labor market pursuits. In other words, persons with low self-efficacy would suffer much psychic distress by ignoring their feelings and forcing themselves into the formal labor market, a psychic distress that is perhaps best avoided. The larger question of interest, however, is whether class members would be better served by instead liberating themselves from this "low-efficacy" personality type, thereby eliminating misperceptions of the likelihood of success (in the labor market) and freeing themselves from the poor decisions that distress-avoidance engenders. Although Wilson would presumably argue that the underclass would indeed be well-served by such a liberation (at least in the long run), the larger point that he of course stresses is that, absent fundamental structural change (e.g., elimination of discrimination, reversal of the job-destroying effects of deindustrialization), it is unlikely that the maladaptive personality types can indeed be excised. In this regard, the "low-efficacy" personality type is yet another adaptation (to the institutional context), albeit in this case an adaptation that in the end is a dysfunctional one.

By way of conclusion, it should therefore be stressed that "second-phase" sociologists began to engage quite seriously with the idea of adaptive preferences, although in the context of their own idiosyncratic language that features (or reifies?) classes as the sources of such preferences. We have likewise argued that "first-stage" sociologists have engaged quite directly with such economic concepts as multidimensionality, capabilities, and social isolation. These engagements all occur through the distinctively sociological device of representing inequality and poverty in class-based terms. Although there is, then, an emerging overlap between the conceptual concerns of sociologists and those of economists, these shared concerns have clearly been addressed in ways that are quite idiosyncratic and discipline specific.[4] The question that then emerges, and one to which we turn in the conclusion, is whether anything useful might be achieved by bringing together the two disciplinary approaches more explicitly than has heretofore been the case.

The Third Phase: Revisiting the Foundations of Class Analysis

It should by now be clear that sociologists operating within the class-analytic tradition have adopted very strong assumptions about how inequality and poverty are structured. As we have noted, intrinsic to the class concept are such claims as (1) the space of outcomes and capabilities has a (low) dimensionality equaling the number of social classes, (2) the class locations of individuals become master statuses that dominate (or at least supplement) the effects of individual-level endowments, and (3) such class locations are socially closed and come to be associated with adaptive or maladaptive cultures. The foregoing claims have been unstated articles of faith among class analysts in particular and sociologists more generally. In this sense, we have suggested that class analysts have behaved rather like stereotypical economists, the latter frequently being criticized (and parodied) for their willingness to assume most anything provided that it leads to an elegant model.

The third phase of conceptual work within sociology has been marked, however, by an increased willingness to challenge the class-analytic status quo. In recent years, criticisms of the class-analytic enterprise have escalated, with many scholars now feeling sufficiently emboldened to argue that the concept of class should be abandoned altogether (see Clark and Lipset 2001; Kingston 2000; Pakulski and Waters 1996; Lee and Turner 1996). Although this retreat from class analysis was anticipated in the late 1950s by Nisbet (1959) and again in the 1980s by Gorz (1982) and other recanting Marxians (e.g., Offe 1985), the present round of anticlass rhetoric is unprecedented in its popularity, especially in Europe where class analysis has historically enjoyed a privileged position. As Wilson outlines in his contribution (Chapter 5), the underclass concept has come under especially strong criticism, much of it challenging the claim that a maladaptive culture has emerged at the bottom of the class structure.

How has the discipline reacted to such criticism? The most common response has been to simply reaffirm the importance of class models and to carry on with class analysis in the usual way. There is, after all, good reason to be skeptical of criticism that has to date rested on largely unsubstantiated claims. For the most part, the critics of class analysis have simply asserted that class models are built on problematic assumptions, but such assertions are no more or less convincing than the equally unsubstantiated presumption in favor of class models. This impasse has, however, been broken by a small band of scholars who have taken the criticisms seriously and sought to assess the empirical foundations of class models. The following research questions, most quite new to the field, may be understood as critical tests of this kind:

Does the space of endowments and outcomes indeed have low dimensionality? The most fundamental assumption of class analysis is that multidimensional characterizations of inequality and poverty are more tractable than most development economists would probably suppose. Although the multidimensional space of endowments and outcomes could in theory be quite complicated, class analysts have presumed that in practice a small number of social classes are institutionalized in the labor market, each comprising a characteristic combination of endowments and outcomes. In its simplest form, this assumption may be tested by examining whether endowments (e.g., education) and outcomes (e.g., income) tend to be combined in a small number of characteristic ways, with each such combination mapping onto a postulated social class (see Grusky and Weeden 2001:234–

235). This type of analysis, crucial though it is in defending class models, has only recently been taken on (e.g., Evans and Mills 1998; Birkelund, Goodman, and Rose 1996).

Is class a master status? The viability of class models also rests on the claim that class membership affects behavior, attitudes, and outcomes independently of individual-level attributes (e.g., human capital). As Wilson (Chapter 5) discusses, there is a burgeoning research literature on "neighborhood effects," with the main objective of this literature being to establish that members of the underclass (i.e., residents of poverty-stricken neighborhoods) are disadvantaged by virtue of true class (i.e., neighborhood) effects that arise from such mechanisms as a maladaptive class culture, a limited number of positive role models, and otherwise restricted social networks. To date, tests of this sort have equated class effects with neighborhood effects, but of course the same analytic approach could be used to assess whether contextual effects also emerge for classes defined in other ways (e.g., occupationally).

Are there class cultures? The foregoing analyses may be understood as an indirect test of the maladaptive effects of class culture. That is, insofar as members of the underclass are exposed to a maladaptive culture, a negative contextual effect of class membership should appear (net of individual-level controls). The latter test, which proceeds by inferring a culture from its presumed effects, might be usefully supplemented with a more direct measurement of the culture itself. Although there is a long tradition of simple descriptive research documenting differences in attitudes and values across presumed class categories (e.g., Kohn 1969), the case for class cultures would be strengthened by identifying the mechanisms (e.g., social closure) through which such class differences obtain. There has been renewed interest in identifying these mechanisms and the associated conditions under which class cultures can be expected to emerge (e.g., Weeden and Grusky 2004).

Are such class cultures maladaptive? It is yet another matter to show that such class cultures, insofar as they can be teased out, are in some cases maladaptive. If class cultures are, as Goldthorpe (2000) contends, merely rules of thumb that encode optimizing responses to the institutional environment that class members face, then such cultures can scarcely be understood as maladaptive. Clearly, it is child's play to redefine any particular culture as adaptive (by arguing, for example, that it simply reveals the idiosyncratic preferences of class members), but at minimum it is still useful to clarify the conceptual gymnastics that are (or are not) needed to make sense of a class culture and to interpret it as adaptive. Moreover, some leverage on the adaptiveness of class cultures can be gained empirically (see Goldthorpe 2000), even if a definitive critical test is logically impossible. As yet, such issues have not been directly addressed in the literature, although an increasing number of scholars have suggested that class scholars would do well to confront them (e.g., Goldthorpe 2000; Grusky and Weeden 2001).

This third phase of analysis involves, then, a reexamination of one of the core conceptual commitments of the field. In carrying out this reexamination, much would be gained if sociologists engaged more directly with the relevant literatures in behavioral and development economics, as doing so would at least clarify the problems (e.g., multidimensionality, adaptive preferences) to which class-based measurement is a possible answer. The long-standing commitment to class models within sociology may be understood as a path-dependent artifact of the extraordinary role that Marx and Weber have played in the discipline. Indeed, because Marx and Weber became such celebrated figures in the history of sociology, the tendency was to default to Marxian and Weberian class formulations without a sufficiently careful demonstration of their analytic virtues. The current reevaluation of this commitment provides an opportunity to demonstrate either that class analysis does solve fundamental measurement problems or that it fails to do so and should therefore be modified or even discarded.

CONCLUSIONS

The question that naturally arises at this point is whether we should follow convention by chastising all involved for their narrowly disciplinary orientation and by issuing the usual call for more collaborative interdisciplinary research. When academics (endlessly!) discuss the possibility of engaging in interdisciplinary research, the usual mantra is that of course more would be better, almost as if such research could be produced at no cost. Unfortunately, the world of academic research is more likely zero sum in character, meaning that a greater investment in interdisciplinary research could only be generated through a diminished investment in narrowly disciplinary pursuits. It is worth asking, then, whether we come out ahead by trading off conventional disciplinary work for additional investments in interdisciplinary research.

This question is usefully approached by distinguishing between two possible levels of investment in interdisciplinary work, a minimalist one involving increased interdisciplinary reading and other limited forms of exchange and engagement, and a maximalist one involving a more substantial experiment in truly collaborative research. Are either of these investments warranted? The cost-benefit calculus for a minimalist investment seems straightforward, as it is hard to imagine that a small amount of additional interdisciplinary reading would fail to pay off, even assuming that a comparable amount of within-discipline reading would be foregone. As best we can tell, scholars read narrowly in their own discipline not out of some full-information calculation that discipline-specific reading is optimizing but rather because information about relevant readings in other disciplines is limited, thus leading to the incorrect inference that the high costs of searching for relevant interdisciplinary work would not likely be compensated by high returns. We hope that the present volume serves in some small way to reduce the search costs that cross-disciplinary forays typically entail and, moreover, to inform about the substantial returns to search. The latter returns are, we suspect, especially substantial because economists and sociologists have developed shared interests in a variety of issues (e.g., multidimensionalism, capabilities, adaptive preferences) without evincing any corresponding convergence in methodological approaches. As a result, interdisciplinary readers can rest assured that they will encounter research that is both relevant (i.e., motivated by similar concerns) and different (i.e., methodologically and conceptually distinctive), a combination that is presumably tailor-made for creative and successful poaching.

Should true interdisciplinary collaboration (i.e., a "maximalist investment") likewise be encouraged? Here too, one has to be optimistic about the returns to interdisciplinary investment, if only because the convergence of interests around such issues as multidimensionality, social exclusion, and adaptive preferences provides an obvious foundation for collaboration. In the more typical case of "forced" interdisciplinary collaboration, the participants must first develop consensus around a shared project, a daunting task given that research questions tend to be so discipline specific. The present convergence of interests means that all such preliminary discussion could be safely skirted and that collaborators could move straightforwardly to the task of solving shared problems. This is, then, a propitious moment in the history of the two disciplines in which more deeply collaborative work seems likely to pay off.

Although we are accordingly forced into the standard platitude about the virtues of interdisciplinary research, we can at least make that platitude more concrete than usual by identifying some research questions that seem especially likely to profit from collaborative efforts. In the preceding sections of this essay, we have discussed several research problems that have, to date, been pursued independently by sociologists and economists but that stem from very similar underlying interests and might therefore be usefully pursued in collaboration. We are referring, for example, to the development of new measures of inequality that factor out the biasing effects of discrepant preferences, that correct for the perversely equality-enhancing effects of poverty-induced death, and that otherwise reflect the multidimensionality of inequality. The foregoing research efforts, while important, clearly do not exhaust the potential for interdisciplinary collaboration within the field of inequality and poverty. We therefore conclude this introductory essay with a sampling of three additional projects that are likewise good candidates for more sustained collaborative research.

International shifts in the division of labor (i.e., "deindustrialization," "globalization"): The processes of globalization and deindustrialization, arguably the most fundamental forces for change in inequality, have been studied in rather different ways by economists and sociologists. For the most part, economists have examined the effects of these processes on income and in-come inequality (e.g., Danziger and Gottschalk 1995), whereas sociologists have examined their effects on nonincome aspects of inequality, such as the rise of a socially excluded underclass (e.g., Wilson, Chapter 5). This difference reflects, of course, a long-standing disciplinary division of labor in which economists have privileged the income distribution and sociologists have privileged other aspects of inequality (e.g., stigma, social exclusion, class formation). If scholars are truly serious about weighing in on social policy, it is surely high time to bring together these approaches and evaluate the short- and long-term effects of deindustrialization and globalization in some comprehensive way, perhaps ultimately in terms of a unitary index that reconciles the various dimensions of inequality that are affected. A daunting task to be sure, but without attempting to move in this direction we are left with policy recommendations that, by virtue of their narrow assumptions about the objective function (e.g., national income), are often quite unsatisfying (see Bourguignon, Chapter 4).

Maladaptive cultures, irrational behavior, and behavioral economics: There are striking, albeit largely unexamined, parallels between (1) the premise elaborated by some behavioral economists (e.g., Rabin 1998) that cognitive functioning in humans can generate irrational or self-destructive behavior, and (2) the premise elaborated by some sociologists (e.g., Wilson, Chapter 5) that class-based subcultures can develop that encourage or reward maladaptive personalities and practices. In both formulations, simple rational action formulations are questioned, although the sources of the presumed irrationality or nonrationality differ. For economists, the presumption is that humans are not cognitively hard-wired to reason and decide in ways that rational action models require, thus undermining the micro-level foundations of such models. By contrast, sociologists have been fascinated with the social sources of maladaptation, most notably the tendency for underclass subcultures to provide incentives for maladaptive or destructive behavior. There may well be returns to developing a more comprehensive account of nonrational behavior and maladaptation that unifies these sociological and economic approaches.

Capabilities and inequality measurement: There is also good reason for sociologists and economists to collaborate in the development of a capabilities-based measure of inequality. It may be recalled that a capabilities approach shifts attention from inequality of outcomes (e.g., income) to inequality in the endowments (e.g., education) that may be converted into outcomes. Because outcomes reflect individual preferences (e.g., tastes for leisure) as well as endowments, the proper focus of policy, it is argued, should be the equalization of endowments themselves, not the equalization of outcomes. This approach implies that inequality is best measured by calculating for each individual the total "social value" of their endowments. In estimating this total value, one reasonable approach would be to regress income (and other outcomes of interest) on endowments, as the resulting estimated income for each individual constitutes the expected value of their endowments. The latter models are, of course, identical to those that sociologists studying processes of intergenerational transmission have long estimated (see Bourguignon, Chapter 4), thus suggesting that sociologists have a potentially important role to play in developing a capabilities-based measure of inequality.

We are struck, then, by the confluence of interests in such topics as the multidimensionality of inequality, the nonrational and self-destructive aspects of social behavior, and a "capabilities" approach to inequality measurement. Indeed, the conceptual challenges emerging within the field of poverty and inequality have an increasingly interdisciplinary feel to them, thus allowing us to reissue the usual platitude about the virtues of interdisciplinary research with less embarrassment than might otherwise be the case. Although this confluence of interests has, for the most part, escaped the notice of scholars from either discipline, the chapters that follow cast it in especially sharp and useful relief.

CHAPTER TWO

Conceptualizing and Measuring Poverty

Amartya Sen

THEORY AND PRACTICE

The period of intense exploration of conceptual foundations of normative measurement that Tony Atkinson's (1970) classic paper on the evaluation of inequality initiated seems to have given way to a relative neglect of conceptual issues, replaced by greater involvement with actual measurement and estimation, applying well-established approaches and measures. It is not that these empirical exercises have not been worthwhile. Certainly, we know a great deal more about the state of inequality and poverty in the world than used to be the case. But there is room for more conceptual questioning and greater foundational scrutiny at this time, both for reexamining old problems (they rarely go away) and for addressing new questions that have emerged in the contemporary world. Indeed, the practical world is a constant source of conceptual challenge, and it is right that we should try to reassess our concepts and ideas in the light of the manifest problems that empirical work identifies.

Let me illustrate with the recent factual debates on the state of inequality and poverty in China—a subject that has engaged much high-powered attention in the last few years. Over the last two decades China has had an altogether exceptional record of rapid economic growth, which has boosted the country's average income faster than anywhere else in the world. The impact of China's fast economic growth can be seen also in the swift reduction in China of the number of poor people—the population below what is agreed to be the minimally acceptable income level. Although the exact estimates of the extent of the decline of poverty in China remain an important subject of debate as well as further empirical research, the fact of a sweeping poverty reduction is not under dispute. In fact, China is recognized to be the principal factor behind whatever downward trend that can be seen in the incidence of poverty in the world as a whole. Indeed, the trend of world poverty looks totally different depending on whether or not China is included in the world statistics.

Despite such success, there are reasons for concern that demand further investigation and scrutiny. First, the poverty-removing character of Chinese economic expansion was much sharper in the early post-reform period than it was later. Second, although the concern in the field of poverty is comparative deceleration, in the related but distinct perspective of inequality, the problem takes the form of an actual increase in income inequality. For example, the Gini coefficient, a commonly used measure of the extent to which the actual income distribution differs from a hypothetical distribution in which each person receives an identical share, seems to have jumped from 0.382 to 0.452 between 1988 and 1995, a remarkably speedy increase in light of international historical experience.[1]

There have been other estimates as well, and for slightly different periods, but the basic result that there has been quite a large increase in income inequality in China seems hard to dispute. For example, Ravi Kanbur and Xiaobo Zhang (2001), using a somewhat different method, calculate that the Gini coefficient for income inequality in China went up from 0.217 in 1985 to 0.303 in 1999—again a remarkably big jump.[2] Kanbur and Zhang find similar results also with another measure of inequality, namely, a "generalized entropy index" from a class of measures that Theil (1967) first explored (another measure on which I will comment further, later on in this chapter).

This development has a profound influence not just for China, but also for the world.[3] Again, concentrating on the Gini coefficient as a measure of inequality, Branko Milanovic (2002) finds, using household surveys across the world, that the Gini coefficient for the world as a whole (based on a broad sampling of countries) has gone up from 0.628 in 1988 to 0.660 in 1993. In explaining the causation of this retrograde movement, Milanovic identifies the powerful influence of the contrast between the "slow growth of rural per capita incomes" in China (among other populous Asian countries) compared with the "fast growth of urban China" (along with the OECD countries). Indeed, the rural-urban contrast in Chinese income growth alone is responsible for a sizeable share of the rise of the world Gini coefficient.

So there is an important issue to be addressed here in discussing poverty and inequality in China. The continued great achievements in income growth seem to have been accompanied, in the more recent years, with an intensification of inequality, and even the tremendous accomplishment in poverty reduction has been uneven over time and regionally disparate.

CRITICAL EVALUATION ISSUES: SPACE AND MEASURES

The statistics with which the inequality literature is concerned have been primarily that of incomes. This focus is the case with the recent Chinese discussions on inequality and poverty as well. The "space" of incomes has been the principal—often the unique—focus of attention of those who have to examine the trend of inequality and poverty in the world, including these trends in China. The dominance of the income perspective has been remarkably large in empirical works on inequality and poverty.

Within that space of incomes, the specific measure that has been most widely used is the Gini coefficient. This is especially so in the literature related to Chinese inequality, even though it is sometimes supplemented by other measures, such as the generalized entropy index. The choice of an exact measure is a subject matter that needs to be identified for further scrutiny.

The measure of poverty most commonly used in examining poverty in the world in general, and specifically in assessing poverty in China, is the headcount measure of poverty. It has been used both in terms of the absolute number of the "poor" people below the poverty line, and in proportionate terms: as the fraction of the total population who have below-poverty-line income. This measure has sometimes been supplemented by other measures, such as the aggregate size of the income shortfall of the poor (expressed as a fraction total income), and also "aggregate squared poverty gap" (P_2) as the proportionate sum of the squared gaps between the poverty line threshold and the actual income of poor persons respectively (a measure that was, in fact, devised by Cornell economists Foster, Greer, and Thorbecke).[4]

Questions can be raised both about (1) the appropriateness of the *space* of incomes, and about (2) the specific *measures* used in the income space. It is useful to address these conceptual issues not just to see how robust the recent findings are, but also—and indeed much more importantly—to place future assessments of inequality and poverty in the world, including in China, on a robust intellectual footing. We have to see how the choice of space and that of measure tallies with the motivation that makes us interested in evaluating inequality and poverty in the first place. The measurement of inequality and poverty has to be in line with the motivating concerns related to equity and justice.

SPACE: INCOMES AND CAPABILITIES

I begin with the choice of space, that is, the determination of the variables in terms of which inequality and poverty are to be assessed. Is income the right space? In fact, in many ways it must be so. Inequality of incomes cannot but be relevant to evaluative assessment, because income is a general-purpose means the shortage of which can reduce a person to serious deprivation. Furthermore, in explaining major economic catastrophes, sudden downturns of incomes of the vulnerable population have great explanatory power.

This connection is well illustrated, for example, by the recent "Asian economic crisis," beginning in 1997, which afflicted countries such as South Korea, Indonesia, and Thailand, where the income decline of those who lost jobs (and who had no social security support) served as the prime mover for the tremendous hardship that ensued. Similarly, the Russian economic crisis of the late 1980s and the 1990s with its botched attempt at sudden privatization and marketization, can be, to a considerable extent, explained by how incomes took a sudden downturn.

To turn to a different—and an enormously distressing—matter, in a troubled period in China's own history, in the causal process that led to the starvation and massive mortality that followed the failure of the "Great Leap Forward," a central role was played by declines in incomes and entitlements, properly estimated. Although a fall in food output and availability was a major factor behind the sharp drop in entitlements (as is the case in some famines but not in others), a fuller understanding of the *pattern* of deprivation and its distribution over the population requires us to go beyond the food availability statistics (while taking due note of them). Indeed, failures of entitlement closely linked with declines in incomes and economic solvency provide a more effective perspective on starvation than concentration on food alone can provide.[5]

The entitlement approach to famines takes food supply to be one factor among many that can influence a collapse of entitlements and drastically reduce the command that vulnerable groups have over food needed for consumption and survival. The command over food depends on income levels, appropriately assessed, including taking note inter alia of the influence of production (including food production) and distribution arrangements (including that of food). It is important to see food availability as one influence among others that affect entitlements, without its being the only influence, nor necessarily the most important causal factor. Because this point is often missed (and it is often wrongly presumed that entitlements must be independent of food availability), the fact that food availability figures among other factors in the determination of entitlements is worth stressing.[6]

The analysis of Justin Lin and Dennis Yang (2000) has shown precisely how the perspective of entitlements, in which incomes (when they are adequately characterized) play a major role, can provide an illuminating explanation of the pattern and intensity of the deprivation that occurred in China during 1959–1961.[7] No matter what other space we use for assessing inequality and poverty, there will almost always be room for discriminating use of incomes and income-related statistics, particularly in explaining major deprivations related to economic causes.

However, having said that, it is also necessary to ask whether the space of incomes, despite its relevance, can really be the appropriate informational basis for assessing *equity and social justice in general,* and if it is inadequate, why it is so? These questions relate to our understanding of what the underlying goals of development are, and how, in particular, the quality of human life and substantive freedoms enjoyed by people can be best assessed. Whereas income is merely one of the *means* of good living, we have reason enough to look directly at the quality of life that people are able to lead, and the freedom they enjoy to live the way they would like. If life consists of various things that people are able to do or be (such as being able to live long, to be in good health, to be able to read and write, and so on), then it is the capability to function that has to be put at the center stage of assessment.

It is precisely the distinction between incomes, on the one hand, and well-being and freedom of persons, on the other, that drives a wedge between income information and the evaluative foundations of justice and equity.[8] Not only can the interest in capability influence the assessment of inequality, but also poverty has to be seen, in this perspective, as failures of certain basic capabilities (rather than of lowness of income per se).

Indeed, in the fourth century BC, Aristotle had pointed out, at the very beginning of his *Nicomachean Ethics*, that income and wealth are only instrumentally valued, and we have to go deeper to understand what makes human life rich and human freedoms effective. As he put it, "wealth is evidently not the good we are seeking; for it is merely useful and for the sake of something else."[9] That distinction had, in fact, been noted, in one way or another, in other ancient civilizations as well, including China (for example in the writings of Confucius). Similarly, in India, Gautama Buddha's famous quest in search of enlightenment, two centuries earlier than Aristotle, was directly linked to his recognition that income and wealth (which, as a prince of a prosperous kingdom, he plentifully had) could not prevent, for anyone, the adversities of illness, old age, and death, nor the penalty of ignorance, illiteracy, and lack of enlightenment.[10]

If we see development in terms of enhancement of human living and the freedom to live the kind of life that we have reason to value, then there is a strong case for focusing on "functionings" and the "capability" to function. The capabilities of relevance are not only those that relate to avoiding premature mortality, being in good health, being schooled and educated, and other such basic concerns, but also various social achievements, including—as Adam Smith (1776) emphasized—being able to appear in public without shame and being able to take part in the life of the community.[11]

It cannot, of course, be doubted that having a higher income will, *given other things*, help the achievement of a larger capability to function. But income is only one input among many (our capabilities also depend, for example, on social and political opportunities), and furthermore, given the level of income, our capability prospects depend also on personal factors (such as proneness to inherited diseases) and on the environment (including the epidemiological environment) in which people live.

CAPABILITY POVERTY AND RELATIVE DEPRIVATION

The connection between income and capability is also made more complex by the relevance of relative deprivation. As Adam Smith noted, the social capabilities may depend on a person's relative income vis-à-vis those of others with whom he or she interacts. A person's ability to be clothed appropriately (or to have other items of consumption goods that have some visibility or social use), given the standards of the society in which he or she lives, may be crucial for the capability to mix with others in that society. This relates directly to relative income vis-à-vis the general level of prosperity in that community. A relative deprivation in terms of income can, thus, lead to absolute deprivation in terms of capabilities, and in this sense, the problems of poverty and inequality are closely interlinked. For example, being relatively poor in a rich country can be a great capability handicap, even when one's absolute income is high in world standards. In a generally opulent country, more income is needed to buy enough commodities to achieve the *same social functioning*. This foundational idea relates to a number of contemporary concerns, for example "social exclusion." [12]

Some implications of Smith's focus on relative income in assessing poverty are worth separating out because of their extensive reach. First, because the absolute deprivation of social capabilities depends on relative deprivation of incomes, clearly the assessment of poverty in the space of capabilities cannot be divorced from the extent of income inequality. This connection indicates that the increasingly common global tendency in public discussion (and sometimes in public policy analysis) to argue in favor of an exclusive concentration on poverty removal, rather than being concerned also about inequality, is intellectually hard to sustain. Although it is easy to see that income poverty and income inequality are distinct phenomena, nevertheless capability poverty relates inseparably to income inequality. An often-articulated political attitude, which takes the form of saying, "I do care about poverty, but don't give a damn about inequality," not only reflects a remarkably narrow approach to morality but also raises issues of inconsistency, given the causal linkages that make inequality and poverty so interdependent.

Second, Smithian reasoning indicates why poverty is hard to eradicate just by raising the average level of income, without also addressing issues of inequality of incomes. In particular, the phenomenon of poverty in rich countries can be better understood through the perspective of relative deprivation. Adam Smith analyzed the relevance of relative position vis-à-vis others in society in the following way:

A linen shirt, for example is, strictly speaking, not a necessary of life. The Greeks and Romans lived, I suppose, very comfortably though they had no linen. But in the present times, through the greater part of Europe, a creditable day-labourer would be ashamed to appear in public without linen shirt, the want of which would be supposed to denote that disgraceful degree of poverty which, it is presumed, nobody can well fall into without extreme bad conduct. Custom, in the same manner, had rendered leather shoes a necessary of life in England. The poorest creditable person of either sex would be ashamed to appear in public without them. (Smith 1776, Vol. 2, Book V, ch. 2)

Similarly, today, a person in New York may well suffer from poverty despite having a level of income that would make him or her immune from poverty in Bangladesh or Ethiopia. This is not only because the capabilities that are taken to be minimally basic tend to change as a country becomes richer, but also because even for the same level of capability, the needed minimal income may itself rise, along with the incomes of others in the community. For example, in order to take part in the life of the community, or for children to be able to communicate with others in the same school, the bundle of commodities needed may include a telephone, a television, a car, and so on, in New York, in a way that would not apply in Addis or in Dhaka (where an adult may be able to participate in social affairs and children can talk to each other without these implements).

Thus, even the same minimal capability has varying commodity demands and divergent requirements of minimal income in different societies, involving systematic connection with incomes of others in the community in which a person lives. One further implication of this linkage is that given the peer pressure that operates in favor of social capabilities (often at the expense of other needs), even physical deprivation, such as undernourishment, can occur in richer countries at levels of family income at which elementary nutritional deprivation would be very rarely seen in poorer countries. The social pressure operating particularly on adult consumption patterns also helps to explain the much discussed odd phenomenon of "hunger in America," particularly given the levels of income of families with hungry members (often the children), which can be much above income levels at which hunger can be observed in poorer economies.[13]

Third, the pivotal role of the consumption patterns of others in the same community, or in a group with which a person interacts, also indicates why poverty cannot but be assessed in purely individual terms. The understanding that no person is an island is quite central to the assessment of poverty, and correspondingly, to the appropriate evaluation of the bite and reach of inequality. I shall have to come back to this issue when discussing the axiomatic demands on formal measures of inequality and poverty, in particular the requirement of decomposability.

How does the choice of space affect our assessment of inequality and poverty in China? Involvement in the space of some elementary functionings and capabilities has been an important feature of Chinese economic policy right from the founding of communist China. Through a visionary commitment to basic education, elementary health care, and social epidemiology, China made early achievements in levels of schooling, literacy, basic health, and longevity that far outshone those of many countries with much higher levels of GNP or real national income per head.

This early accomplishment of China related, from one perspective, to the average of the country, but it also reflected a sharp decline in the traditional inequalities in education, health, and life expectancy as well as a sharp reduction in the deprivation of basic economic capabilities (and in this sense, of capability poverty). It is worth recollecting also that these achievements predate the economic reforms, because China already had an extended base of elementary education and basic health care when the reforms were initiated in 1979. Income poverty still remained very high, because China's real economic growth was not particularly comprehensive or spectacular before the reforms, but it would be a serious mistake not to note the great achievements of China in reducing capability poverty and capability inequality in the *pre-reform* period.

As it happens, when the economic reforms were ultimately introduced, China's astonishing performance was inter alia drawing on what it had already achieved in health and education, because its economic expansion is greatly facilitated by the educational achievements and quality of health of the working population.[14] Nevertheless, there is no question that the pre-reform achievements in health and education, accomplished by 1979, badly needed the supplement of the enhancement of real incomes, because many other capabilities depend greatly on economic means. There is also no doubt that rapid economic growth—with fast decline in income poverty—after 1979 would not have occurred but for a radical economic reform. It is in this light that the poverty reduction in post-reform China, with its particular focus on income poverty, has to be appropriately assessed. The post-reform experience of China, especially in the early years, was both drawing on pre-reform achievements and also changing its special involvement with health and education, compared with income levels and the economic means of families and individuals.

There is a case, I believe, for reexamining the focus of research on inequality and poverty in contemporary China, with greater concentration on disparities and deprivations of basic capabilities. There is a very strong case for supplementing the powerful work that has occurred—and is continuing to occur—on income inequality and income poverty with a similarly extensive investigation of the trends of inequality and poverty in such variables as mortality, morbidity, education, and other indicators of capability that may or may not relate closely to income inequality and income poverty. To some extent this investigation is already happening, and even in this book, there are a number of chapters on issues that link closely with capability inequality and capability deprivation. It would be very useful to integrate a capability-based overall assessment of the attainments and adversities in contemporary China.

I might mention that there may be some prima facie reason to think that China's situation can be an important area of investigation. The rise in income in the post-reform period has been so exceptionally fast that the slowness of progress in other areas has tended to receive comparatively little attention. For example in the field of life expectancy, when China introduced economic reforms in 1979, China was ahead of India by about 14 years (with a life expectancy at birth in India of around 54 years and in China of about 68 years). The gap seems now to have narrowed to perhaps 7 years or so (with India's life expectancy at 64 years and China's at 71 years). Of course, it gets harder to expand life expectancy further as the absolute level rises. But nevertheless it is perhaps of some significance that the state of Kerala in India (with a good educational base and an extensive system of health services, and effective multi-party, participatory politics) now has substantially higher life expectancy than China, namely 74 years (with 72 years for men and 76 years for women), even though in 1979, Kerala was well behind China. Similarly, while Kerala had an infant mortality comparable to China's around 1979, that rate has continued to drop in Kerala in a way it has not quite happened in China, so that today Kerala's infant mortality rate of 10 per thousand is about a third of China's infant mortality of around 30 per thousand.[15]

Although these are mainly aggregative statistics, they have proximate connections with capability poverty, and indirect ones even with capability inequalities. Also, a number of policy questions can be better evaluated with more explicit and definitive studies on the inequality and poverty of basic capabilities, and these questions could aid the making of public policy. The financing of medical care and health insurance may be one such field. I should perhaps also add that one of the positive influences on the success of health care and the reach of school education (especially for girls) in Kerala is the nature of public discussion on this issue. So the issue of public participation is not only of interest as a constitutive component of a basic capability, but also as a strong influence on other capabilities, related to longevity, health, and education.

DECOMPOSABILITY: GINI COEFFICIENT AND OTHER MEASURES

Let me now move away from the issue of space (and the importance of capabilities) and come back to the more familiar income perspective that is central to so much of the current work on inequality and poverty. As was mentioned earlier, no matter what other perspectives are introduced and pursued in this field, interest remains in the assessment of income inequality and income poverty. It is in this context particularly worth asking whether the specific measures of income inequality and income poverty that are standardly used are indeed appropriate. It is also relevant to inquire whether the distinction as well as the connections between incomes and capabilities have any bearing on this complex question.

As I noted earlier, the most commonly used measure of income inequality in China—and indeed also elsewhere—is the Gini coefficient. Some economists have argued that this measure is defective because it is not decomposable, and many applied economists hold a quite well-developed opinion that non-decomposable measures should be, as far as possible, avoided.

What exactly, we must ask, is decomposability? Why is it taken to be important? And is that reasoning correct?[16] The interest in decomposability, related particularly to inequality measures, can be traced to the *analysis of variance*, a traditional method of evaluating "how much" of the variance in a variable (such as income) can be "explained" by relevant characteristics that—directly or indirectly—influence income (such as age, sex, race, schooling, or work experience). Any population can be seen to be divided between different groups, for example, the Chinese population can be divided between coastal and non-coastal residents (or more finely between residents of particular provinces), or between different occupation groups, or between women and men, and so on. The exercise of decomposition is typically invoked to relate the overall income inequality to "between-group" and "within-group" components in any measure of inequality we happen to use. The former, that is the between-group measure, is the inequality that would be seen if all the individual observations within one group were replaced by the average income of that group, so that the concentration would then be only on variations *between* these distinct groups (with no within-group inequality). The within-group term, on the other hand, is the weighted sum of the inequality *within* all the different groups, taken respectively on their own (with no account being taken of between-group inequality).

Decomposability is the requirement that the two constitutive parts, namely the between-group and the within-group components (thus defined), should add up exactly to the total inequality of the distribution of the variable in question. Indeed, formal decomposability demands—and this is a critically important issue—that this must hold for *every* way of partitioning the total population.

For those who would want a more formal statement of these issues, let me cater a little to their demand. An inequality measure $I(a)$ of a distribution (say, of incomes) is called additively decomposable (for short, decomposable) if for any two disjoint population groups with income distribution vectors x and y:

$$I(x, y) = I\,(x^*, y^*) + [w_x I(x) + w_y I(y)],$$

where w_x and w_y are the respective population shares of the two groups (used as weights), and x^* and y^* are the "smoothed" group distributions with each member of the respective group having the mean income of that group. In the right-hand expression, the first item is the between-group component (given by inequality for the two smoothed group distributions taken together, with no within-group inequality) and the second the within-group component (given by the population-weighted average of the respective inequalities within each group). In the analysis of inequality, such decompositions are often invoked, and also attention is confined to inequality measures that satisfy decomposability.

Sometimes a somewhat weaker requirement in the general direction of decomposability is used, called "subgroup consistency," which requires that for two distributions x and x' with the same population size and mean income, and similarly y and y':

$$\text{if}\quad \text{I}(x) = \text{I}(x')\quad \text{and}\quad \text{I}(y) = \text{I}(y'),\quad \text{then}\quad \text{I}(x, y) = \text{I}(x', y').$$

Even though this seemingly undemanding condition is indeed less demanding in general than decomposability, nevertheless for normalized and continuous measures of relative inequality, subgroup consistency must also yield decomposability.[17]

Some inequality measures satisfy decomposability, and others—such as the Gini coefficient—famously do not. This is because the Gini coefficient uses weights on incomes of individuals that reflect the relative deprivation of that individual vis-à-vis those of others in the group in question, so that the weights depend on the group that is chosen for comparison.[18] The results thus depend on which group is taken for reference, and also on how a particular group is partitioned into different components. So the Gini coefficient can violate decomposability, and so do many other proposed measures of inequality.

Indeed, Anthony Shorrocks (1980; 1984) established remarkable results showing that for the class of inequality measures that satisfy certain "desirable" characteristics standardly demanded from inequality measurement,[19] the only decomposable inequality measures consist of one very specific measure, namely Theil's generalized entropy index, and positive multiples thereof. I referred earlier to Kanbur and Zhang's (2001) use of the generalized entropy measure with Chinese statistics. The attraction of decomposability would have been among the factors suggesting that choice.

Decomposable poverty measures have similar requirements. However, because the concern here is with poverty rather than with inequality, there is obviously no between-group term. Rather, this case focuses on arriving at aggregate poverty as a weighted sum of poverty within different groups, adding exactly to total poverty for the population as a whole. Again, the formal requirement of decomposability insists that this method should work for *every* way of partitioning the total population into distinct groups.

As far as poverty is concerned, the old and most used measure, namely the head count of poverty, is indeed easily decomposable. But it is also extremely crude, because it takes no account of the *extent* of deprivation of the poor below the threshold "poverty line" income: it simply counts the number of people below that line. In order to correct this crudity, and to bring in both the extent of income shortfalls of the poor, and the distribution of this shortfall among the poor, various distribution-sensitive poverty measures have been proposed. The measure I proposed in 1976, which others have called the "S measure" (S stands, I believe, for simpleminded), which is axiomatically derived through a concentration on the normative perspective of relative deprivation, ends up having, as one of its components, the Gini coefficient of the distribution of income among the poor.[20] Despite being a distribution-sensitive measure of poverty (and having some other virtues in reflecting the extent of poverty), the S measure is not decomposable for much the same reason as the Gini coefficient violates decomposability.

An identifiable class of poverty measures that satisfies decomposability includes the previously mentioned "aggregate squared poverty gap" (P_2), defined as the proportionate sum of the squared gaps between the poverty line threshold and the actual income of every poor person, respectively (taken separately).[21] Particularly because of appeal of decomposability, aggregate squared poverty gap has become a widely used measure, especially by the World Bank.[22] This measure applies, to some extent, to the accounting of poverty in China as well.[23]

If decomposability is taken to be a necessary virtue of measures of inequality and poverty, the class of permissible normative indicators would be severely restricted. The much used Gini coefficient, in particular, as a measure of inequality must be abandoned. Similarly, distribution-sensitive poverty measures that make use of the Gini method of taking account of inequality among the poor, such as the "S measure" (or its variations), must also be rejected.[24] It is, therefore, important to ask whether decomposability is indeed a necessary—or at least a desirable—characteristic of the indicators to be chosen to reflect poverty or inequality in the income space.

It is easy to see why decomposability has such a strong appeal. It is "nice" to be able to "break down" the overall poverty of a total population into poverty in different subgroups of people that make up the total population. It gives, I suppose, some forensic satisfaction in solving a "whodunit" (and by how much respectively). For example, it may be interesting to see the overall poverty in China as being a weighted average of poverty in the different provinces, such as Beijing, Guangdong, Shandong, Hunan, Sichuan, and so on. And in this particular case, such a breakdown would also make considerable intuitive sense.

The problem, however, arises from the fact that decomposability is supposed to work *no matter how the population is divided* (that is, into what subgroups—whether the subgroups are coherent entities or not). It is because decomposability is supposed to work for *every* possible partitioning, the adding requirement would have to work even if we divided the total population into, say, subgroups according to the first letter of their first names, for example, "those with names beginning with A," "those with names beginning with B," and so on. But unlike people living in, say, a province, such as Hunan, people with names beginning with A need not have any relation with each other. The entire perspective of relative deprivation, as Smith had emphasized (in a different context), depends on defining groups according to interactions between them (such as those whose clothing or consumption patterns one compares with one's own). If the cogency of the relative deprivation is to be captured, the breakdown should work for some partitioning—according to interactive communities—and not for others. By insisting that the breakdown should work for every logically possible partitioning, a demand is imposed on measures of poverty and inequality that makes little intuitive sense.

On the other hand, mathematically the demand that the breakdown works for every logically possible classification has the effect that the only measures of inequality or poverty that survive treat every individual as an island. This is why the entropy measure works, because no one's income is assessed by comparing it with anyone else's. This is also why the "aggregate squared poverty gap" (P_2) satisfies the decomposability requirements, because everyone's income shortfall from the poverty line income is considered separately, without making any relative comparison with the incomes or shortfalls of others. The mathematical form of decomposability has had the odd result of ruling out any comparative perspective (and the corresponding sociological insights), which is, in fact, fatal for both inequality evaluation and poverty measurement. Indeed, the very insight of Adam Smith, which—as was discussed earlier—links relative deprivation in the space of incomes to absolute deprivation in terms of capabilities, is completely ignored by decomposable measures of poverty and inequality.

What we really need is a measure that would satisfy the decomposition requirement for *some* partitions (for example, splitting the Chinese population into provincial populations) and *not* for others (for example, splitting them according to the first letters of one's first name). The search for such measures has very radical implications, because it would require that even in measuring income inequality or income poverty, we must not confine our attention only to the income information, but also look at other characteristics of persons that link—or delink—them with each other. This idea implies that we cannot identify the extent of even "income inequality" for a group on the basis of the income vector of that group, because other information— other than incomes—about the group would be needed to assess the extent of income inequality itself.

I would like to conclude that all the measures of inequality and poverty so far used are defective, but their defects lie in different directions. The Gini coefficient as an inequality index, or the S measure (or any of its variations) as a measure of poverty, concentrates only on one kind of social relationship (one's relative position vis-à-vis others in whatever group we select), but whether this makes acceptable sense or not must depend on the nature of the groups involved. On the other side, the generalized entropy measure (and its variations) and the aggregate squared poverty gap (and its variations) tend to *ignore* every kind of group relation by treating each individual as an isolated island, uninfluenced by associations with particular comparison groups. If we want a properly satisfactory measure of inequality or poverty, we cannot define it over the income space alone, and have to supplement the income data by information about social relations between people and about comparison groups whose consumption patterns influence what is taken to be "necessary consumption" in a particular social context. Economic data cannot be interpreted without the necessary sociological understanding.

The attempt to see social beings as isolated islands works particularly badly in a world in which information about others' living conditions spreads rapidly, as it does in the contemporary world of easy travel and rapid communication (much more so than the world with which Adam Smith was familiar when he already emphasized the importance of social interactions). The linkages can work powerfully also across borders of states and nations. The relatively rich in China may be influenced by the consumption habits of people in more affluent countries, and in turn, the consumption patterns of the relatively rich in China can bring a sense of relative deprivation among the less affluent *within* China itself. It is hopeless to try to capture the essential features of inequality or poverty, including the relevance of relative deprivation, within measures that treat every individual's income just on its own, without any reference to incomes of others in comparison groups. The generalized index of entropy or the aggregate squared poverty gap deny the use of vital social information in the pursuit of decomposability.

The philosophical dilemma that ultimately troubles this particular literature is the tension between the desire to "split up" aggregate poverty and aggregate inequality between different components related to various partitions of population and the need to have non-income information to be able to make sure when such a "split up" would make sense and when it would not. There is no more reason a priori to be less skeptical of the use of the entropy class of universally decomposable inequality measures and the universally decomposable poverty measures than of the use of the non-decomposable Gini coefficient, or of poverty indicators that inter alia invoke the Gini coefficient.

Empirical work can proceed along each of these lines, provided it is borne in mind that each type of measure is most likely making some mistake by either ignoring social relations (with too much decomposability) or presuming social relations of very particular types (with a very specific view of relative deprivation). The old idea that while theorists argue, the empirical economists must give each claimant measure a fair shot has some rough wisdom.[25] There is a long way to go still to make adequate social sense of economic measures.

CHAPTER THREE

Poverty and Human Functioning: Capabilities as Fundamental Entitlements

Martha C. Nussbaum

THE CAPABILITIES APPROACH AND SOCIAL JUSTICE

For many years, approaches to poverty in the international development and policy-making world were obtuse in human terms. They focused on economic growth as the primary goal of development and measured quality of life simply by looking at GNP per capita. That crude measure, of course, did not even take distribution into account, and thus was utterly useless in confronting nations with a lot of poverty and high rates of inequality. And it was actually worse than useless, because it gave high marks to nations that contained huge inequalities, encouraging people to think that such nations (for example, South Africa under apartheid) had done things right. Moreover, as that example shows, the GNP approach also failed to take cognizance of other aspects of the quality of life that are not well correlated with economic advantage, even when distribution is factored in: aspects such as health, education, gender, and racial justice. And once again, by suggesting that things were well done when nations increased their GNP, it positively distracted attention from these factors, so crucial to taking the full measure of poverty.

Today, a different approach is prominent: the capabilities approach, represented in the *Human Development Reports* of the UNDP. As the late Mahbub Ul Haq wrote in the first of those reports, in 1990 (p. 9), "The real wealth of a nation is its people. And the purpose of development is to create an enabling environment for people to enjoy long, healthy, and creative lives. This simple but powerful truth is too often forgotten in the pursuit of material and financial wealth." Amartya Sen, of course, has been the primary architect of this approach; I have also developed it, focusing particularly on women's poverty and the relationship between poverty and sex inequality.

Sen and I argue that if we ask not about GNP only, but about what people are actually able to do and to be, we come much closer to understanding the barriers societies have erected against full justice for women and the poor. Similarly, we criticize approaches that measure well-being in terms of utility by pointing to the fact that deprived people frequently exhibit "adaptive preferences," preferences that have adjusted to their second-class status. Thus, the utilitarian framework, which asks people what they currently prefer and how satisfied they are, proves inadequate to confront some pressing issues of justice. We can only have an adequate theory of gender justice, and of social justice more generally, if we are willing to make claims about fundamental entitlements that are to some extent independent of the preferences that people happen to have—preferences shaped, often, by unjust background conditions.

In this chapter I suggest that the capabilities approach is indeed a valuable way to approach the question of fundamental entitlements, one that is especially pertinent to issues of sex equality. (One way of using it, which I discuss elsewhere, is as a basis for constitutional accounts of fundamental entitlements of all citizens.[1] I argue that it is superior to other approaches to social justice in the Western tradition when we confront it with problems of sex equality. It is closely allied to, but in some ways superior to, the familiar human rights paradigm, in ways that emerge most vividly in the area of sex difference. And it is superior to approaches deriving from the Western notion of the social contract, because of the way in which it can handle issues of care, issues fundamental to achieving sex equality, as recent feminist work has demonstrated.[2]

I argue, however, that the capabilities approach supplies definite and useful guidance, and proves an ally in the pursuit of sex equality, only if we formulate a definite list of the most central capabilities, even one that is tentative and revisable, using capabilities so defined to elaborate a partial account of social justice, a set of basic entitlements without which no society can lay claim to justice.

SEN AND SOCIAL JUSTICE

We must begin by laying out the aspects of Sen's work that are most pertinent to thinking about justice in the area of basic social entitlements. Throughout his career, Amartya Sen has been preoccupied with questions of social justice. Inequalities between women and men have been especially important in his thinking, and the achievement of gender justice in society has been among the most central goals of his theoretical enterprise. Against the dominant emphasis on economic growth as an indicator of a nation's quality of life, Sen has insisted on the importance of *capabilities*, what people are actually able to do and to be.[3] Frequently his arguments in favor of this shift in thinking deal with issues of gender.[4] Growth is a bad indicator of life quality because it fails to tell us how deprived people are doing; women figure in the argument as people who are often unable to enjoy the fruits of a nation's general prosperity. If we ask what people are actually able to do and to be, we come much closer to understanding whether full justice for women has been secured. Similarly, Sen is dissatisfied with measuring well-being in terms of utility because women often come to want merely what they think they can have, the classic problem of adaptive preferences to which I alluded above (Sen 1990, 1995). It follows that an adequate theory of gender justice, and of social justice more generally, requires us to lay out fundamental entitlements to which we can commit regardless of the preferences that people come to develop.

This critique of dominant paradigms in terms of ideas of gender justice is a pervasive feature in Sen's work, and it is obvious that one central motivation for his elaboration of the "capabilities approach" is its superior potential for developing a theory of gender justice. But the reader who looks for a fully formulated account of social justice generally, and gender justice in particular, in Sen's work will not find one; she will need to extrapolate one from the suggestive materials Sen provides.

Development as Freedom develops one pertinent line of thought, arguing that capabilities provide the best basis for thinking about the goals of development (Sen 1999). Both when nations are compared by international measures of welfare and when each nation strives internally to achieve a higher level of development for its people, capabilities provide us with an attractive way of understanding the normative content of the idea of development. Thinking of development's goal as increase in GNP per capita occluded distributional inequalities, particularly central when we are thinking about sex equality. It also failed to disaggregate and separately consider important aspects of development, such as health and education, that are demonstrably not very well correlated with GNP, even when we take distribution into account. Thinking of development's goal in terms of utility at least has the merit of looking at what processes do for people. But utility, Sen argues, is inadequate to capture the heterogeneity and non-commensurability of the diverse aspects of development. Because it fails to account for adaptive preferences, it also biases the development process in favor of the status quo, when used as a normative benchmark. Finally, it suggests that the goal of development is a state or condition of persons (e.g., a state of satisfaction), and thus understates the importance of agency and freedom in the development process.

All these failings, he stresses, loom large when we confront the theory with inequalities based on sex: for women's lives reflect a striving after many different elements of well-being, including health, education, mobility, political participation, and others. Women's current preferences often show distortions that are the result of unjust background conditions. And agency and freedom are particularly important goals for women, who have so often been treated as passive dependents. This line of argument has close links with the feminist critique of utilitarianism and dominant economic paradigms (e.g., Anderson 1993, Agarwal 1997). It also connects fruitfully with writings by activist-scholars who stress the importance of women's agency and participation (e.g., Chen 1983, Agarwal 1994).

Not surprisingly, I endorse these arguments. But they do not take us very far in thinking about social justice. They give us a general sense of what societies ought to be striving to achieve, but because of Sen's reluctance to make commitments about substance (which capabilities a society ought most centrally to pursue), even that guidance remains but an outline. And they give us no sense of what a minimum level of capability for a just society might be. We typically measure capabilities in comparative terms, as in the UNDP's *Human Development Reports*. Thus, nations are compared in areas such as health and educational attainment. But concerning what level of health service, or what level of educational provision, a just society would deliver as a fundamental entitlement of all its citizens, the view is suggestive, but basically silent.

Another famous line of argument that Sen pursued in works from "Equality of What?" to *Inequality Reexamined* seems more closely related to concerns of social justice. This argument begins from the idea of equality as a central political value (Sen 1992). Most states consider equality important, Sen argues, and yet they often do not ask perspicuously enough what the right space is within which to make the relevant comparisons. With arguments closely related to his arguments about the goals of development, Sen argues that the space of capabilities provides the most fruitful and ethically satisfactory way of looking at equality as a political goal. Equality of utility or welfare falls short for the reasons I have already summarized. Equality of resources falls short because it fails to account for individuals' having differing needs for resources if they are to come up to the same level of capability to function. They also have differing abilities to convert resources into actual functioning.

Some of these differences are straightforwardly physical: a child needs more protein than an adult to achieve a similar level of healthy functioning, and a pregnant woman more nutrients than a nonpregnant woman. But the differences that most interest Sen are social, and connected with entrenched discrimination of various types. Thus, in a nation where women are traditionally discouraged from pursuing an education, it will usually take more resources to produce female literacy than male literacy. Or, to cite Sen's famous example, a person in a wheelchair will require more resources connected with mobility than will the person with "normal" mobility, if the two are to attain a similar level of ability to get around (Sen 1980). (Although Sen tends to treat this example as one of straightforward physical difference, I believe that we should not so treat it: for the reasons that a person in a wheelchair is not able to get around are thoroughly social. We know that in a marathon the wheelchair contestants always finish more quickly than those without wheelchairs. What impedes their mobility in life generally is the lack of social provisions: ramps, wheelchair access lifts on buses, and so on. The social world is made for people with an average set of abilities and disabilities, and not for the person whose condition is non-average.[5])

Sen's arguments about equality seem to have the following bearing on issues of social justice and public policy: to the extent that a society values the equality of persons and pursues that as among its social goals, equality of capabilities looks like the most relevant sort of equality to aim at. And it is clear that equality is a central goal for women who pursue social justice; once again, then, the arguments have particular force and relevance in the context of feminism. But Sen never says to what extent equality of capability *ought* to be a social goal,[6] or how it ought to be combined with other political values in the pursuit of social justice. Thus, the connection of his equality arguments with a theory of justice remains as yet unclear.

CAPABILITIES AND RIGHTS

The capabilities that Sen mentions in illustration of his approach, and those that I include in my more explicit list, include many of the entitlements that are also stressed in the human rights movement: political liberties, freedom of association, free choice of occupation, and a variety of economic and social rights. And capabilities, like human rights, supply a moral and humanly rich set of goals for development, in place of "the wealth and poverty of the economists," as Marx so nicely put it. Thus, capabilities have a very close relationship to human rights, as understood in contemporary international discussions. In effect, they cover the terrain covered by both the so-called first-generation rights (political and civil liberties) and the so-called second-generation rights (economic and social rights). And they play a similar role, providing both a basis for cross-cultural comparison and the philosophical underpinning for basic constitutional principles.

Both Sen and I connect the capabilities approach closely to the idea of human rights, and in *Women and Human Development* I have described the relationship between the two ideas at some length (Nussbaum 2001a: Ch. 1; see also Nussbaum 1997). Feminists have frequently criticized the human rights approach for being male-centered and for not including as fundamental entitlements some abilities and opportunities fundamental to women in their struggle for sex equality. They have proposed adding to international rights documents such rights as the right to bodily integrity and the rights to be free from violence in the home and from sexual harassment in the workplace. My list of capabilities explicitly incorporates that proposal, and Sen's would appear to do so implicitly.[7] But the theoretical reasons for supplementing the language of rights with the language of capabilities still require comment.

Capabilities, I would argue, are very closely linked to rights, but the language of capabilities gives important precision and supplementation to the language of rights. The idea of human rights is by no means a crystal clear idea. Rights have been understood in many different ways, and difficult theoretical questions are frequently obscured by the use of rights language, which can give the illusion of agreement where there is deep philosophical disagreement. People differ about what the *basis* of a rights claim is: rationality, sentience, and mere life have all had their defenders. They differ, too, about whether rights are prepolitical or artifacts of laws and institutions. (Kant held the latter view, although the dominant human rights tradition has held the former.) They differ about whether rights belong only to individual persons, or also to groups. They differ about whether rights are to be regarded as side constraints on goal-promoting action, or rather as one part of the social goal that is being promoted. They differ, again, about the relationship between rights and duties: if A has a right to S, then does this mean that there is always someone who has a duty to provide S, and how shall we decide who that someone is? They differ, finally, about what rights are to be understood as rights *to*. Are human rights primarily rights to be treated in certain ways? Rights to a certain level of achieved well-being? Rights to resources with which one may pursue one's life plan? Rights to certain opportunities and capacities with which one may make choices about one's life plan?

The capabilities approach has the advantage of taking clear positions on these disputed issues, while stating clearly what the motivating concerns are and what the goal is. The relationship between the two notions, however, needs further scrutiny, given the dominance of rights language in international feminism.

When thinking about fundamental rights, I would argue that the best way of thinking about what it means to secure them to people is to think in terms of capabilities. The right to political participation, the right to religious free exercise, the right of free speech—these and others are all best thought of as secured to people only when the relevant capabilities to function are present. In other words, to secure a right to citizens in these areas is to put them in a position of capability to function in that area. To the extent that rights are used in defining social justice, we should not grant that the society is just unless the capabilities have been effectively achieved. Of course people may have a prepolitical right to good treatment in this area that has not yet been recognized or implemented; or it may be recognized formally and yet not implemented. But by defining the securing of rights in terms of capabilities, we make it clear that a people in country C do not really have an effective right to political participation, for example, a right in the sense that matters for judging that the society is a just one, simply because this language exists on paper: they really have been given the right only if there are effective measures to make people truly capable of political exercise. Women in many nations have a nominal right of political participation without having this right in the sense of capability: for example, they may be threatened with violence should they leave the home. In short, thinking in terms of capability gives us a benchmark as we think about what it is really to secure a right to someone. It makes clear that this involves affirmative material and institutional support, not simply a failure to impede.

We see here a major advantage of the capabilities approach over understandings of rights—very influential and widespread—that derive from the tradition within liberalism that is now called "neoliberal," for which the key idea is that of "negative liberty." Often fundamental entitlements have been understood as prohibitions against interfering state action, and if the state keeps its hands off, those rights are taken to have been secured; the state has no further affirmative task. Indeed, the U.S. Constitution demonstrates this conception directly in that negative phrasing concerning state action predominates, as in the First Amendment: "Congress shall make no law respecting an establishment of religion, or prohibiting the free exercise thereof; or abridging the freedom of speech, or of the press; or the right of the people peaceably to assemble, and petition the Government for a redress of grievances." Similarly, the Fourteenth Amendment's all-important guarantees are also stated in terms of what the state may not do: "No State shall make or enforce any law which shall abridge the privileges or immunities of citizens of the United States; nor shall any State deprive any person of life, liberty, or property, without due process of law; nor deny to any person within its jurisdiction the equal protection of the laws." This phraseology, deriving from the Enlightenment tradition of negative liberty, leaves things notoriously indeterminate as to whether impediments supplied by the market, or private actors, are to be considered violations of fundamental rights of citizens (Nussbaum forthcoming).

The Indian Constitution, by contrast, typically specifies rights affirmatively.[8] Thus for example: "All citizens shall have the right to freedom of speech and expression; to assemble peaceably and without arms; to form associations or unions; . . . [etc.]" (Art. 19). These locutions have usually been understood to imply that impediments supplied by non-state actors may also be deemed violative of constitutional rights. Moreover, the Constitution is quite explicit that affirmative action programs to aid the lower castes and women are not only not incompatible with constitutional guarantees, but are actually in their spirit. Such an approach seems very important for gender justice: the state needs to take action if traditionally marginalized groups are to achieve full equality. Whether a nation has a written constitution or not, it should understand fundamental entitlements in this way.

The capabilities approach, we may now say, sides with the Indian Constitution, and against the neoliberal interpretation of the U.S. Constitution.[9] It makes it clear that securing a right to someone requires more than the absence of negative state action. Measures such as the recent constitutional amendments in India that guarantee women one-third representation in the local *panchayats*, or village councils, are strongly suggested by the capabilities approach, which directs government to think from the start about what obstacles there are to full and effective empowerment for all citizens, and to devise measures that address these obstacles.

A further advantage of the capabilities approach is that, by focusing from the start on what people are actually able to do and to be, it is well placed to foreground and address inequalities that women suffer inside the family: inequalities in resources and opportunities, educational deprivations, the failure of work to be recognized as work, insults to bodily integrity. Traditional rights talk has neglected these issues, and this is no accident, I would argue: for rights language is strongly linked with the traditional distinction between a public sphere, which the state regulates, and a private sphere, which it must leave alone.

The language of capabilities has one further advantage over the language of rights: it is not strongly linked to one particular cultural and historical tradition, as the language of rights is believed to be. This belief is not very accurate, as Sen has effectively argued: although the term "rights" is associated with the European Enlightenment, its component ideas have deep roots in many traditions (Sen 1997a, Nussbaum 2000a). Nonetheless, the language of capabilities enables us to bypass this troublesome debate. When we speak simply of what people are actually able to do and to be, we do not even give the appearance of privileging a Western idea. Ideas of activity and ability are everywhere, and there is no culture in which people do not ask themselves what they are able to do, what opportunities they have for functioning.

If we have the language of capabilities, do we also need the language of rights? The language of rights still plays, I believe, four important roles in public discourse, despite its unsatisfactory features. First, when used as in the sentence "A has a right to have the basic political liberties secured to her by her government," it reminds us that people have justified and urgent claims to certain types of urgent treatment, no matter what the world around them has done about that. It imports the idea of an urgent claim based on justice. This is important particularly for women, who may lack political rights. However, the capabilities approach can make this idea of a fundamental entitlement clear in other ways, particularly, as I argue, by operating with a list of capabilities that are held to be fundamental entitlements of all citizens based on justice.

Rights language also has value because of the emphasis it places on people's choice and autonomy. The language of capabilities, as both Sen and I employ it, is designed to leave room for choice, and to communicate the idea that there is a big difference between pushing people into functioning in ways you consider valuable and leaving the choice up to them. Sen makes this point very effectively in *Development as Freedom* (Sen 1999). But we make this emphasis clear if we combine the capabilities analysis with the language of rights, as my list of capabilities does at several points, and as the Indian Constitution typically does.

On one issue concerning the relationship between capabilities and rights, I differ to some extent with Sen, and I can only briefly record that difference here (see Nussbaum 1997). Both earlier and in *Development as Freedom*, Sen takes issue with the idea that rights should be regarded as side constraints on the pursuit of social well-being. He uses Bob Nozick's version of this claim as his target, and he makes the very plausible claim that Nozick is wrong to hold that property rights, construed in Nozickian fashion, are side constraints on the pursuit of social well-being, always to be respected no matter what disasters befall. But there are two ways of making this objection. I think that Sen should emphasize that Nozick has the wrong account of what fundamental rights people have, including property rights. But if he makes this criticism, he need not object to Nozick's contention that rights are side constraints (Sen 1999:65–67). They may still be so: only Nozick has got hold of the wrong account of rights. Nozick's account of property rights is implausible in all sorts of ways. But if we really have correctly identified the fundamental entitlements of all citizens, then it does seem right to say that those entitlements (in my account, the central capabilities) function as side constraints on the pursuit of overall well-being: that is, we should not pursue greater well-being by taking away any citizen's freedom of religion, freedom of speech, and so forth. Now, of course, in emergencies some of the fundamental entitlements have to be suspended (although politicians from Indira Gandhi to

George W. Bush[10] have done a great deal to discredit this idea). But in general, it seems right that we cannot pursue the good by violating one of these basic requirements of justice.

A feature of the Indian Constitution illuminates that idea. As a reaction against the suspension of fundamental civil rights during the Emergency, the Indian Supreme Court has evolved a doctrine of the "essential features" of the Constitution: features that represent the most fundamental entitlements, such that they cannot be removed even by a constitutional amendment (of the sort that Indira Gandhi's large parliamentary majority so easily passed, removing crucial civil liberties).[11] To say that the fundamental entitlements of citizens are like side constraints is to say something like that: they are essential features of the structure of a just society (or one that aspires to justice), such that they cannot be abrogated for the sake of greater prosperity or even security.

ENDORSING A LIST

One obvious difference between Sen's writings and my own is that for some time I have endorsed a specific list of the Central Human Capabilities as a focus both for comparative quality-of-life measurement and for the formulation of basic political principles of the sort that can play a role in fundamental constitutional guarantees.

The basic idea of my version of the capabilities approach, in *Women and Human Development*, is that we begin with a conception of the dignity of the human being, and of a life that is worthy of that dignity—a life that has available in it "truly human functioning," in the sense described by Marx in his 1844 *Economic and Philosophical Manuscripts*. With this basic idea as a starting point, I then attempt to justify a list of ten capabilities as central requirements of a life with dignity. These ten capabilities are supposed to be general goals that can be further specified by the society in question, as it works on the account of fundamental entitlements it wishes to endorse (Nussbaum 2000a, Ch. 1). But in some form all are part of a minimum account of social justice: a society that does not guarantee these capabilities to all its citizens, at some appropriate threshold, falls short of being a fully just society, whatever its level of opulence. (One way of implementing such a list would be through a written constitution with its account of fundamental rights [Nussbaum forthcoming]. But this is not a necessary feature of the idea.) Moreover, the capabilities are held to be important for each and every person: each person is treated as an end, and none as a mere adjunct or means to the ends of others. And although in practical terms priorities may have to be set temporarily, the capabilities are understood as both mutually supportive and all of central relevance to social justice. Thus, a society that neglects one of them to promote the others has shortchanged its citizens, and there is a failure of justice in the shortchanging (Nussbaum 2001b). (Of course someone may feel that one or more of the capabilities on my list should not enjoy this central status, but then she will be differing with me about what ought to be on the list, not about the more general project of using a list to define a minimal conception of social justice.)

The list itself is open-ended and has undergone modification over time; no doubt it will undergo further modification in the light of criticism. But here is the current version.

The Central Human Capabilities

1. Life. Being able to live to the end of a human life of normal length; not dying prematurely, or before one's life is so reduced as to be not worth living.

2. Bodily Health. Being able to have good health, including reproductive health; to be adequately nourished; to have adequate shelter.

3. Bodily Integrity. Being able to move freely from place to place; to be secure against violent assault, including sexual assault and domestic violence; having opportunities for sexual satisfaction and for choice in matters of reproduction.

4. Senses, Imagination, and Thought. Being able to use the senses, to imagine, think, and reason—and to do these things in a "truly human" way, a way informed and cultivated by an adequate education, including, but by no means limited to, literacy and basic mathematical and scientific training. Being able to use imagination and thought in connection with experiencing and producing works and events of one's own choice, religious, literary, musical, and so forth. Being able to use one's mind in ways protected by guarantees of freedom of expression with respect to both political and artistic speech, and freedom of religious exercise. Being able to have pleasurable experiences and to avoid non-beneficial pain.

5. Emotions. Being able to have attachments to things and people outside ourselves; to love those who love and care for us, to grieve at their absence; in general, to love, to grieve, to experience longing, gratitude, and justified anger. Not having one's emotional development blighted by fear and anxiety. (Supporting this capability means supporting forms of human association that can be shown to be crucial in their development.)

6. Practical Reason. Being able to form a conception of the good and to engage in critical reflection about the planning of one's life. (This entails protection for the liberty of conscience and religious observance.)

7. Affiliation.

A. Being able to live with and toward others, to recognize and show concern for other human beings, to engage in various forms of social interaction; to be able to imagine the situation of another. (Protecting this capability means protecting institutions that constitute and nourish such forms of affiliation, and also protecting the freedom of assembly and political speech.)

B. Having the social bases of self-respect and non-humiliation; being able to be treated as a dignified being whose worth is equal to that of others. This entails provisions of nondiscrimination on the basis of race, sex, sexual orientation, ethnicity, caste, religion, national origin.

8. Other Species. Being able to live with concern for and in relation to animals, plants, and the world of nature.

9. Play. Being able to laugh, to play, to enjoy recreational activities.

10. Control over One's Environment.

A. Political. Being able to participate effectively in political choices that govern one's life; having the right of political participation, protections of free speech and association.

B. Material. Being able to hold property (both land and movable goods), and having property rights on an equal basis with others; having the right to seek employment on an equal basis with others; having the freedom from unwarranted search and seizure. In work, being able to work as a human being, exercising practical reason and entering into meaningful relationships of mutual recognition with other workers.

Because considerations of pluralism have been on my mind since the beginning, I have worked a sensitivity to cultural difference into my understanding of the list in several ways.

First, I consider the list as open-ended and subject to ongoing revision and rethinking, in the way that any society's account of its most fundamental entitlements is always subject to supplementation (or deletion).

I also insist, second, that the items on the list ought to be specified in a somewhat abstract and general way, precisely in order to leave room for the activities of specifying and deliberating by citizens and their legislatures and courts that I have outlined in the section, "Sen and Social Justice." Within certain parameters it is perfectly appropriate that different nations should do this somewhat differently, taking their histories and special circumstances into account. Thus, for example, a free speech right that suits Germany well might be too restrictive in the different climate of the United States.

Third, I consider the list to be a free-standing "partial moral conception," to use John Rawls's phrase: that is, it is explicitly introduced for political purposes only, and without any grounding in metaphysical ideas of the sort that divide people along lines of culture and religion.[12] As Rawls says: we can view this list as a "module" that can be endorsed by people who otherwise have very different conceptions of the ultimate meaning and purpose of life; they will connect it to their religious or secular comprehensive doctrines in many ways.

Fourth, if we insist that the appropriate political target is capability and not functioning, we protect pluralism here again.[13] Many people who are willing to support a given capability as a fundamental entitlement would feel violated were the associated functioning made basic. Thus, the right to vote can be endorsed by believing citizens who would feel deeply violated by mandatory voting, because it goes against their religious conception. (The American Amish are in this category: they believe that it is wrong to participate in political life, but they endorse the right of citizens to vote.) The free expression of religion can be endorsed by people who would totally object to any establishment of religion that would involve dragooning all citizens into some type of religious functioning.

Fifth, the major liberties that protect pluralism are central items on the list: freedom of speech, freedom of association, freedom of conscience.[14] By placing them on the list we give them a central and nonnegotiable place.

Sixth and finally, I insist on a rather strong separation between issues of justification and issues of implementation. I believe that we can justify this list as a good basis for political principles around the world. But this does not mean that we thereby license intervention with the affairs of a state that does not recognize them. It is a basis for persuasion, but I hold that military and economic sanctions are justified only in certain very grave circumstances involving traditionally recognized crimes against humanity (Nussbaum 2003). So it seems less objectionable to recommend something to everyone, once we point out that it is part of the view that state sovereignty, grounded in the consent of the people, is a very important part of the whole package.

Where does Sen stand on these questions? I find a puzzling tension in his writings at this point. On the one hand, he speaks as if certain specific capabilities are absolutely central and nonnegotiable. One cannot read his discussions of health, education, political, and civil liberties, and the free choice of occupation without feeling that he agrees totally with my view that these human capabilities should enjoy a strong priority and should be made central by states the world over, as fundamental entitlements of each and every citizen (although he says little about how a threshold level of each capability would be constructed). In the case of liberty, he actually endorses giving liberty a considerable priority, though without giving an exhaustive enumeration of the liberties that would fall under this principle. His role in the formulation of the measures that go into the *Human Development Reports*, moreover, clearly shows his endorsing of a group of health- and education-related capabilities as the appropriate way to measure quality of life across nations.

On the other hand, Sen has conspicuously refused to endorse any account of the central capabilities. Thus, the examples mentioned above remain in limbo: clearly they are examples of some things he thinks very important, but it is not clear to what extent he is prepared to recommend them as important goals for all the world's people, goals connected with the idea of social justice itself. And it is equally unclear whether other capabilities not mentioned so frequently might be equally important, and, if so, what those capabilities might be. The reason Sen has not addressed this topic appears to be his respect for democratic deliberation.[15] He feels that people should be allowed to settle these matters for themselves. Of course, as I have said above, I do too, in the sense of implementation. But Sen goes further, suggesting that the endorsement of a set of central entitlements inhibits democracy in international political debate, as when feminists insist on certain requirements of gender justice in international documents and in deliberative forums.

In *Development as Freedom* things become, I believe, even more problematic. For Sen speaks throughout the work of "the perspective of freedom" and uses language, again and again, suggesting that freedom is a general all-purpose social good, and that capabilities are to be seen as instances of this more general good of human freedom. Such a view is not incompatible with ranking some freedoms ahead of others for political purposes, of course. But it does seem to go in a problematic direction.

First of all, it is unclear whether the idea of promoting freedom is even a coherent political project. Some freedoms limit others. The freedom of rich people to make large donations to political campaigns limits the equal worth of the right to vote. The freedom of businesses to pollute the environment limits the freedom of citizens to enjoy an unpolluted environment. The freedom of landowners to keep their land limits projects of land reform that might be argued to be central to many freedoms for the poor. And so on. Obviously these freedoms are not among those that Sen considers, but he says nothing to limit the account of freedom or to rule out conflicts of this type.

Furthermore, even if there were a coherent project that viewed all freedoms as desirable social goals, it is not at all clear that this is the sort of project someone with Sen's political and ethical views ought to endorse. The examples I have just given show us that any political project that is going to protect the equal worth of certain basic liberties for the poor, and to improve their living conditions, needs to say forthrightly that some freedoms are central for political purposes, and some are distinctly not. Some freedoms involve basic social entitlements, and others do not. Some lie at the heart of a view of political justice, and others do not. Among the ones that do not lie at the core, some are simply less important, but others may be positively bad.

For example, the freedom of rich people to make large campaign contributions, though defended by many Americans in the name of the general good of freedom, seems to me not among those freedoms that lie at the heart of a set of basic entitlements to which a just society should commit itself. In many circumstances, it is actually a bad thing, and constraint on it a very good thing. Similarly, the freedom of industry to pollute the environment, though cherished by many Americans in the name of the general good of freedom, seems to me not among those freedoms that should enjoy protection; beyond a certain point, the freedom to pollute is bad, and should be constrained by law. And although property rights are certainly a good thing up to a point and in some ways, the freedom of large feudal *zamindars* in India to hold onto their estates—a freedom that some early Supreme Court decisions held to enjoy constitutional protection (wrongly, in my view, and in the view of subsequent decisions)—is not part of the account of property rights as central human entitlements that a just society would want to endorse. To define property capabilities so broadly is actually a bad thing, because land reform can be essential to social justice (see generally Agarwal 1994).

To speak more generally, as the example of land reform shows us, justice for the poor cannot be pursued without limiting the freedom of the rich to do as they like. Similarly, gender justice cannot be successfully pursued without limiting male freedom. For example, the "right" to have intercourse with one's wife whether she consents or not has been understood as a cherished male prerogative in most societies, and men have greatly resented the curtailment of liberty that followed from laws against marital rape — one reason why about half of the states in the United States still do not treat nonconsensual intercourse within marriage as genuine rape, and why many societies the world over still lack laws against it. The freedom to harass women in the workplace is a cherished prerogative of males the world over: the minute sexual harassment regulations are introduced, one always hears protests invoking the idea of liberty. Terms like "feminazis" are used to suggest that feminists are against freedom for supporting these policies. And, of course, in one sense feminists are indeed insisting on a restriction of liberty, on the grounds that certain liberties are inimical both to equalities and to women's liberties and opportunities.

In short, no society that pursues equality or even an ample social minimum can avoid curtailing freedom in very many ways, and what it ought to say is those freedoms are not good, they are not part of a core group of entitlements required by the notion of social justice, and in many ways, indeed, they subvert those core entitlements. Of other freedoms, for example the freedom of motorcyclists to drive without helmets, they can say, these freedoms are not very important; they are neither very bad nor very good. They are not implicit in our conception of social justice, but they do not subvert it either.

In other words, all societies that pursue a reasonably just political conception have to evaluate human freedoms, saying that some are central and some trivial, some good and some actively bad. This evaluation also affects the way we assess an abridgment of a freedom. Certain freedoms are taken to be entitlements of citizens based on justice. When any one of these entitlements is abridged, that is an especially grave failure of the political system. In such cases, people feel that the abridgment is not just a cost to be borne; it is a cost of a distinctive kind, involving a violation of basic justice. When some freedom outside the core is abridged, that may be a small cost or a large cost to some actor or actors, but it is not a cost of exactly that same kind, one that in justice no citizen should be asked to bear. This qualitative difference is independent of the amount of cost, at least as figured in terms of standard subjective willingness-to-pay models. Thus, men may mind greatly a law that tells them that they may no longer harass women in the workplace; they may feel that it severely burdens their lives. In terms of standard willingness-to-pay models, they might be willing to pay quite a lot for the right to drive without a helmet. On the other hand, many citizens probably would not think that not being able to vote was a big cost. In terms of standard willingness-to-pay models, at least, they would not pay much for the right to vote, and some might have to be paid for voting. And yet I would want to say that the right to vote is a fundamental entitlement based on justice, whereas the right to drive without a helmet is not (Nussbaum 2001b).

Sen's response to these questions, in discussion, has been to say that freedom per se is always good, although it can be badly used. Freedom, he said, is like male strength: male strength is per se a good thing, although it can be used to beat up women. I am not satisfied by this reply. For obviously enough, so much depends on how one specifies the freedoms in question. Some freedoms include injustice in their very definition: thus, the freedom to rape one's wife without penalty, the freedom to hang out a sign saying "No Blacks here," the freedom of an employer to discriminate on grounds of race or sex or religion. Those are freedoms all right, and some people zealously defend them. But it seems absurd to say that they are good per se, and bad only in use. Any society that allows people these freedoms has allowed a fundamental injustice, involving the subordination of a vulnerable group. Of other freedoms, for example, the freedom of the motorcycle rider to ride without a helmet, we should not say, "good in itself, bad only in use," we should say "neutral and trivial in itself, probably bad in use." Once again, attention to the all-important issue of content is vital.

I would argue that Sen cannot avoid committing himself to a core list of fundamental capabilities, once he faces such questions. If capabilities are to be used in advancing a conception of social justice, they will obviously have to be specified, if only in the open-ended and humble way I have outlined. Either a society has a conception of basic justice or it does not. If it has one, we have to know what its content is, what opportunities and liberties it takes to be fundamental entitlements of all citizens. One cannot have a conception of social justice that says, simply, "All citizens are entitled to freedom understood as capability." Besides being wrong and misleading in the ways I have already argued, such a blanket endorsement of freedom and capability as the goal would be hopelessly vague. It would be impossible to say whether the society in question was just or unjust.

Someone may now say, sure, there has to be a definite list in the case of each nation that is striving for justice, but why not leave the list making to them? Of course, as I have already said, in the sense of *implementation*, and also in the sense of *more precise* specification, I do so. So, to be a real objection to my proposal, the question must be, why should we hold out to all nations a set of norms that we believe justified by a good philosophical argument, as when feminists work out norms of sex equality in documents such as CEDAW (The Convention on the Elimination of All Forms of Discrimination against Women), rather than letting each one justify its own set of norms? The answer to this question, however, is given in all of Sen's work: some human matters are too important to be left to whim and caprice, or even to the dictates of a cultural tradition. To say that education for women, or adequate health care, is not justified just in case some nation believes that it is not justified seems like a capitulation to subjective preferences, of the sort that Sen has opposed throughout his career. As he has repeatedly stated: capabilities have intrinsic importance. But if we believe that, we also believe that it is right to say to nations that do not sufficiently recognize one of them: you know, you too should endorse equal education for girls, and understand it as a fundamental constitutional entitlement. You too should provide a certain level of health care to all citizens, and view this as among their fundamental constitutional entitlements. Just because the United States does not choose to recognize a fundamental right to health care, that does not make the United States right or morally justified.

In short: it makes sense to take the issue of social justice seriously, and to use a norm of justice to assess the various nations of the world and their practices toward the poor, toward women, and toward other vulnerable groups. But if the issue of social justice is important, then the content of a conception of justice is important. Social justice has always been a profoundly normative concept, and its role is typically critical: we work out an account of what is just, and we then use it to find reality deficient in various ways. Sen's whole career has been devoted to developing norms of justice in exactly this way, and holding them up against reality to produce valuable criticisms. It seems to me that his commitment to normative thinking about justice requires the endorsement of some definite content. One cannot say, "I'm for justice, but any conception of justice anyone comes up with is all right with me." Moreover, Sen, of course, does not say that. He is a radical thinker, who has taken a definite stand on many matters, including matters of sex equality. He has never been afraid to be definite when misogyny is afoot, or to supply a quite definite account of why many societies are defective. So it is somewhat mysterious to me why he has recently moved in the direction of endorsing freedom as a general good. Certainly there is no such retreat in his practical policies regarding women. In recent writing such as "The Many Faces of Misogyny," he is extremely definite about what is just and unjust in laws and institutions, and one can infer a rich account of fundamental human entitlements from his critique (Sen 2001). But then it would appear that he cannot actually believe that the content of an account of fundamental entitlements should be left up for grabs.

Such leaving-up-for-grabs is all the more dangerous when we are confronting issues of poverty and sexism. For obviously enough, many traditional conceptions of social justice and fundamental entitlements have made women, and the poor, second-class citizens, if citizens at all. Women's liberties, opportunities, property rights, and political rights have been construed as unequal to men's, and this has been taken to be a just state of affairs. Nor have traditional accounts of justice attended at all to issues that are particularly urgent for women, such as issues of bodily integrity, sexual harassment, and, as my next section will describe, the issue of public support for care to children, the disabled, and the elderly. Similarly, the poor have often had rights that in the sense of capability are very unequal to those of the rich, and issues particularly pertinent to their lives have similarly been avoided.

Some supporters of a capabilities approach might be reluctant to endorse a list because of concerns about pluralism.[16] But here we may make two points that pertain specifically to the norm of respect for pluralism. First, the value of respect for pluralism itself requires a commitment to some cross-cultural principles as fundamental entitlements. Real respect for pluralism means strong and unwavering protection for religious freedom, for the freedom of association, and for the freedom of speech. If we say that we are for pluralism, and yet refuse to commit ourselves to the nonnegotiability of these items as fundamental building blocks of a just political order, we show that we are really halfhearted about pluralism.

I am sure that Sen would agree with this. I am sure, too, that he would say the same about other items on my list, such as health and education: if a nation says that they are for human capabilities, but refuses to give these special protection for all citizens, citing reasons of cultural or religious pluralism, Sen will surely say that they are not making a good argument, or giving genuine protection to pluralism. Instead, they are, very often, denying people (often, women in particular) the chance to figure out what culture and form of life they actually want. So they are actually curtailing the most meaningful kind of pluralism, which requires having a life of one's own and some choices regarding it. And that goal surely requires a certain level of basic health and education.

But then we are both, in effect, making a list of such entitlements, and the only question must be what shall go on the list, and how long it will be.

The second argument is one that derives from the Rawlsian idea of political liberalism, and I am not certain that Sen would endorse it. The argument says that classical liberalism erred by endorsing freedom or autonomy as a general good in human life. Both earlier liberals such as Mill and modern comprehensive liberals such as Joseph Raz hold that autonomy and freedom of choice are essential ingredients in valuable human lives, and that society is entitled to promote freedom across the board. Rawls, and I with him, hold that this general endorsement of freedom shows deficient respect for citizens whose comprehensive conceptions of the good human life do not make freedom and autonomy central human values. People who belong to an authoritarian religion cannot agree with Raz or Mill that autonomy is a generally good thing. Mill responds, in Chapter 3 of *On Liberty*, by denigrating such people (he understands Calvinists to be such people) (Mill 1859). Presumably the Millean state would denigrate them too, and would design education and other institutions to disfavor them, although their civil liberties would not be restricted. Rawls and I agree that this strategy shows deficient respect for a reasonable pluralism of different comprehensive conceptions of the good life. We should respect people who prefer a life within an authoritarian religion (or personal relationship), so long as certain basic opportunities and exit options are firmly guaranteed.

I hold that this respect for pluralism is fostered both by making capability and not functioning the appropriate political goal and also by endorsing a relatively small list of core capabilities for political purposes. Thus, we say two things to religious citizens. We say, first, that endorsing the capabilities list does not require them to endorse the associated functioning as a good in their own lives, a point I have stressed earlier in this section. And we say, second, that the very fact that it is a short list shows that we are leaving them lots of room to value other things in mapping out their life plan. We do not ask them to endorse freedom as a general good—as we might seem to do if we talk a lot about freedom but fail to make a list. Instead, we just ask them to endorse this short list of freedoms (as capabilities), for political purposes and as applicable to all citizens. They may then get on with the lives they prefer.

The expectation is that a Roman Catholic citizen, say, can endorse this short list of fundamental liberties for political purposes, without feeling that her view of Church authority and its decisive role in her life is thereby being denigrated. Even an Amish citizen, who believes that all participation in public life is simply wrong, can still feel that it is all right to endorse the capabilities list for political purposes, because no general endorsement of autonomy as an end tells her that her life is less worthwhile than other lives. And, as I argued in *Women and Human Development*, even a woman who believes that the seclusion of women is right may endorse this small menu of liberties and opportunities for all women, though she herself will use few of them— and she will feel that the conception is one that respects her, because it does not announce that only autonomous lives are worthwhile (Nussbaum 2000a, Chs. 1, 3).

I am not certain whether Sen is in this sense a comprehensive liberal like Raz, or a political liberal like Rawls and me. But to the extent that he finds Rawls's arguments on this score persuasive, he has yet a further reason to endorse a definite and relatively circumscribed list of capabilities as political goals, rather than to praise freedom as a general social good.

The question of how to frame such a list, and what to put on it, is surely a difficult one, in many ways. But I have argued that there is no way to take the capabilities approach forward, making it really productive for political thought about basic social justice, without facing this question and giving it the best answer one can.

CAPABILITIES AND THE SOCIAL CONTRACT TRADITION[17]

One further issue, fundamental to concerns about justice for women and the disadvantaged, will help us to see both why the capabilities approach is superior to other approaches to social justice within the liberal tradition, and why a definite list of entitlements is required if the approach is to deliver an adequate conception of justice. This is the all-important issue of care for people who are physically or mentally dependent on others: children, the disabled, the elderly. This is a central issue for gender justice, because women do most of the caregiving for such dependents, often without any public recognition that it is work. The time spent on this caregiving disables women from many other functions of life, even when a society has in other respects opened those functions to them. For this reason, a large body of feminist writing has developed pursuing this issue; and the 1999 *Human Development Report* devoted special attention to it as an issue of gender justice. To appreciate why this problem has not been adequately addressed, and why the capabilities approach does better, we must now contrast it with approaches familiar within the social-contract tradition.

Insofar as the capabilities approach has been used to articulate a theory of social justice, or part of such a theory, it has been in dialogue from the start with the ideas of John Rawls and the Western liberal social contract tradition (Rawls 1971, 1996). In "Equality of What?" Sen already argued for the capabilities approach by contrasting it with Rawls's approach, which defines justice in terms of the distribution of "primary goods," prominently including wealth and income (Sen 1980).[18] My account of capabilities in *Women and Human Development* takes the argument further, comparing capabilities to Rawlsian primary goods at several points and endorsing the idea of an overlapping consensus (Nussbaum 2000a, Ch. 1). Sen and I both argue that Rawls's theory would be better able to give an account of the relevant social equalities and inequalities if the list of primary goods were formulated as a list of capabilities rather than as a list of things.[19]

But another problem ought to trouble us, as we ponder the social contract tradition as a source of basic principles of justice, particularly with women's lives in view. All well-known theories in the social contract tradition imagine society as a contract for mutual advantage. They therefore imagine the contracting parties as rough equals, none able to dominate the others, and none asymmetrically dependent on the others. Whatever differences there are among the different founders of that tradition, all accept the basic Lockean conception of a contract among parties who, in the state of nature, are "free, equal, and independent."[20] Thus, for Kant persons are characterized by both freedom and equality, and the social contract is defined as an agreement among persons so characterized. Contemporary contractarians explicitly adopt this hypothesis. For David Gauthier (1986: 18), people of unusual need are "not party to the moral relationships grounded by a contractarian theory."[21] Similarly, the citizens in Rawls's Well Ordered Society are "fully cooperating members of society over a complete life" (Rawls 1980:546, 1996:183).

Life, of course, is not like that. Real people begin their lives as helpless infants, and remain in a state of extreme, asymmetrical dependency, both physical and mental, for anywhere from ten to twenty years. At the other end of life, those who are lucky enough to live on into old age are likely to encounter another period of extreme dependency, either physical or mental or both, which may itself continue in some form for as much as twenty years. During the middle years of life, many of us encounter periods of extreme dependency, some of which involve our mental powers and some our bodily powers only, but all of which may put us in need of daily, even hourly, care by others. Finally, and centrally, many citizens never have the physical or mental powers requisite for independence. These lifelong states of asymmetrical dependency are in many respects isomorphic to the states of infants and the elderly.

In short, any real society is a caregiving and care-receiving society, and must therefore discover ways of coping with these facts of human neediness and dependency that are compatible with the self-respect of the recipients and do not exploit the caregivers. This, as I have said, is a central issue for gender justice.

In this area a Kantian starting point, favored by Rawls and other modern contractarians, is likely to give bad guidance. For Kant, human dignity and our moral capacity, dignity's source, are radically separate from the natural world. Morality certainly has the task of providing for human neediness, but the idea that we are at bottom split beings, both rational persons and animal dwellers in the world of nature, never ceases to influence Kant's way of thinking about how these deliberations will go.

What is wrong with the split? Quite a lot. First, it ignores the fact that our dignity just is the dignity of a certain sort of animal. It is the animal sort of dignity, and that very sort of dignity could not be possessed by a being who was not mortal and vulnerable, just as the beauty of a cherry tree in bloom could not be possessed by a diamond. Second, the split wrongly denies that animality can itself have a dignity; thus it leads us to slight aspects of our own lives that have worth, and to distort our relation to the other animals.[22] Third, it makes us think of the core of ourselves as self-sufficient, not in need of the gifts of fortune; in so thinking we greatly distort the nature of our own morality and rationality, which are thoroughly material and animal themselves; we learn to ignore the fact that disease, old age, and accident can impede the moral and rational functions, just as much as the other animal functions. Fourth, it makes us think of ourselves as atemporal. We forget that the usual human life cycle brings with it periods of extreme dependency, in which our functioning is very similar to that enjoyed by the mentally or physically handicapped throughout their lives. Feminist thought has recognized these facts about human life more prominently, at any rate, than most other political and moral thought.

Political thought in the Kantian social contract tradition (to stick with the part of the tradition I find deepest and most appealing) suffers from the conception of the person with which it begins. Rawls's contracting parties are fully aware of their need for material goods. Here Rawls diverges from Kant, building need into the foundations of the theory.[23] But he does so only to a degree: for the parties are imagined throughout as competent contracting adults, roughly similar in need, and capable of a level of social cooperation that makes them able to make a contract with others. Such a hypothesis seems required by the very idea of a contract for mutual advantage.

In so conceiving of persons, Rawls explicitly omits from the situation of basic political choice the more extreme forms of need and dependency human beings may experience. His very concept of social cooperation is based on the idea of reciprocity between rough equals, and has no explicit place for relations of extreme dependency. Thus, for example, Rawls refuses to grant that we have any duties of justice to animals, on the grounds that they are not capable of reciprocity (1971: 504–505); they are owed "compassion and humanity," but "[t]hey are outside the scope of the theory of justice, and it does not seem possible to extend the contract doctrine so as to include them in a natural way" (1971: 512). This makes a large difference to his theory of political distribution. For his account of the primary goods, introduced, as it is, as an account of the needs of citizens who are characterized by the two moral powers and by the capacity to be "fully cooperating," has no place for the need of many real people for the kind of care we give to people who are not independent.[24]

Now of course Rawls is perfectly aware that his theory focuses on some cases and leaves others to one side. He insists that, although the need for care for people who are dependent is "a pressing practical question," it may reasonably be postponed to the legislative stage, after basic political institutions are designed:

> So let's add that all citizens are fully cooperating members of society over the course of a complete life. This means that everyone has sufficient intellectual powers to play a normal part in society, and no one suffers from unusual needs that are especially difficult to fulfill, for example, unusual and costly medical requirements. Of course, care for those with such requirements is a pressing

practical question. But at this initial stage, the fundamental problem of social justice arises between those who are full and active and morally conscientious participants in society, and directly or indirectly associated together throughout a complete life. Therefore, it is sensible to lay aside certain difficult complications. If we can work out a theory that covers the fundamental case, we can try to extend it to other cases later. (Rawls 1980:546)

This reply seems inadequate. Care for children, the elderly, and the mentally and physically handicapped is a major part of the work that needs to be done in any society, and in most societies it is a source of great injustice. Any theory of justice needs to think about the problem from the beginning, in the design of the most basic level of institutions, and particularly in its theory of the primary goods.[25]

What, then, can be done to give the problem of care and dependency sufficient prominence in a theory of justice? The first thing we might try, one that has been suggested by Eva Kittay (1999, 102–103) in her fine book, is to add the need for care during periods of extreme and asymmetrical dependency to the Rawlsian list of primary goods, thinking of care as among the basic needs of citizens.

This suggestion, if we adopt it, would lead us to make another modification: for care is hardly a commodity, like income and wealth, to be measured by the sheer amount of it citizens have. As Sen has long suggested (see "The Capabilities Approach and Social Justice" section, page 47), we would do well to understand the entire list of primary goods as a list not of things but of central capabilities. This change would not only enable us to deal better with people's needs for various types of love and care as elements of the list, but would also answer the point that Sen has repeatedly made all along about the unreliability of income and wealth as indices of well-being. The well-being of citizens will now be measured not by the sheer amount of income and wealth they have, but by the degree to which they have the various capabilities on the list. One may be well off in terms of income and wealth, and yet unable to function well in the workplace, because of burdens of caregiving at home (see Williams 2000).

If we accepted these two changes, we would surely add a third, relevant to our thoughts about infancy and old age. We would add other capability-like items to the list of basic goods: for example the social basis of health, adequate working conditions, and the social basis of imagination and emotional well-being, items that figure on my list (Nussbaum 2000a, Ch. 1).

Suppose, then, we do make these three changes in the list of primary goods: we add care in times of extreme dependency to the list of primary goods; we reconfigure the list as a list of capabilities; and we add other pertinent items to the list as well. Have we done enough to salvage the contract doctrine as a way of generating basic political principles? I believe that there is still room for doubt. Consider the role of primary goods in Rawls's theory. The account of primary goods is introduced in connection with the Kantian political conception of the person, as an account of what citizens characterized by the two moral powers need.[26] Thus, we have attributed basic importance to care only from the point of view of our own current independence. It is good to be cared for only because care subserves moral personality, understood in a Kantian way as conceptually quite distinct from need and animality. This seems like another more subtle way of making our animality subserve our humanity, where humanity is understood to exclude animality. The idea is that because we are dignified beings capable of political reciprocity, therefore we had better provide for times when we are not that, so we can get back to being that as quickly as possible. I think that this is a dubious enough way to think about illnesses in the prime of life; but it surely leads us in the direction of a contemptuous attitude toward infancy and childhood, and, a particular danger in our society, toward elderly disability. Finally, it leads us strongly in the direction of not fully valuing those with lifelong mental disabilities: somehow or other, care for them is supposed to be valuable only for the sake of what it does for the "fully cooperating." They are, it would seem, being used as means for someone else's ends, and their full humanity is still being denied.

So I believe that we need to delve deeper, redesigning the political conception of the person, bringing the rational and the animal into a more intimate relation with one another, and acknowledging that there are many types of dignity in the world, including the dignity of mentally disabled children and adults, the dignity of the senile demented elderly, and the dignity of babies at the breast. We want the picture of the parties who design political institutions to build these facts in from the start. The kind of reciprocity in which we humanly engage has its periods of symmetry, but also, of necessity, its periods of more or less extreme asymmetry—and this is part of our lives that we bring into our situation as parties who design just institutions. And this may well mean that the theory cannot be a contractarian theory at all.

So I believe we need to adopt a political conception of the person that is more Aristotelian than Kantian,[27] one that sees the person from the start as both capable and needy—"in need of a rich plurality of life-activities," to use Marx's phrase, whose availability will be the measure of well-being. Such a conception of the person, which builds growth and decline into the trajectory of human life, will put us on the road to thinking well about what society should design. We do not have to contract for what we need by producing; we have a claim to support in the dignity of our human need itself. Because this is not just an Aristotelian idea, but one that corresponds to human experience, we have good reason to think that it can command a political consensus in a pluralistic society. If we begin with this conception of the person and with a suitable list of the central capabilities as primary goods, we can begin designing institutions by asking what it would take to get citizens up to an acceptable level on all these capabilities. Although Sen refrains from specifying a political conception of the person, I believe that this suggestion is squarely in line with his ideas.

In *Women and Human Development* I propose that the idea of central human capabilities be used as the analogue of Rawlsian primary goods, and that the guiding political conception of the person should be an Aristotelian/ Marxian conception of the human being as in need of a rich plurality of life activities, to be shaped by both practical reason and affiliation (Nussbaum 2000a, Ch. 1). I argue that these interlocking conceptions can form the core of a political conception that is a form of political liberalism, close to Rawls's in many ways. The core of the political conception is endorsed for political purposes only, giving citizens a great deal of space to pursue their own comprehensive conceptions of value, whether secular or religious. Yet more room for a reasonable pluralism in conceptions of the good is secured by insisting that the appropriate political goal is capability only: citizens should be given the option, in each area, of functioning in accordance with a given capability or not so functioning. To secure a capability to a citizen it is not enough to create a sphere of noninterference: the public conception must design the material and institutional environment so that it provides the requisite affirmative support for all the relevant capabilities.[28] Thus, care for physical and mental dependency needs will enter into the conception at many points, as part of what is required to secure to citizens one of the capabilities on the list.

Although Sen has not commented explicitly on issues of mental disability and senility, I believe that the view I have just mapped out is squarely in line with his emphasis on freedom as a goal. We see, then, here again, that the capabilities approach solves some problems central to a theory of social justice that other liberal theories seem unable to solve well; the capability-based solution seems to be an attractive way of thinking about fundamental entitlements.

But now we must observe that the capabilities approach does these good things only in virtue of having a definite content. The capabilities approach provides us with a new way of understanding the *form* of "primary goods," and that is one part of the work that it does in providing a more adequate theory of care. But getting the *form* right was not all that had to be done: we also had to add the need for care in times of acute dependency to the existing list of primary goods. And then, I argued, we would also need to add other capabilities as well to the list, in areas such as health care, work conditions, and emotional well-being. My own list of capabilities provides for these things already, in areas such as emotions, affiliation, and health. A shift from the space of resources to the space of capabilities would not go far in correcting the deficiencies of the Rawlsian framework unless we had a list with a definite content, one that prominently includes care. Moreover, I also argued that we need to associate the list with a specific political conception of the person, one that conceives of dignity and animality as related rather than opposed. This is another piece of definite content, one that suffuses the capabilities list as I conceive it.

The capabilities approach is a powerful tool in crafting an adequate account of social justice. But the bare idea of capabilities as a space within which comparisons are made and inequalities assessed is insufficient. To get a vision of social justice that has the requisite critical force and definiteness to direct social policy, we need to have an account, for political purposes of what the central human capabilities are, even if we know that this account will always be contested and remade.

CHAPTER FOUR

From Income to Endowments:
The Difficult Task of Expanding
the Income Poverty Paradigm

François Bourguignon

INTRODUCTION

Much of the economic literature on poverty relies on what may be referred to as the "income poverty paradigm." In this paradigm, poor people are defined by their standard of living expressed in some money metric, typically income or consumption expenditure per capita, falling short of an arbitrary predetermined level, the "poverty line." The extent of poverty is then measured by the proportion of people in the population below this line, possibly combined with the average distance they are from it and inequality among them. The goal of the anti-poverty policy is therefore to reduce the extent of poverty so defined as much as possible.

This paradigm has generated a lot of work over the last thirty years. At present, it may be considered as almost fully mastered. It proved to be extremely useful, sometimes indispensable, in numerous applications. Yet, as it was being built and improved on, limitations of the basic concepts behind the paradigm were noticed. Paradoxically, now that this research program is technically close to completion, scholars as well as policymakers acknowledge that it does not permit a satisfactory analysis of all relevant issues related to poverty and inequality.

The principal critique of the poverty income paradigm comes from social justice theory. It calls into question the use of current income or expenditure as the only basis to define poverty. Income or expenditure may be seen as resulting from decisions that ultimately depend on the preferences of an individual as well as from factors beyond their control. Poverty and inequality should preferably be defined on the basis of the latter and not, for instance, on the preferences of a person regarding work or leisure. In the words of Amartya Sen, what matters is the set of "capabilities" or the "choice set" an individual faces, not the choice he or she actually makes. Likewise, some authors of the inequality literature consider it more appropriate to define inequality on the basis of the "opportunities" open to people rather than the results they obtain (Roemer, 1998). An important difference in the income poverty paradigm is that capabilities or opportunities must be measured in several dimensions, some of which may differ fundamentally from traditional income or expenditure concepts: educational achievements, inherited financial wealth, health status, or power to affect political decisions on collective goods. A second limitation and illustration of this point is found in several developed countries that successfully reduced income poverty but could not prevent the existence of a strong feeling of "social exclusion" in some parts of their population.

The development of a broad redistribution and social insurance system aimed at reducing inequality or "relative" income poverty—that is defined by a poverty line dependent on the overall mean income of the population—may thus not be enough to eradicate social and economic hindrances.

Although the concept of social exclusion is far from precise,[1] it means that eradicating poverty simply through income redistribution policy may not be enough to eliminate the "feeling" of poverty. To some extent, income transfers may even worsen the situation as they may stigmatize their beneficiaries. In short, reducing income poverty is certainly desirable but it may fail to eliminate a feeling of social deprivation that may be rooted in deeper causes.

These arguments are normative or sociological. The income poverty paradigm also exhibits weaknesses of a positive nature. The following would seem to apply more to developing countries but they also have some relevance for developed countries. First, if poverty is defined with respect to an "absolute" poverty line that does not change over time, then it is often held that economic growth probably is the most effective cure to poverty.[2] There is truth to this argument but the recent literature on growth and inequality—as summarized in Aghion et al. (1999)—also suggests various channels through which "relative poverty" or inequality may negatively affect growth. Owing to these channels of relative poverty, redistribution may be as effective as growth per se in reducing absolute poverty.

However, the problem is that the kind of redistribution considered in this literature is not as concerned with current income or expenditure as with tangible assets such as land or wealth or intangible ones like education or democracy. In this case as well, the income poverty paradigm may not allow dealing fully satisfactorily with this type of anti-poverty or redistribution policy. The way redistribution is analyzed in developing countries provides an example of this unsatisfactory existing condition. It is generally accepted in the literature that governments in these countries redistribute mostly through social public expenditures, i.e., spending essentially on education and health. Following the income poverty paradigm, it is then normal to accept that this spending is strictly equivalent to transferring current income to the beneficiaries. But spending on the education of children is not commensurate with the income that the family may rely on. Education and health are above all assets, hopefully allowing children to be more productive and possibly more "socially included" in the future. Evaluating this kind of policy thus requires taking an intergenerational perspective somewhat distant from the income poverty paradigm.

All these critiques of the income poverty paradigm revolve around the same basic idea. The analysis of poverty and inequality should not bear so much on income or expenditure per se but on those multiple attributes, mostly assets of different kinds that determine it.and are beyond the control of individuals. The focus should thus move from *income* to *endowment*. Several questions then arise about the status of the income poverty paradigm. In particular, why was it not progressively extended to another, more general paradigm, based on a broader concept, viz. "poverty of opportunities," "poverty of endowments," or "social inclusion"?

The answer to these questions is not surprising. The old income poverty paradigm is relatively easy to understand and implement both from an analytical and a policy-making point of view. On the other hand, a poverty paradigm based on opportunities or endowments is conceptually complex. There may be multiple definitions of who is poor, not all of them being unambiguous, and quantifying them is difficult, if not impossible. Understandably, policies would be difficult to evaluate in such an extended framework.

With this background, the key challenge in the field of poverty analysis is clear. It consists of building a set of instruments, starting with a satisfactory definition of poverty, that would meet part or all of the critiques of the dominant paradigm described above, *while retaining at least part of its "operationality."* Current economic analysis of poverty clearly falls short of this objective. Actually, the situation resembles the proverbial person looking for her keys under a lamppost because it is too dark where she actually lost them. Helping her requires not searching with her under the lamppost, but bringing some light in dark spots around it. The poverty income paradigm is presently often used in situations calling for alternative definitions of poverty, essentially because instruments to handle these definitions are not available. The challenge is to create those instruments, rather than trying to make the initial paradigm artificially fit a different conceptual basis.

This chapter reviews the scenarios where the income poverty paradigm appears most ill-adapted and analyzes the difficulties in designing instruments that could fit modified poverty concepts while retaining a quantitative or policy-oriented framework. It is hoped that this exploration will be useful to identify directions for a better understanding and handling of poverty issues.

The discussion is organized as follows. The first section, "The Income Poverty Paradigm: A Brief Review," provides a background for the analysis included in the rest of the paper by briefly summarizing the income poverty paradigm, its achievements and its major uses. The second section, "On the Need to Go Beyond the Income Poverty Paradigm," includes a formal identification of the reasons behind the unsatisfactory nature of the paradigm and points towards various research directions for improvement of the same. Four salient issues are then dealt with in some detail in the third section, "Problems in Expanding the Income Poverty Paradigm." These issues are (1) the multidimensionality of poverty and its implications for poverty measurement, (2) the generic difficulty of defining or observing endowments or opportunities, (3) specific issues in dealing with poverty and inequality in educational endowments, and (4) the generalization of the optimal redistribution framework to include in it both endowments and current income.

A few caveats should be noted before proceeding with this exercise. This chapter, having been written by an economist, bears the distinct mark of economics, although it deals with issues that go much beyond the realm of economics and touches on philosophy, anthropology and sociology. This however is not necessarily a bias. It is simply like looking at these issues in a particular perspective and emphasizing some aspects over others. Next, the chapter deals more with poverty than with inequality, although we will see that both issues are closely linked to each other. Dealing successively with poverty and inequality would have led to many repetitions, whereas dealing simultaneously with both poverty and inequality would have made the discussion somewhat confusing. A third point to note is that poverty, and possibly, inequality will sometimes be discussed with clear reference to the case of developing countries. This is partly because of the abundance of literature on (absolute) poverty in developing countries, but also because of my current interest.

THE INCOME POVERTY PARADIGM: A BRIEF REVIEW

The objective of this section is not to give an extensive account of the economics of income (expenditure) poverty from the definition of poverty to its measurement and to policies for reducing it. Instead, we will present the main assumptions, analytical achievements and policy implications of that stream of the literature.[3] Such an objective implies a largely oversimplified view, but may be sufficient for the understanding of developments in the rest of this chapter.

The starting point is our assumption that differences in individual welfare or standard of living within a population may be summarized by differences in income or consumption expenditures. Implicitly, this assumption implies that all individuals transform income into welfare in the same way. Differences in the set of prices they face and differences in the composition of households they belong to may be taken into account through deflating total income or expenditure by the appropriate price index and equivalence scale. With this exception, all individuals, or households depending on the unit of analysis, are assumed to be identical.

Poor people are defined by the condition that, after the correction described above, their income falls short of some arbitrarily predetermined "poverty line." This limit may be defined in *absolute* terms, as the US\$1 or US\$2 a day per person minimum used by several international organizations. It may also be defined in *relative* terms as some percentage of the median or the mean income of the whole population.

Various considerations may be behind an absolute poverty line, like the minimum cost of the diet ensuring the intake of calories and other nutrients necessary for survival, the corresponding amount being corrected by some coefficient representing the weight of non-food components of consumption.[4] Things are more arbitrary in the case of a relative line. This arbitrariness or the looseness of the justification of the poverty line implies some fuzziness in that concept. With "poor" being defined, the issue is then to measure the extent of poverty within the population, an operation that Sen (1976) called "aggregation." A simple aggregate measure of poverty, probably the most widely used, is "headcount," which is simply the proportion of people below the poverty line. The inadequacy of this measure is that it does not take into account the extent of poverty, as measured by the shortfall of actual income over the poverty line. The "poverty gap" intends to remedy this problem. It is defined as the product of the headcount and the average shortfall among the poor. It measures the cost per person to fully eradicate poverty by bringing all the poor up to the poverty line. Although more precise than the headcount, this measure does not take into account the distribution of income among the poor or, in other words, individual differences in the extent of poverty. Sen (1976) launched an important literature by proposing an index with that property. A simpler, but possibly more restrictive way of introducing that sensitivity is to define the "welfare cost" of poverty as some increasing and convex function of the poverty shortfall for each individual—using same function for everybody. Then, a poverty measure may be defined as the product of the headcount and the average welfare cost among the poor. This measure defines a kind of total "intensity" of poverty where intensity is in some sense defined by the function that maps the shortfall into the welfare cost. All of these poverty measures have the property that redistributing income among the poor from the least poor to the poorest reduces the poverty measure, even though it leaves the head count or the poverty gap unchanged.

The problems of using a single poverty measure, or several, to compare two distributions of income—across two countries, in the same country at two points of time, or under two different policy scenarios—are well known. It may be the case that distribution A appears to have more poverty than distribution B with poverty measure P1 but with less poverty with poverty measure P2. Poverty dominance is a simple solution in this case, although it leads to a partial rather than complete ordering of distributions. A simple definition of dominance (1st order) is as follows: distribution A is said to unambiguously exhibit less poverty than distribution B if and only if the total intensity of poverty is less in A than in B for all increasing functions that map the poverty shortfall into welfare cost. A very interesting equivalence result is that the poverty head count must be less with A than with B *for all possible poverty lines* below the one that was arbitrarily selected—for example, all possible poverty lines below $2 a day. A more restrictive dominance condition (2nd order) is obtained when it is requested that the function mapping poverty shortfall into welfare cost be increasing and convex—the marginal welfare cost of $1 less of income increases with the extent of poverty. Then, the same equivalence result holds after replacing the poverty headcount by the poverty gap.[5]

The reason why this result is interesting is that it gives some prominence to the simplest poverty measures, the head count and the poverty gap, and to the fuzziness of the poverty line. Roughly speaking, dominance is obtained under the following intuitive argument. "The poverty line is set at *L* but, actually this must be taken as an upper limit. Practically, it is thus desirable to compare poverty in *A* and in *B* for all poverty lines below *L*. If it found to be less in *A* for all poverty lines then it may be concluded unambiguously that there is less poverty in *A* than in *B*."

These concepts lead to simple policy applications. Poverty minimization seems to be a natural objective for a government with anti-poverty preferences. If a government has decided on normative grounds to use some specific poverty measure, it may be looking for the optimal policy that will minimize that specific measure under some constraints defined by the redistribution instruments at its disposal. Say that the government observes incomes and is able to redistribute a given budget on the basis of pre-transfer incomes. The optimal policy then consists of transferring income from the non-poor to the poor. Depending on which inequality measure is chosen, the latter may be the richest or the poorest of the poor.[6] Many other situations are possible. For instance, if the government is unable to precisely target the poor, it must then use some kind of geographic targeting. Here again simple allocation rules of a budget may be derived under the condition that all individuals in a region benefit equally, or in the same proportion of their initial income of the government transfer.[7]

A more complex situation arises when pre-transfer incomes depend on the very possibility of receiving a transfer. For instance, individuals who know they will receive some transfer from the government if their income falls short of some limit, may act in a way—work less or report less—that their pre-transfer income does fall below that limit. If the redistribution authority is familiar with this behavior, its objective becomes that of minimizing a specific poverty measure under both a budget constraint and this endogenous response of potential beneficiaries. Mirrlees (1971) in his seminal paper first studied the general problem of maximizing social welfare under these constraints. An application of the same framework to poverty was proposed by Kanbur, Keen, and Tuomala (1994).

A host of other policy applications of this basic one-dimension static poverty income framework could be cited, for instance all empirical analyses of redistribution that seek to find out the effect of a specific policy on poverty. Equipped with a simple definition of poverty—income or consumption expenditure per capita below some limit—aggregate measures of poverty, or possibly a simple ordering of distributions, and micro- or macro-economic models that describe reactions to policy changes, it is conceptually simple, although often analytically intricate, to evaluate the effect of these policies on poverty. It is in that sense that this chapter refers to an "income poverty paradigm," that is a set of analytical instruments linked to a common concept or a common assumption. It took twenty years to go from the recognition of (and a first solution to) the problem of (income) poverty measurement (Sen 1976) to dominance analysis and the full integration of income poverty measures into economic analysis. The paradigm is probably not complete yet. There are very few optimization results using the dominance concept available. Yet, research on this paradigm seems advanced, and from some points of view, close to completion.

ON THE NEED TO GO BEYOND THE INCOME POVERTY PARADIGM

It is becoming increasingly evident that the applications of the income poverty paradigm are limited to a subset of poverty issues. Limitations of this paradigm have long been stressed, in particular by Sen ever since his 1980 piece on the "equality of what." [8] In recent times, there has been widespread recognition of these limitations and of the relative lack of instruments that would actually permit dealing efficiently with them. That these limitations may be of a positive as well as a normative kind is also something that became evident only recently.

Starting with normative arguments, the main critiques of the income poverty paradigm may be formulated as follows. Let Q be the multiple determinants of individual welfare. [9] These determinants include income or consumption expenditure as one component, health conditions, public goods consumed, and so on. The components of vector Q are considered as the outcomes of a complex process through which an individual relates to the economy and the rest of society. Denote that dependency by:

$$Q = F(A; Z; P) \tag{1}$$

where $F(\ )$ is a (vector) function the arguments of which are (1) the endowments or productive assets (A) of the individual being considered, that is, wealth, education, initial health, etc ; (2) a set of parameters (Z) conditioning the individual's choices and imposed on him or her by society, for example, the price of goods, access to some specific markets (credit, labor) or public goods, the kind of social institutions the individual lives in, etc; (3) his or her preferences (P).

In very general terms, welfare may be defined as a function

$$W = G(Q)$$

where W may be a scalar index, or possibly a vector of such indices. In such a general framework, poverty income may be seen as reducing the vector of outcomes to a single component, for example, real income or expenditures, and $G(\ )$ to some transformation of that component. A first generalization of that paradigm would thus consist of enriching this representation of outcomes so as to include other determinants of welfare in it. This would mean switching from a *one-dimensional* view of welfare focused on income to a *multidimensional* view including other welfare attributes.

A more fundamental question is whether interpersonal comparisons should be based on the vector of outcomes, Q, as with the welfare function $G(Q)$ or on some other concept. Indeed, it is easy to imagine cases where evaluating equity or poverty on the basis of the outcome vector, Q, or some component of it, may be quite misleading. Consider the case where a person who works only a few hours a week is compared to a full-time worker. On the basis of the income component of Q, the first person may be much poorer than the second. But the opposite might well hold if the comparison were made on the basis of equal working time. If the observed difference in income only reflect differences in individual preferences for work, it is irrelevant from a social point of view. The first person is poorer than the second one because she decided to work less or because the second one chose to work more. This example suggests the following principle. If individual preferences, P, are assumed to be under the full responsibility of individuals then social justice requires evaluating poverty, or more generally equity, independently of them. Conceptually, this may be done by considering the set K of outcomes Q that is generated when preferences in (1) are allowed to vary but A and Z are kept constant. This set may be formally represented by:

$$K = F^\circ(A; Z; .) \tag{2}$$

It represents the set of possible outcomes for an individual with the endowment vector A and facing an environment Z. The same set is referred to as the set of "capabilities" by Sen and the set of "opportunities" by other writers.[10] What is important is that interpersonal comparisons should ultimately be based on the size and the shape of this set, or equivalently in terms of A and Z, rather than in terms of Q. By focusing on multiple outcomes or even on a single outcome, the income poverty paradigm leads to some confusion. Outcome *determinants beyond the control of individuals*, rather than outcomes per se should be the basis for defining poverty or for measuring inequality. In other words, education, inherited wealth, or access to specific markets or public goods, rather than observed current income, should be the main ingredients of poverty and inequality analysis. The emphasis recently placed on various developed countries on the concept of social exclusion, as opposed to or independent of poverty, illustrates the distinction and also exhibits its relevance from a sociological perspective.

Many developed countries are equipped with a redistribution system such that no individual can fall below some poverty line. Thus, even if an individual is not working and cannot obtain any income, the state transfers enough so as to keep him or her over the poverty line. There is almost no income poverty in such societies. Yet, a feeling of social exclusion is often reported among the beneficiaries of minimum income guarantee programs.

A possible explanation of this apparent paradox is that the lack of access to the labor market is in itself the source of social injustice and social exclusion, independent of income. Thus, the safety net solves only part of the problem of long-run unemployment. It eradicates poverty in the sense of the welfare function $G(\ )$ above, but it does not correct the disparities in the opportunity sets K that come from unequal access to the labor market in the population. Doing so would require modifying that component of Z that stands for labor market access in the case of pure discrimination or improving the endowments A of those individuals whose low productivity is the cause of their exclusion from the labor market. This situation is different from the one considered above where low income is the result of personal preferences being biased toward leisure. That argument may be generalized to other markets like the credit market or even to the market for certain goods.[11] In all cases, the difficulty of identifying the causes of the exclusion must be stressed. In the labor market, social justice requires distinguishing whether unemployment is voluntary, due to some preference for leisure, or involuntary, and thus due to low endowments, A, or access restrictions in Z. Practically, this distinction is not clear, as will be seen below. The switch of emphasis from outcome variables Q to outcome determinants A and Z, or from income to endowments and other welfare determinants was justified in the preceding argument on purely normative grounds. It may also be justified on positive grounds. The recent literature on growth, efficiency, and inequality provides a good illustration of this point. It was seen in the previous section that the redistribution of current income may entail a loss of economic efficiency. This loss would probably be the case for the redistribution of wealth and other economic endowments, if such a direct redistribution were possible. There are several reasons to believe that such redistribution could also generate efficiency gains. If redistribution caused gains, then endowment poverty or inequality would in fact emerge as a more relevant concept than income poverty. An important mechanism through which a more equal distribution of wealth may enhance economic efficiency goes through the credit market. Imperfections in that market often prevent poor people from borrowing and undertaking investment projects that may well have an expected return much higher than in the rest of the economy. If it were possible to redistribute some wealth to the poor, it would give them the collateral they lacked for accessing the credit market, thereby enhancing economic efficiency and growth.

A second example of the importance of the distribution of wealth for economic efficiency is provided by the intensity of income redistribution. In societies where redistribution is decided through voting it may be shown that redistribution, and the inefficiency accompanying it, will be the strongest, the more distant the economic endowments—including human capital—of the decisive voter is from the mean. Gaining in efficiency and accelerating growth may thus be obtained by redistributing endowments and wealth—but not current income—because this practice is known to generate inefficiency. Wealth, rather than income poverty or inequality, is therefore what really matters.

Endowment redistribution is not easy, so equalizing the distribution of wealth is to be sought through policies that bias asset accumulation in favor of the poor. These policies might involve some redistribution of current income, despite the efficiency loss it may produce, if it is thought that this redistribution will indeed induce a more equal distribution of endowments in the medium or long run. Also, targeting the accumulation of human capital, infrastructure, or market reforms more systematically in favor of the poor may more directly achieve redistribution of assets.

The evaluation of redistribution policies based on social public spending channels provides yet another example of the application of the income poverty paradigm and of the need to go beyond it. Consider the case of a tax levied on the rich, or possibly the whole population to finance the accumulation of an asset, e.g., education, among the poor. Following the income poverty paradigm, it is customary in tax-benefit "incidence analysis" to lump all these transfers together as if they were all income. For instance, the public cost of education is simply divided among beneficiaries, that is households with children in school, and the corresponding amount is considered as an implicit cash transfer to these households.[12] Then, income poverty or inequality may be re-evaluated accounting for these positive transfers as well as the taxes levied to finance them. The contribution of public spending towards poverty and inequality reduction can thus be easily computed.

This type of calculation is misleading because it confuses the children who are the true beneficiaries of educational spending as well as their households. It makes sense only under very special assumptions, namely, the case of parents who would increase their own consumption by forecasting the future income gains that more spending in public education would bring to their children. If parents are not altruistic or if they are liquidity constrained, the benefits of public educational spending accrue only to children when they enter the labor force.[13]. Their distributional effect should be evaluated applying equation (1) above to the cohort of children once they become adults. As their preferences are not known, however, the inequality or poverty concept to be used should in effect be close to the capability or opportunity set K in equation (2), which precisely abstracts from these preferences. Interestingly enough, one is thus brought back to the social justice critique of the income poverty paradigm but *from within this paradigm itself*. Income poverty or inequality is still the concept being used but the uncertainty on the future preferences of the individuals being considered forces concentration on endowment poverty or inequality.[14]

In sum, both normative and positive reasons suggest that the income poverty paradigm may sometimes be of limited interest when analyzing poverty and inequality policy issues. These limitations are of a diverse nature, and do not imply that the paradigm is unhelpful. They point to necessary additions to this paradigm instead of its rejection. The social justice arguments suggesting that capabilities and opportunities, rather than income per se, should be taken as the focus of the analysis are well founded and may be justified on grounds other than social justice. Yet, this justification does not necessarily make the income poverty paradigm irrelevant. First, an alternative approach is called for only insofar as income and capabilities or opportunities are sufficiently uncorrelated—leaving aside the case where income itself is not observed as in the example of future inequality in a cohort of children. This ultimately is an empirical issue. Second, the arguments which suggest focusing on the distribution and redistribution of assets or endowments—social exclusion, imperfect credit markets, endogeneity of income redistribution—do not imply that income should be excluded from the analysis. As redistributing assets and endowments is difficult without some redistribution of current income, there should be some complementarity between the two approaches. This balance suggests that an extension of the poverty paradigm instead of its abandonment is the need of the hour. Some of the issues related to such an extension are now discussed.

PROBLEMS IN EXPANDING THE INCOME POVERTY PARADIGM

The previous section has shown that despite its simplicity and practicality, the income poverty paradigm in its existing form is not sufficient to deal with several important issues appearing in a more general definition or a more general analysis of poverty and inequality. This section focuses on issues encountered in trying to extend the paradigm to overcome these weaknesses. Among the various points discussed in the previous section, the following are analyzed in more detail: (1) handling the multidimensionality of poverty; (2) the difficulty of identifying the role of endowments and preferences;

(3) specific issues linked to human capital endowment; and (4) the integration of asset accumulation in an optimal redistribution framework.

Measuring Multidimensional Poverty

The need for a multidimensional approach to poverty and inequality analysis comes directly from the social justice critique of the income poverty paradigm. A vector of attributes describes the set of opportunities or capabilities that should be substituted to the income concept. These are the various types of assets and endowments, including access to certain markets or goods—that is, A and Z above. Let $X = (A, Z)$ denote this vector.

A first approach towards describing poverty or inequality in the space of the X vector is to define an aggregator scalar function, $V(\ )$, that permits comparing individuals with different X vectors. Inequality within a population may then be defined on the basis of that function, and poverty may be defined by the condition that its value, assuming it may be given some meaningful interpretation, falls short of some threshold. Clearly, everything is then as if some "hyper-income" concept, $Q^* = V(X)$, had been defined and inequality and poverty analysis were conducted in terms of this Q^* magnitude. Most of the income poverty paradigm may then be applied to Q^*. In effect, this one-dimensional aggregator function simply bypasses the original multidimensionality.

Such an approach would certainly lead to an evaluation of poverty and inequality different from what the same type of analysis would yield if it were applied to the money income component of observed outcomes, Q. The danger, however, is the absence of a consensus on what the aggregator function $V(\ )$ should be, or in the arbitrariness of a particular choice about the way of aggregating education, inherited wealth, health status, access to the credit market, and so on, into a single index. The function $V(\ )$ therefore must clearly be related to the definition of the opportunity set, $K=F°(A, Z, .\ )$. In effect, it should be a specific generic point of the frontier of that set.[15] As such, it should include some features of the "production function" implicit in $F(A; Z; P)$ that describes how endowments, market access, and variables under individual control are transformed into the outcome variables Q. The problem is that these functions are very imperfectly observed. Because of this imperfect observation, it is thus very unlikely that a consensus may be established on the aggregator function, $V(\ )$.

A second approach that generalizes the notions of dominance or poverty orderings in the income poverty paradigm consists of considering not a single function $V(\ )$ but a set of such functions. For instance, one could use linear functions and allow the weight of the various arguments of $V(\ )$ to vary within some given range.[16] It is not difficult to show that, in this case, a distribution of the vector X within the population unambiguously leads to less (multidimensional) poverty if and only if there is less poverty for each component of the vector X, considered independently of each other, and with all possible poverty lines below some threshold.

In this case, multidimensional poverty measurement reduces to one-dimensional poverty measures in each dimension that define the set of opportunities or capabilities. Consider the case where the set of opportunities has two dimensions, education and inherited wealth. Suppose then that one wants to compare two policies that modify the distribution of these two characteristics within the population. According to the criterion, one will conclude that there is less poverty overall with the first policy if it leads to less poverty in inherited wealth on the one hand and less poverty in education on the other.[17] "Less poverty" in this statement must be understood in the sense of dominance. In other words, there must be a smaller number of poor in each dimension for all poverty lines defined within some pre-specified range.

More truly multidimensional criteria may be obtained in the preceding framework by assuming some complementarity or some substitutability among the various arguments of the $V(\ )$ function. We have (Atkinson and Bourguignon 1982) generalized the inequality dominance criterion mentioned above with income as a single variable to the multidimensional case by making assumptions successively on the sign of the second, third, and even fourth cross-derivatives of $V(\ )$. These criteria are more restrictive than the preceding one, which is dominance on each dimension. But, of course, the problem is whether it is possible to get some consensus on the sign of the cross-derivatives of $V(\ )$.

A third approach to multidimensional poverty is to specify a poverty line on each dimension of vector X. This approach is in line with the suggestion of considering all dimensions independently of each other and with their own poverty line. It is also much closer to the concept of a minimum set of opportunities or capabilities or of minimum rights. To "function" optimally any individual needs to have a minimum of each component of X, a minimum educational level, minimum health condition, and so on. A natural definition of poverty is then to consider as poor all individuals who are poor according to at least one component of X. Such a definition implicitly assumes some limited substitutability among the components of X because an individual will remain poor if one of his or her endowments falls short of the poverty line irrespective of the size of the other components. It is much more difficult to define the intensity of poverty in such a situation. The short-falls observed along the various dimensions need to be combined into an overall shortfall. It may be assumed that an individual with positive short-falls in the first and the second endowment is poorer than somebody with the same shortfall in the first endowment and no shortfalls in all the other endowments. This assumption does not permit going very far. In Bourgui-gnon and Chakravarty (2003) we propose a set of multidimensional poverty measures that parameterizes the shortfalls along the various dimensions in a simple way and combines them into an overall poverty intensity. However, it is not clear if it would be easier to obtain a consensus on the value of these parameters than on the function $V(\ )$. In a subsequent paper, we derive dom-inance criteria under the sole assumption of complementarity or substi-tutability of the shortfalls in the various endowments.[18] These criteria gen-eralize income poverty dominance: there is less poverty in distribution A than in distribution B if there are less poor—in the multidimensional sense— for all combinations of poverty lines below the actual poverty lines in each dimension. This criterion nests the one-dimensional dominance criteria. In other words, multidimensional poverty dominance requires dominance in each dimension but the converse is not true.

Rather than defining a poverty line in each dimension irrespective of what the other dimensions are, it is also possible to have poverty lines de-fined conditionally on other dimensions. For instance, if the vector X has two dimensions, wealth and education, one could define a wealth poverty line conditionally on the level of education of an individual and an education poverty line conditional to his or her wealth. This definition requires speci-fying a priori the way in which the poverty line in one dimension depends on the other dimension. Once these functions have been chosen, poverty dom-inance criteria of the same type as the one discussed above can be defined. These criteria are formally derived in Duclos, Sahn, and Younger (2001).

As with income poverty or inequality, the criteria just reviewed lead to a partial ordering of various multidimensional distributions of endowments in the population. The problem is to identify the partialness of this ordering and the extent to which the preceding criteria may permit evaluating multidimensional trade-offs.

It is not difficult to get the intuition of these criteria and the restrictions necessary to deal unambiguously with trade-offs. Coming back to the wealth and education example, consider a wealth redistribution policy that would unambiguously reduce (one-dimensional) wealth poverty for all groups of individuals with the same education. Such a policy would clearly reduce poverty in a multidimensional sense. Second, consider a policy that unambiguously reduces wealth poverty only for certain educational levels. Whether this policy reduces overall poverty will now clearly depend on how wealth and education are supposed to combine to define overall poverty, that is, on whether less wealth poverty at low educational level does or does not compensate more poverty at a higher educational level. This is where the issue of whether wealth and education are complements or substitutes comes in. Overall dominance criteria alluded to above are based on this kind of argument. How often they permit an unambiguous ranking of policies ultimately depends on the policies being evaluated and is an empirical issue. Situations where policy rankings are ambiguous are easy to imagine, and they cover a wide spectrum. Consider the case where the distribution of wealth is modified to unambiguously reduce wealth poverty for all educational levels. Now compare this wealth redistribution policy to the reciprocal educational policy that would unambiguously reduce education poverty for all possible levels of wealth. Comparing those two policies requires making precise assumptions either on the first derivatives of the aggregator function, $V(\ )$, or on the derivatives of the overall intensity of multidimensional poverty with respect to wealth and education. In the case where these functions are linear, this indeed requires choosing the weight of the two dimensions in the aggregator function or the overall intensity of poverty. A consensus may well exist on the sign of these derivatives and on that of the cross-derivatives. It is more challenging to reach a consensus on the relative size of these derivatives. In other words, it seems unlikely that the comparison criteria discussed above could permit choosing between a policy that would reduce multidimensional poverty by redistributing wealth—possibly conditionally on education—and a policy that would change the distribution of education. Yet, this is the kind of question policymakers facing the issue of the multidimensionality of poverty would like to answer, although perhaps not in such a crude form.

Before concluding the discussion on these issues, it is worth stressing that the issue of defining and measuring multidimensional poverty does not arise only when dealing with the set of capabilities and opportunities. They are also present when poverty is defined on the vector of individual outcomes, Q. As a matter of fact, the best illustration of the need for a multidimensional approach to poverty analysis is provided by such an example.[19]. In the introduction to this book, Kanbur mentions the problem that arises when life duration is introduced into income poverty measurement. If the poorest part of the population is dying prematurely, income poverty measured within cohorts of individuals would be decreasing with time. There clearly is something alarming in such a result. But, of course, things are totally different if poverty is defined as a multidimensional concept in the space of (average lifetime) income and life expectancy. In such a framework, increasing the proportion of people with a low life expectancy cannot unambiguously reduce poverty, as would be the case with one-dimensional income poverty. This example shows that even simple extensions of the income poverty paradigm lead quite directly to the issue of multidimensionality and the difficulty of satisfactorily dealing with it.

The dominance of the income poverty paradigm in the theoretical and applied literature may explain why experience with criteria adapted to a multidimensional concept of poverty is presently limited.[20] Acquiring such an experience probably is the best way for testing and improving comparison criteria to be used in analyzing poverty and inequality in the space of outcomes, opportunities, or capabilities.

The Empirical Difficulty of Distinguishing Opportunities and Preferences

Social exclusion could reveal a lack of opportunities and should be considered independently of income poverty. The typical example is that of an individual who, for some reason, is unemployed but benefits from an income safety net that prevents him or her to fall below the poverty line. This person is not (income) poor but may feel socially excluded if unemployed involuntarily.

The important issue that this example raises is that of distinguishing between voluntary and involuntary unemployment. Is unemployment due to a lack of opportunities, that is, the lack of access to the labor market, or to individual preferences? In the general discussion, it was assumed that the vector Z of access to markets and some public goods was readily observable. The fact that the voluntary or involuntary nature of unemployment is not observed means that the components of Z may not be perfectly known, and therefore that the set of capabilities may be very ambiguously defined.

Consider a country where there exists both a minimum income scheme for all people whose resources fall below that minimum and a minimum wage rate, $w°$, which must be paid to all employed people. Consider, then, an individual who is unemployed and benefits from the minimum income scheme. The issue is whether this individual is voluntarily unemployed and would get back to work if the minimum income scheme were less generous, or whether he or she is simply unemployable because his or her productivity falls short of the minimum wage, $w°$. The presumption that voluntary unemployment was frequent among the long-run unemployed is what justified the creation of back to work incentive programs like the EITC system in the United States and several other countries.[21]

Knowing the frequency of voluntarily and involuntarily unemployed among the long-run unemployed requires having some information on the actual productivity, w, of individuals and on their preference for leisure, as formally summarized by their reservation wage, w^*. Two cases are to be considered. First, if the reservation wage of an unemployed individual is below the minimum wage, then unemployment is de facto involuntarily. Indeed, if the person's productivity were above the minimum wage, he or she would be hired by an employer and would accept a job at a wage above the reservation wage. Second, if the reservation wage is above the minimum wage, then two situations may arise. Unemployment is voluntary if productivity is below the minimum wage. It is involuntary in the opposite case. In short, unemployment is voluntary only in the case where:

$$w° < w < w^*$$

It is involuntary—or both[22]—in all other situations. Practically, w^*, which summarizes the preferences of an individual for leisure—or more exactly non-market time—is never directly observed and w is observed only for those individuals who are employed. Under these conditions, it is practically impossible to observe whether an individual is long run unemployed because of lack of opportunities or preferences. The best econometrics can do is to give some probability of the two states, under some necessarily arbitrary assumptions about the statistical distribution of w and w^*.

This ambiguity arises in more general situations. In fact, any rationing on the labor market, due to the presence of some efficiency wage—as often hypothesized for the formal labor market of developing countries for instance—leads to the situation just described. But it also applies to other markets. In the credit market, the problem is to know whether an individual who is not observed as a borrower did not wish to borrow or was prevented to do so through some kind of rationing. The same can be said of the access to public goods in presence of cost recovery schemes. Attempts at asking direct questions about rationing situations are sometimes made through surveys. This is certainly useful but not very much use is presently made of that kind of information. These simple examples show that moving from the space of outcomes, Q, to that of capabilities and opportunities is not an easy thing. Observation restrictions may prevent identifying the role of endowments and that of preferences in producing a specific vector of outcomes. Of course, this problem comes on top of whether preferences are truly under individuals' control or whether they are endogenous. In the preceding case, for instance, one may wonder whether the reservation wage, w^*, is not affected by the time an individual spent on unemployment benefits.

In view of that ambiguity, the issue arises of whether the vector Z of access to markets and public goods should be defined in a stochastic way. This would add a new dimension to poverty measurement and anti-poverty analysis, which as yet remains to be undertaken.[23] Extending poverty measurement and analysis to take into account the uncertainty about some basic poverty determinant is something that remains to be done.

Dealing with Human Capital

Several reasons have been mentioned above for considering poverty and inequality independently for each dimension in the space of endowments. In particular, it was seen that multidimensional dominance of a vector's distribution of endowments over another generally implying the dominance of marginal distributions for each endowment. It was also seen that redistributing from the rich to the poor under the form of better education for the children of the poor should logically be evaluated by considering the inequality of the educational endowment this implies for children when they become adults. Paradoxically, studying the inequality of the educational endowment distribution or analyzing "educational poverty" is infrequently undertaken in economic analysis. The reason is probably that transposing directly the income poverty paradigm to education is not obvious. Thomas et al. (2001) analyze in detail the evolution of the distribution of education in a large number of countries over the last three decades or so. Despite its relevance and originality, however, their study illustrates that extending standard tools of income poverty and inequality measurement to an endowment like human capital raises several difficulties. Some of these difficulties are discussed below.

The first difficulty is the unit of measurement. Consider the case where human capital is reduced to formal education. What unit should be used here? The number of years of schooling, as used in Thomas et al. (2001)? Or should these years be weighed by some coefficient so as to represent the social value of education or its income generation potential? One could use the estimated marginal returns to successive years of schooling obtained in a conventional econometric earning equation. As these weights are not constant, evaluating inequality or poverty using the number of years of schooling or the number of *weighted years* would clearly lead to different results. One could also use alternative sets of weights and then simply order educational distributions rather than define specific poverty or inequality measures.

A second difficulty is, of course, that the human capital endowment can hardly be reduced to formal education. This is true even when one is willing to restrict this concept to what may be transmitted from parents to children, thus disregarding innate differences and the capital that may be voluntarily acquired by individuals later in life. In particular, informal human capital transmitted by parents in addition to formal schooling is unobservable. But, here again, a detour through earnings equation permits obtaining indirect estimates. This method requires introducing the characteristics of parents among the earning determinants of an individual. This practice has already a long tradition in economics starting with Bowles (1972) or Griliches and Mason (1972). Formally, the idea is to estimate an earning equation in a cross-section of individuals with the following specification:

Earning rate = a * Schooling level + b * Parents' education and other
characteristics + c * age + . . . + residual term standing
for all unobserved determinants

where a, b, and c are coefficients, or vectors of coefficients. The sum of the first two sets of terms in the right-hand side of this equation yield an estimate of inherited human capital. This estimate is commensurate with income and lends itself to standard treatment in terms of poverty and inequality measurement.[24]

It is interesting that this simple extension of the definition of the human capital endowment actually establishes a bridge between poverty and inequality analysis and the literature on intergenerational income and educational mobility.[25] In this respect, it may be noted that the schooling variable in the earlier equation may itself be related to parents' characteristics and thus may be decomposed into inherited determinants and a residual term standing for unobserved determinants of schooling achievements. With such a model, intergenerational transmission mechanisms that have been the subject of intense independent scrutiny in the sociological literature find themselves integrated into a common quantitative framework aimed at analyzing poverty and inequality of the human capital endowment.

One limitation of this framework is the incomplete description of human capital endowment. The residual term in the earlier earnings equation includes unobserved components of an individual's human capital endowment, as well as the effect of his or her preferences or random events. The same impossibility of distinguishing between the effect of opportunities or sheer luck and preferences stressed above in connection with the accessibility to the formal labor market is also present here. In effect, the earnings equation, possibly coupled with an equation that explains schooling achievements, only permits a partial analysis of inequality in human capital endowment, restricted to the influence of *observed* parents' characteristics in earnings and schooling achievements. Whether it may be considered as yielding a lower bound of estimated poverty or inequality is open to discussion.[26] The above discussion is essentially inspired by the objective of analyzing poverty and inequality in terms of the human capital endowment. This objective requires aggregating various elements together to quantify that endowment. But one may question the relevance of the weights used in this summation, or even consider that the human capital endowment is itself multidimensional with schooling achievements as one dimension, parents' education as another, and parents' financial wealth still another. Adopting such an approach implies studying these various dimensions independently of each other as well as jointly through their mutual correlation. Much of the literature on intergenerational mobility—of education, occupation or income—may be considered as explorations of these various dimensions. As such, they yield very valuable information. For instance, an increase in educational mobility, as measured by the elasticity of schooling with respect to the schooling of parents, seems to imply *some* equalizing of the human capital endowment in the youngest generation. Whether this is quantitatively important or not is another story. For example, mobility may be taking place in a range of educational levels with very limited marginal returns on the labor market and may therefore be of little interest.

Part of the challenge in evaluating poverty and inequality in the human capital endowment dimension consists of integrating these different perspectives. In this respect, it is interesting that the general economic framework for income generation mechanisms provides in many instances a useful reference and possibly a partial solution to this integration problem.

Redistribution of Assets and Income

Equalizing endowments or opportunities involves redistributing assets rather than income. But transferring authoritatively and instantaneously the ownership of assets is unlikely to be a feasible option, unless at a prohibitive social cost. Under these conditions, the redistribution required is mostly from *income* among the rich, or even the whole population, to asset *accumulation* among the poor. In some cases, this asset accumulation may take the form of an easier access to the credit market—as for instance with market-based land reforms in some developing countries.[27] Most often, however, it simply consists of making sure that poor people may access public services that permit accumulating assets, and human capital in the first place. As a matter of fact, some authors recommend that "progressive" redistribution simply takes the form of a flat tax on all incomes and an egalitarian distribution of public social expenditures like education, health care, and other infrastructures.[28]

Of course, if poverty in endowments is really what matters, one should go further than this recommendation and develop a conceptual framework equivalent to that of optimal redistribution in the income poverty paradigm. In such a framework, the problem of anti-poverty policy would be stated as follows: "find the optimal structure of tax and public spending, given existing constraints in targeting the poor, the excess return of the assets invested in them, and the distortion effects of taxes." This problem is far from trivial. Moreover, its empirical basis is, for the moment, extremely weak for the various reasons emphasized above: multidimensionality, imperfect observability of endowments, and so on. It should thus come as no surprise that little has been done in that direction.

Another important point to take into account is that, even though it focuses on improving the endowments of the poor, such an objective cannot be taken independently of pure income redistribution. Thus, it would be incorrect to believe that the pure income redistribution paradigm becomes irrelevant when taking an endowment view at poverty and inequality. There are three reasons for this. First, income safety nets may be necessary to cushion the poor and prevent asset decumulation when facing temporary adverse shocks. Second, income transfers may be complementary of accelerated asset accumulation. Third, income transfers may be a necessary condition for an efficient use of public social services. These three points will be considered in turn.

Much of what is called income redistribution in developed countries may actually be considered pure income insurance mechanisms. The need for this type of insurance in developing countries certainly great, even when one recognizes that the protection of existing endowments and the accumulation of new assets among the poor may matter more than current income. A succession of adverse shocks and the lack of access to the credit market may force some households to stop accumulating endowments and even sell those with monetary value. This may make them unable to recover their initial functioning when good times return. At the same time, this may produce a loss of endowment that is irreversible—for instance, when children are taken out of school during crisis periods. Under these conditions, developing current income redistribution schemes acting as safety nets in periods of hardship may be an effective way of preventing a slowing down of asset accumulation and reduction in endowment poverty.[29]

Outside crisis periods, current income transfers toward the poor may also contribute to an improvement of their future endowment. This potential improvement will be the case when part of the additional income is spent on improved nutrition of the children or sending them to school. Of course, it is most likely that some part of the income transfer will also be devoted to increasing other types of expenditures and may thus be considered as "lost" if the focus is exclusively on asset accumulation. The problem is then to know what proportion of the transfer will be devoted to each use.[30]

It is also possible to design incentives that will increase the portion of the income transfer devoted to asset accumulation. Such transfers could be used to induce poor households to make efficient use of public infrastructure in schooling or health care. Indeed, it is not necessarily that households will use these facilities more intensively if the geographical density of schools or health care units is increased. The opportunity cost of sending a child to school, including market or domestic child labor, rather than the proximity of a school, may be the binding constraint for schooling.[31] If this is the case, helping the accumulation of assets among the poor would necessarily involve income transfers that would ease their budget constraint. But such transfers will be more efficient from an endowment perspective if they are made conditional on effective asset accumulation.

Mexico's Progresa program (now called Oportunidades) provides an excellent illustration of this kind of policy. It consists of means-tested transfers to poor households with children at schooling age conditionally on these children going to school and undergoing two medical examinations a year. Even though the transfers have been computed to compensate households for the opportunity cost of child labor, not all of them are devoted to asset accumulation among children. Some households would have sent their kids to school whether they received the transfers or not. In their case, the Progresa transfer is thus a pure income complement. There is evidence, however, that it contributed to a significant improvement of the health status of the population.[32]. Other programs like Progresa exist or are being introduced in other countries in Latin America and in Asia. They increasingly appeal to policy makers precisely because of their orientation toward human capital accumulation among poor children.

These arguments show that both for normative and positive reasons, redistribution policy should be concerned exclusively with asset accumulation—but not because the emphasis of poverty and inequality evaluation should be put on endowments rather than current income or consumption. Even outside the income poverty paradigm, income redistribution may be an important means of achieving a more equitable distribution of endowments in the future. The optimal income redistribution model briefly summarized above does not lose all its relevance in this context, but it would have to be seriously amended to fit the endowment view at poverty and inequality.

CONCLUSION

Critiques of the conceptual basis of the income poverty and inequality paradigm started to develop at the same time as the paradigm itself. Where do we stand some twenty-five years later? The income poverty paradigm has reached a high level of elaboration and operationality, thanks to several major technical advances. The critique to the paradigm has also become much clearer and more elaborate. There is now little doubt that defining poverty and inequality in terms of a multidimensional set of endowments and access to markets or goods is in many instances essential. This conclusion has been stated repeatedly and explicitly in major reports.[33]. The justification for that evolution is to be found not only in social justice theory, as it was originally the case, but also in sociological trends or attitudes and, as shown in this chapter, increasingly in positive economic analysis.

The challenges of making alternative concepts to the income poverty paradigm truly operational remain great. Some progress has been made to meet them. This is true of poverty and inequality evaluation. Not only are multidimensional views increasingly common, but analysts and policy makers are more prepared to accept the inconclusiveness of partial orderings of multidimensional distributions. In particular, progress in education, health status, or access to the credit market are now seen as at least as important as—though not necessarily commensurate with—changes in income when evaluating changes in poverty and inequality. Yet, the multidimensionality of the phenomena under study is such that orderings based on these broader concepts may prove to be extremely partial. Thus, there may be a need to reduce the dimensionality of the problem and to have a more unified view that would allow easier decision-making about important trade-offs—for example, investing a marginal dollar in education or in health care. Using a more or less systematic reference to some generalized income generation model, as suggested in this chapter, could be useful. The same applies to the identification of individual endowments that permit going beyond the concept of income. This is a challenging task, which has made little analytical or operational progress in the last decades: data on intergenerational transmission remain scarce; distinguishing preferences from endowments or pure random events remains very imprecise. Yet, as suggested in this chapter, some improvements are possible.

Finally, this alternative view of poverty only marginally reduces the relevance of the general optimal income redistribution question that is central to the income poverty paradigm. Seen as a means to facilitate endowment accumulation among the poor, income redistribution schemes gain even more importance. But redistribution must be analyzed in a framework that differs substantially from the old income poverty minimizing paradigm. In particular, new challenges appear in designing appropriate redistribution schemes or reforming the existing ones.

CHAPTER FIVE

Social Theory and the Concept "Underclass"

William Julius Wilson

INTRODUCTION

The use of the concept "underclass" has been the subject of considerable debate among scholars of urban poverty. Many question the meaning of the term and its value as a social category, and react critically to the way the term has been appropriated by those intellectuals and journalists whose ideological views and orientations strongly influence their perceptions of the urban poor (Hughes 1989; Aponte 1990; Katz 1993; Gans 1995; and O'Connor 2001).[1] However, in their critical commentary the scholars of urban poverty do not address, in theoretical terms, the scientific import of the concept "underclass," that is, its role in the description, explanation, and prediction of social behavior. Rather they object to the way the term is used to label a subgroup of the urban poor whose cultural traits are thought to differ from those of the larger society.

In this chapter, I consider whether a theoretically defined concept of underclass—as opposed to the nonsystematic and atheoretical usages—can be helpful in social scientific discourse. But first, by way of background, let me examine briefly the various ways the term "underclass" has been used in published writings down through the years.

THE UNDERCLASS IN HISTORICAL PERSPECTIVE

Invidious comparisons between the cultural traits of certain segments of the poor and those of the larger society have a long history in western industrialized countries. For many decades, the British establishment publicly expressed concerns about those elements among the poor—variously labeled "the lumpen," "the rabble," "the vagrants," and "the dangerous" classes— who were described as morally deficient and a potential threat to the social order of British society. Moreover, these "social outcasts" were seen as different from other poor British citizens who, despite their poverty, tended to conform to societal norms. Likewise, in the United States, the early poor laws clearly distinguished two groups among the poor—the incapacitated and the able-bodied. The amount and type of aid the able-bodied poor could receive was limited as the laws drew distinctions between the "deserving" and "undeserving" poor (Katz 1989).

With the dawn of the industrial revolution, European social scientists began to associate the experiences of poverty with the technological revolution, which had changed the processes of work, especially manual labor. Gunnar Myrdal, a Swedish economist, first used the label "underclass" in this connection to describe the increasing polarization of American society (Myrdal 1962). Myrdal argued that because of inadequate schooling and a paucity of marketable skills, as well as a lack of government support, a growing segment of the disadvantaged were consigned to the very bottom of the economic class structure. Myrdal never intended the concept of "underclass" to be a generic label for a host of cultural and behavioral traits that supposedly differentiate a certain segment of the poor from the rest of society.

In the 1960s, a number of liberal scholars in the United States associated the impact of economic restructuring and long-term joblessness not only with the limited life chances of the most disadvantaged segments of urban America but also with cultural behavior (i.e., the sharing of outlooks and modes of conduct) in the inner-city ghetto (Clark 1965; Rainwater 1966; Liebow 1967; and Hannerz 1969). These writers demonstrated that it is possible to be aware of the importance of macro-structural economic constraints (i.e., avoid the extreme notion of a "culture of poverty") and still "see the merits of a more subtle kind of cultural analysis of life in poverty" (Hannerz 1969:182).

A cultural analysis of life in poverty is perhaps best captured through the kind of ethnographic research conducted by scholars such as Hannerz (1969), Liebow (1967), and Rainwater (1966), where an attempt was made to study empirically the influence of cultural patterns on individual and group outcomes, given certain social and economic constraints. However, the controversy over the Moynihan Report (1965) on the black family in the late 1960s abruptly interrupted such studies. Indeed, in the aftermath of the controversy, empirical research on the inner-city ghetto in general decreased sharply throughout the 1970s and first half of the 1980s (Wilson 1987).

The harsh criticism of the Moynihan Report—which devoted far more attention to his unflattering depiction of the inner-city African-American family than to his historical analysis of the special plight of black families and his proposed remedies—proved to be too intimidating to scholars, especially to liberal scholars. Accordingly, in the early 1970s, social scientists were hardly motivated to research the structural and cultural roots of ghetto social dislocations. In an effort to protect themselves from the charge of "blaming the victim" or of racism, liberal social scientists tended to avoid describing any behavior that could be construed as stigmatizing or unflattering to people of color. Accordingly, for several years, and well after this controversy had subsided, the problems of social dislocation in the inner city received scant research attention (Wilson 1996).

Until the mid-1980s, the void was partially filled by journalists and conservative intellectuals who tended to highlight and reach conclusions about the behavioral and cultural "deficiencies" of the inner-city poor—frequently referred to as the "underclass"—without the benefit of systematic empirical research or carefully constructed theoretical frameworks (The American Underclass 1977; Gilder 1981; Murray 1984; Auletta 1982; and Mead 1986).

Against this setting my book *The Truly Disadvantaged* was published in 1987. The relationship between economic restructuring, long-term joblessness, and cultural behavior—previously highlighted in the writings of the liberal scholars in the 1960s (Clark 1965; Rainwater 1966; Liebow 1967; and Hannerz 1969)—was once again strongly emphasized. However, in spelling out this relationship, I also explicitly used the concept "underclass," described as a heterogeneous grouping of families and individuals who are (1) outside the mainstream of the American occupational system—including those "who lack training and skills and either experience long-term unemployment or are not members of the labor force, individuals who are engaged in street crime and other forms of aberrant behavior, and families that experience long-term spells of poverty and/or welfare dependency"(p. 8)—and (2) share the same social milieu.

Regarding the sharing of the same social environment, I stated: "It is true that long-term welfare families and street criminals are distinct groups, but they live and interact in the same depressed community and they are part of the population that has, with the exodus of the more stable working- and middle-class segments, become increasingly isolated from mainstream patterns and norms of behavior" (Wilson 1987:8). I argued that the existence of maladaptive behavior and culture was a response to social structural constraints, including constraints imposed by the decreased relative demand for low-skilled labor.

I wrote *The Truly Disadvantaged* with two main objectives in mind: (1) to encourage serious scholars to return to a systematic study of ghetto life and (2) to elaborate on a theory of the social transformation of the inner city. In this chapter I present a more refined concept of the "underclass," which derives its meaning from this theory. In the process I show how a theoretically defined concept of underclass can be helpful in social scientific discourse, despite the ongoing controversy and debate concerning its meaning and value as a social category.

A THEORY OF THE SOCIAL TRANSFORMATION OF THE INNER CITY

I advanced the argument in *The Truly Disadvantaged* that historical discrimination combined with migration from the rural South to large metropolises kept the urban black population relatively young and created a problem of weak labor-force attachment that has made them particularly vulnerable to the industrial and geographic changes in the economy since the early 1970s. Innovations in technology, the shift from goods-producing to service-producing industries, the relocation of manufacturing industries out of central cities, the increasing polarization of the labor market into low-wage and high-wage sectors, and periodic recessions have elevated the rate of black joblessness (unemployment and nonparticipation in the labor market), despite the passage of legislation against discrimination and the creation of affirmative action programs.

The growth in joblessness has in turn helped generate a rise in the concentration of poor blacks with accompanying increases in single-parent families, and the receipt of welfare. These problems have been particularly noticeable in the inner-city ghetto neighborhoods of large cities, not only because the vast concentrations of impoverished minority families and individuals there but also because these neighborhoods have become less diversified and isolated in ways that make them more vulnerable to the impact of the continuing economic changes.

Since the early 1970s, a significant out-migration of working- and middle-class families from inner-city neighborhoods combined with rising numbers of poor residents due to escalating rates of joblessness have resulted in heavy concentrations of ghetto poverty. The number of census tracts with poverty rates of at least 40 percent—a threshold definition of "high poverty" areas—has risen precipitously.[2] The diminishing presence of middle- and working-class families has also weakened an important social buffer that served to deflect the full impact of the prolonged high levels of neighborhood joblessness stemming from uneven economic growth and periodic recessions.

In earlier decades, most of the adults in ghetto neighborhoods were employed. And black working and middle classes provided stability in these neighborhoods. They invested their economic and social resources by patronizing neighborhood stores, banks, churches, and community organizations, and by sending their children to the local public schools. In the process they reinforced societal values and norms, and made it meaningful for the more disadvantaged in these segregated enclaves to envision the possibility of some upward mobility.

However, the inner-city ghetto today features a group of residents, the underclass, whose major predicament is rising joblessness, a trend that is strengthened by growing social isolation. The contact between groups of different class and racial backgrounds has decreased because of the out-migration of higher income families, resulting in greater adverse effects from living in impoverished neighborhoods. These concentration effects, reflected, for example, in the self-limiting social dispositions of inner-city residents, are created by inadequate access to job networks and jobs, the lack of access to quality schools, the decreasing availability of suitable marriage partners, and lack of exposure to conventional role models and informal "mainstream" social networks.

Accordingly, the arguments presented in *The Truly Disadvantaged* to account for the recent increases in social dislocations in the inner-city ghetto are complex. They cannot be reduced to the easy explanations of racism advanced by those on the left, or of "culture of poverty" posited by those on the right. Although historic racism created the ghetto and although contemporary discrimination has undoubtedly aggravated the economic and social woes of its residents, an adequate understanding of the sharp increase in these problems requires the specification of a complex web of additional factors, including the impact of shifts in the modern American economy.

It is not explicit in this summary of *The Truly Disadvantaged* that social structural, cultural, and social psychological variables are integrated into my theoretical framework.[3] A more formal statement of this framework is that a structure of inequality has evolved that is linked to contemporary behavior in the ghetto by a combination of opportunities, constraints, and social psychology.

The exogenous factors, representing the sources of the concentration of black ghetto poverty, include racial discrimination, changes in the economy that have restructured occupations and relocated industries, and political processes (affirmative action programs and antibias legislation) that have had the unanticipated consequence of increasing the class divisions among urban African Americans.[4] The endogenous factors created by these exogenous determinants include demographic variables such as urban migration, age structures, and the pool of marriageable men, and economic factors such as employment and income distributions.

The endogenous determinants also include social isolation, which is a characteristic feature of the social environment of the urban underclass. Social isolation deprives inner-city ghetto residents not only of economic and social resources, including conventional role models whose presence buffers the impact of neighborhood joblessness, but also of cultural learning from mainstream social networks that facilitates economic and social mobility in modern society. The lack of economic and social resources in the neighborhood, the declining presence of conventional role models, and circumscribed cultural learning produce outcomes that restrict social advancement. Some of these outcomes are structural (weak labor-force attachment and lack of access to informal job networks) and some are social-psychological (limited aspirations and negative social dispositions).

These theoretical issues should be kept in mind as I attempt to more fully establish the role of the concept "underclass" in the description, explanation, and prediction of social behavior.

LABOR-FORCE ATTACHMENT AND THE
INNER-CITY SOCIAL ENVIRONMENT

I argued in *The Truly Disadvantaged* that the central problem of the under-class is joblessness, a problem that is rendered even more severe by an increasing social isolation in impoverished neighborhoods, as reflected, for example, in the weakening of the informal job information network systems. In Martha Van Haitsma's (1989) conceptual explication of my theory, the relationship between the social environment and experiences in the labor market is more sharply delineated. She distinguishes those persons with weak attachment to the labor force and whose social environment "tends to maintain or further weaken this attachment"(Van Haitsma 1989:28). I would like to incorporate this more explicit conception by referring to the neighborhood as the social environment.

The term "weak labor-force attachment" as used here does not imply a desire or willingness to work. Rather, weak labor-force attachment implies the marginal position of people in the labor force because of restricted job opportunities—including those that result from changes in the demand for labor and from racial discrimination—or limited access to the informal job network systems.

To understand the unique position of members of the underclass, it is important to comprehend how their neighborhood context aggravates their weak attachment to the labor force. "Environments with low opportunity for stable and legitimate employment and high opportunity for alternative income-generating activities, particularly those which are incompatible with regular employment perpetuate weak labor force attachment," states Van Haitsma (p. 7). Poor people who reside in areas that support or foster strong labor-force attachment are in a better position to avail themselves of employment opportunities than those with similar educational training and occupational skills living in neighborhoods that reinforce or promote weak labor-force attachment.

Neighborhoods that have inadequate job information networks, few legitimate employment opportunities, and inferior schools not only feature weak labor-force attachment, they also increase the likelihood that people will turn to deviant or illegal activities for income, resulting in further deterioration of their attachment to the legitimate labor market. The problems associated with the absence of work are most severe for a jobless family in a neighborhood with low rates of employment because they are more likely to be shared and reinforced by other families in this neighborhood through the process of nonconscious or accidental cultural transmission (Wilson 1996; Hannerz 1969). A perception of a lack of self-efficacy is one of these shared problems.

In social cognitive theory, perceived self-efficacy refers to personal beliefs that one has the ability to take the necessary steps to achieve the goals required in a given situation. Such beliefs affect the level of challenge that an individual perceives he or she is able to handle, the amount of effort expended in a given endeavor, and the degree of perseverance when confronting difficulties. As Albert Bandura (1982:140) points out, "Inability to influence events and social conditions that significantly affect one's life can give rise to feelings of futility and despondency as well as to anxiety."

Two sources of perceived futility are identified in self-efficacy theory: people (1) may seriously doubt that they can accomplish what is expected or (2) are confident of their abilities but nonetheless do not try because they feel that their efforts will ultimately fail in an environment that is discriminatory, punitive, or unresponsive. "The type of outcomes people expect depends largely on their judgments of how well they will be able to perform in given situations" (Bandura 1982:140).

I would hypothesize that unstable work and low income will lower a person's perceived self-efficacy. Accordingly, I would expect lower levels of perceived self-efficacy in ghetto neighborhoods than in the more advantaged neighborhoods because of higher levels of underemployment, unemployment, and labor-force dropouts in ghetto areas. I would also expect the level of perceived self-efficacy to be higher among those individuals who are weakly attached to the labor force but who live in working- and middle-class areas than among their counterparts who reside in ghetto neighborhoods.

In the ghetto neighborhoods, networks of kin, friends, and associates are more likely to include a higher proportion of individuals who tend to doubt that they can actually achieve approved societal goals because of their experiences with extreme economic marginality. The self-doubts may exist for either of the two reasons stated above: these individuals may have questions concerning their own preparedness or capabilities, or they may perceive that a hostile society has imposed severe restrictions on their avenues to advancement.

The more extended the period of joblessness, the more likely these self-doubts will be internalized. I think it is reasonable to assume that the longer a neighborhood is plagued with high unemployment and non-labor-force participation, the stronger the association between joblessness and feelings of low self-efficacy. In such neighborhoods a jobless family is influenced by the behavior, social perceptions, beliefs, and orientations of similar families disproportionately concentrated in the neighborhood. In *The Truly Disadvantaged* (1987) I used the term "concentration effects"—that is, the effects of living in an overwhelmingly impoverished environment—to capture this process.

Thus, in my formulation the meaning of the concept of underclass is derived from a theoretical framework on the social transformation of the inner city, a framework that links structural, cultural, and social-psychological propositions. In this theory, what distinguishes members of the underclass from those of other economically disadvantaged groups is that their neighborhood or social milieu uniquely reinforces their marginal economic position or weak attachment to the labor force.

This is not a view that is shared by other social scientists. For example, Christopher Jencks (1992:28) maintained that "what we now call the underclass bears a striking resemblance to what sociologists used to call the lower class." However, I know of no previous studies that define "lower class" in terms of the dual problems of weak attachment to the labor force or marginal economic position, and social isolation in neighborhoods of highly concentrated poverty. The standard designation "lower class" does not capture this important distinction.

What the terms "lower class" and "underclass" have in common is that they connote economic marginality. Where they differ is that unlike the term "underclass," as theoretically defined in this chapter, the term "lower class" does not signify the added dimension of neighborhood or social milieu. In America, the problems this definition of the underclass connotes—economic marginality and neighborhoods of highly concentrated poverty—are more likely to be present in the inner-city ghettos.

In this connection, Jencks (1992) argues that because my definition of the underclass emphasizes location, it refers mainly to a nonwhite population. However, the concept as used in my theoretical framework can be applied not only to different racial and ethnic groups, but also to different societies. In the United States, the concept will more often apply to people of color because whites seldom live in ghetto or extreme poverty areas—that is, neighborhoods with poverty rates of at least 40 percent.[5] For example, the proportion of the poor who reside in ghetto neighborhoods in metropolitan areas varies noticeably by race. Of the 8 million ghetto poor in 1990, 4.2 million were African American, 2 million were Latino, and roughly 1.8 million were white (Jargowsky 1997).[6]

Thus, to speak of the underclass in the United States is to refer primarily to blacks and Latinos.[7] However, there is nothing in my conceptual definition of the underclass that would restrict its application to people of color. In other societies, the combination of weak labor-force attachment and social isolation may exist in certain inner-city neighborhoods even though the levels of concentrated poverty do not match those inherent in American ghettos. For example, there is evidence that the long-term jobless in the Holland inner cities of Rotterdam and Amsterdam—particularly the immigrants with weak labor-force attachment from Surinam and Indonesia—have experienced sharply decreasing contact with conventional groups and institutions in Dutch society despite levels of ethnic and class segregation far below those of large inner cities in the United States. In response to this development, several Dutch social scientists have discussed the formation of an underclass in the Netherlands in precisely the theoretical terms outlined in my book, *The Truly Disadvantaged* (Engbersen 1990; Engbersen, Schuyt, and Timmer 1990; Kloosterman 1990; and Schuyt 1990).

We need a concept that allows us to describe and highlight the important theoretical linkage between a disadvantaged group's position in the labor market and its social environment. I have shown how the term "underclass" can serve this purpose. Social scientists may choose another concept to capture this relationship. I now use the term "ghetto poor" to designate the dual problem of weak labor-force attachment and a social milieu featuring concentrated poverty and social isolation. My concern is that a theoretically derived concept of underclass will be overcrowded in the long run by nonsystematic, arbitrary, and atheoretical usages that often end up as ideological slogans or code words, particularly in journalistic descriptions of patterns of behavior in the inner city (cf. Hamill 1988 and Magnet 1987).

However, regardless of the concept used to describe the theoretical linkage between a disadvantaged group's position in the labor market and its social environment, many may question the strength of this relationship given the recent criticisms of the research on neighborhood effects for not adequately considering the unmeasured differences between inner-city ghetto families and families that reside in non-ghetto communities (Tienda 1991). In other words, it is argued that the effects that we attribute to neighborhoods may be due in large measure to the characteristics of families who end up living in neighborhoods of highly concentrated poverty—families with the weakest job-related skills, with the least awareness of and concern for the effects of the local environment on their children's social development, and with the most personal problems (Jargowsky 1997).

Indeed, some scholars have maintained that neighborhood effects disappear when researchers use appropriate statistical techniques to account for "self-selection bias" (Evans, Oates, and Schwab 1992; Plotnick and Hoffman 1993). I think that such conclusions are often reached because of the crude measures that are used to capture neighborhood effects. Allow me to elaborate. The research that we conducted in Chicago in the late 1980s revealed that the residents in Chicago's ghetto neighborhoods share a feeling that they have little informal social control over their children. A primary reason is a weak institutional resource base that fails to provide a foundation for social organization in their neighborhoods (Wilson 1996).

It is easier for parents to control the behavior of the children when their neighborhood features a strong institutional resource base—that is, when community institutions such as churches, schools, political organizations, businesses, and civic clubs are stable, and their links are strong or secure. The higher the density and stability of community organizations, the less deviant activities such as crime, the formation of gangs, drug trafficking, and prostitution can take root in the neighborhood.

A weak institutional resource base is what distinguishes inner-city ghetto neighborhoods from stable working- and middle-class areas. Parents in ghetto neighborhoods experience much greater difficulty in trying to control the behavior of their adolescents and prevent them from getting involved in activities detrimental to pro-social development, activities that may affect their chances for future success in the labor market. Because our rudimentary measures of neighborhood effects are unable to capture the dynamic impact of differences in the institutional resource base on families and individuals, we are more likely to overemphasize the importance of self-selection bias.

Moreover, our rudimentary measures of neighborhood effects are also unlikely to capture indirect forces that operate to disadvantage individuals and families residing in highly concentrated poverty areas. I am referring to both indirect structural and cultural factors (Smelser, Wilson, and Mitchell 2001). These causal mechanisms are "indirect" because they are mediated by the position of the group in the system of social stratification (i.e., the position the group occupies in terms of power, prestige, influence, and privilege). Take for example, the impact of national economic change on low-skilled African American workers.

In recent years, the growth and spread of new technologies and the growing internationalization of economic activity have changed the demand for different types of workers (Katz 1996; Schwartzman 1997). Although these trends tend to benefit highly educated or highly skilled workers, they have created situations where lower skilled workers face the growing threat of job displacement and eroding wages.

The decreased relative demand for low-skilled labor has had a greater impact on poor black communities because the percentage of low-skilled workers is still disproportionately large. Low-skilled workers in all racial and ethnic groups are likely to be adversely affected by the changes in the relative demand for labor, but the severest dislocations will be felt in the inner-city ghettos. Social isolation in these areas, for example the lack of access to the informal jobs network, exacerbates the problems that low-income workers in all neighborhoods experience from shifts in the demand for labor.

Also, social isolation in ghetto neighborhoods creates mechanisms that affect race-neutral processes that ultimately influence group outcomes. Consider the problem of the flow of information to poor inner-city ghetto neighborhoods. In order to make wise decisions, people have to have good information. However the more socially isolated or segregated the community, the less likely the residents will have ready access to reliable information concerning the labor market, schools, apprenticeship programs, financial markers, and so on.

Our rudimentary measures of neighborhood effects do not capture these indirect structural factors. They also fail to capture indirect cultural factors. Following Ulf Hannerz (1969), I define "culture" as the sharing of modes of behavior and outlook within a community. The study of culture not only involves an analysis of how it is transmitted from generation to generation, but the way in which it is sustained through social interaction in the community.

When individuals act according to their culture, they are following their inclinations as they have been developed by learning or influence from other members of their community (Hannerz 1969). Skills, styles, and habits are often shaped by the frequency in which they are present in the community (Swidler 1986). Accordingly, the point I want to emphasize—which should be kept in mind when considering my theoretically derived definition of the underclass—is that the environment embodies both structural and cultural constraints and opportunities. In order to fully appreciate and explain the divergent social outcomes of human groups, we must take into account their exposure to different cultural influences.

Patterns of behavior in the inner city often represent particular cultural adaptations to the systematic blockage of opportunities in the environment of the inner city and the society as a whole. These adaptations are reflected in habits, skills, styles, and attitudes that are shaped over time. The exposure to different cultural influences in the environment has to be taken into account if one is to really appreciate and explain the divergent social outcomes of human groups. To state the issues more formally, culture provides the tools and creates constraints in patterns of social interaction, including the social interaction that leads to different racial outcomes. Accordingly, culture is closely intertwined with social relations in the sense that its effects on stratified racial outcomes are filtered through social relational processes and are therefore indirect (Tilly 1998).

Imposed or voluntary restrictions on the actions of members of the community increase differences in behavior and outlook and may limit opportunities for economic and social advancement. This limited opportunity creates situations in which social factors, such as a group's economic position in society, interact over time with cultural factors in the formation of observable group traits and characteristics. As noted above, these group traits and characteristics often shape the attributes of individual members of the community—such as their motivations, attitudes, and skills—which in turn affect their social outcomes, including their social mobility.

Among the effects of living in segregated neighborhoods is repeated exposure to cultural traits—styles of behavior, particular skills, habits, orientations, and worldviews—that emanate from or are the products of racial exclusion, traits that may impede successful maneuvering in the larger society. For example, our research in Chicago revealed that many parents in the inner-city ghetto neighborhoods warned their children to avoid eye-to-eye contact with strangers and to develop a tough demeanor when encountering people on the streets. Although such behaviors are helpful for survival in the ghetto, they hinder successful interaction in mainstream society (Wilson 1996).

When I speak of the impact of the environment I am not making an either/or distinction between culture and social structure, rather I am highlighting the interaction between these two variables. In the final analysis, the exposure to different cultural influences in the environment has to be taken into account if one is to really appreciate and explain the divergent social outcomes of human groups.

CONCLUSION

One of the general hypotheses from my theory of the social transformation of the inner city is that a social environment featuring concentrated poverty and social isolation reinforces weak attachment to the labor market (Wilson 1987). A number of the specific hypotheses that embody the notion of concentration effects—the effects of living in highly concentrated poverty areas—specify the mechanisms that create the connection between the social environment and labor-force attachment. For example, one of these hypotheses states that individuals living in high poverty areas are much less likely to be tied into the informal job information network system than those living in marginal or low poverty areas.

The dual problem facing many individuals of weak labor-force attachment and residing in a social environment that further weakens that attachment is conveyed by the concept "underclass." Accordingly, this concept derives its meaning from the theory of the social transformation of the inner city and helps to highlight the importance of the social environment for so many truly disadvantaged individuals.

However, as I have tried to indicate, because our empirical measures of the impact of the environment are rudimentary, as is so clearly revealed in the research on neighborhood effects, we have yet to demonstrate the complex ways that the environment or neighborhood milieu directly and indirectly affects the social outcomes of individuals and families, including the cumulative effects of living in an environment that is overwhelmingly impoverished. But as we work to improve our measures of the social environment's impact on poverty populations, a concept that forces us to keep in focus the role of the environment in weakening attachment to the labor is indispensable, regardless of whether that concept is the "underclass" or some equivalent designation.

CHAPTER SIX

Race, Class, and Markets: Social Policy in the 21st Century

Douglas S. Massey

The concept of the "free market" is one of the most misleading ever devised. The pairing of the words "free" and "market" suggests that markets some-how exist autonomously, as states of nature, and that in the absence of human interference they will operate smoothly and effectively, as natural processes do. The trope of the free market implies that human actions undertaken to influence market outcomes represent unwarranted "interventions" that arti-ficially constrain a naturally functioning system, in the same way that build-ing a dam constitutes a human intervention to create a lake from what used to be a river. Whereas the construction of dams, highways, and bridges are usually viewed positively, however, actions undertaken to influence markets are more commonly seen as detrimental, undermining, however good one's intentions, the market's efficient operation so that it no longer produces the greatest good for the greatest number.

In fact, markets, like dams and highways, are very much human creations (White 1981; Granovetter 1985). Indeed, in the panorama of human exis-tence they are a fairly recent invention (Carruthers and Babb 2000). For the vast majority of the time that humans have walked on earth, they exchanged resources almost exclusively through nonmarket mechanisms (Heilbroner 1962). It was not until the 15th century that markets began unambiguously to grow and for a long time they only covered a tiny share of human transac-tions (Braudel 1979). It has only been within the last 200 years that markets have expanded geographically and socially to circumvent the globe and sub-sume large swaths of human behavior (Massey 2005).

Until around 10,000 years ago virtually all human beings lived in groups no larger than 150–200 persons that were spread fairly uniformly through the environment (Livi-Bacci 1992). The economy was one of subsistence achieved through hunting and gathering and there was little differentiation between people or groups (Bettinger 1991). Although objects could be endowed with symbolic value, money did not exist (Zelizer 1994; Davies 2002). Under these circumstances markets could not emerge and cultural norms and social institutions that specified obligations and behaviors according to age, gender, and kinship governed interpersonal exchanges (Massey 2002).

Well-functioning markets only became feasible with the urbanization of human society. Although the first cities came into existence around 6,000 years ago, it has only been within the last two centuries that more than 5 percent of human beings ever lived in them; and it is only within the current decade that more than 50 percent of the world's population will come to be urban dwellers (Brockerhoff 2000). Paralleling these trends, markets emerged relatively slowly, beginning with the revival of long-distance trade in Europe during the 15th century and continuing steadily through the mercantilist and capitalist eras (Braudel 1979). After 1800 market development accelerated rapidly in tandem with urban industrialism (Weber 1899).

Markets grew quickly during the 19th century because they proved remarkably effective at organizing the production, distribution, and consumption of goods and services under an industrial system (Berry 1973). Early capitalism, however, was associated with regular market failures and a high degree of inequality, leading many observers to a search for alternatives (Heilbroner 1962). Following the demise of the first global market economy in the ashes of World War I, several nations undertook experiments with command economies. They hoped that centralized planning and the rational allocation of resources would preclude the inequalities and vagaries associated with the market. Whether justified by an ideology of the right (fascism) or the left (communism), experiments in state socialism distinctively marked the period from 1917 to 1989.

The fatal flaw in command economies proved to be that they required a concentration of economic and political power within a single bureaucratic structure. In planned economies, decisions about production, distribution, and consumption are made by a central bureaucracy rather than private consumers and producers. The resources of land, capital, and labor are mobilized by administrative fiat rather than market signals. In order for allocation decisions to be effective, planners must have sufficient power and authority to make their decisions stick, and the consequent monopolization of eco nomic and political power within a single social structure meant that whomever controlled the state wielded near-absolute power in society. The resulting dictatorships (Stalin, Hitler, Mao, Pol Pot) proved to be far more destructive and deadly than capitalism had ever been, yielding tens of millions of deaths over the course of the 20th century. One by one the socialist dictatorships have either self-destructed or been abandoned in favor of a return to market mechanisms, though not always straight into a full-blown market economy.

Not all the social experimentation of the 20th century entailed violence, of course. Some European nations peacefully attempted to create mixed economies that combined private enterprise and state ownership within the framework of a parliamentary democracy. In these countries, however, popular demand for state-provided services proved to be virtually inexhaustible, leading over time to the growth of the public bureaucracy at the expense of the private enterprise. Eventually the taxes and bureaucracies became so onerous that in country after country voters rebelled to elect center-right politicians committed to shrinking the size of the state. Planning bureaucracies turned out to be too slow, inflexible, and ponderous to manage a rapidly changing information economy (Castells 1996) and over time bureaucratic decisions came to reflect special interests rather than the public good (Olson 1982).

At the dawn of the new millennium, therefore, markets have come to prevail throughout the globe, embracing ever more remote geographic reaches and more recondite areas of social and economic life. Although markets rule, their evident triumph does not signal a victory of the natural over the human. Markets are human creations and in a very real way citizens have *chosen* them as the least tyrannical and the most effective human-designed system for generating wealth, allocating resources, and ensuring well-being. Citizens do not stand *apart* from markets but by their actions they *constitute* them. The issue is not *whether* to regulate markets. Markets are necessarily regulated by the decisions made (implicitly or explicitly) in creating them. The real issue is whether markets created by past decisions are presently yielding outcomes desired by society, and whether there are actions that might be taken to bring their performance into conformity with democratic preferences.

GOVERNMENT AND THE MARKET

Ultimately, markets are nothing more than competitions between citizens that occur within particular arenas according to specific rules. By building arenas and defining rules, societies necessarily regulate competition and constrain outcomes. The proper role of government in a democratic society is to ensure, on behalf of the citizenry, that needed markets exist, that appropriate arenas are constructed to enable necessary transactions, that all members of society have equal market access, that competition within markets is seen to be "fair," and that citizens are protected against the deleterious consequences of market failure.

Creating Markets

If markets are constituted by societies in which they are embedded, then there is no inherently correct number, distribution, or nature of markets. Markets may take a variety of forms, and as societies change socially, demographically, and culturally, as new technologies emerge, and as new knowledge is created, the nature and number of markets may also be expected to change. As a result, in any society actions must be undertaken periodically to create new markets, modify old ones, and eliminate those that have become obsolete. Historically, the first markets to emerge were associated with finance and trade (Carruthers 1996) and next were insurance markets (Zelizer 1979). Fully functioning labor markets developed only in the 19th century, in concert with the urbanization and industrialization of society (Thompson 1966). Later still to emerge were markets for futures, options, derivatives, and consumer credit.

Within the past two decades, the range and efficiency of markets has expanded dramatically within and between nations, in response to improvements to social organization, transportation, communication, and information processing. Markets are most thoroughly developed in wealthy industrialized nations, of course. Although developing nations are presently being incorporated into global trade and financial networks, their internal markets remain weak and ineffective. Third world countries continue to be hampered by missing or poorly functioning markets in a variety of crucial areas.

A good example is the market for home mortgages—financial instruments that allow people of modest means to purchase homes. Even in the United States, mortgage markets are of very recent origin. Prior to World

War II, they did not exist except for a privileged few (Jackson 1985). Although home-purchase loans existed before the 1940s, home lending markets were incomplete and poorly functioning. Banks typically required half the cost of a home as a down payment and demanded very short amortization periods. To purchase a home, buyers had to post a large amount of cash up front and be in a position to make high monthly payments. As a result, mortgages were available only to those with considerable wealth and income.

After World War II, the U.S. government deliberately moved to create a mass housing market by setting up mortgage guarantee programs through the Federal Housing Administration and the Veteran's Administration. The federal government agreed to underwrite private mortgages for up to 90 percent of assessed home value and extended the amortization period to thirty years. Under these circumstances, as long as a buyer put down 10 percent of the cost of the home, banks experienced no risk whatsoever in making a loan. If a buyer defaulted, the bank retained the equity and collected the outstanding balance from the federal government as insurance. After 1945 banks were eager to offer loans, and the minimal outlay and low monthly payments meant that most Americans could afford to purchase rather than rent. Through its loan guarantee programs, and later through institutions such as Fannie Mae and Freddie Mac (which created a secondary mortgage market to expand the pool of mortgage capital) the U.S. government created a new mass market where none had existed before.

Most developing nations, in contrast, lack well-functioning mortgage markets, and the desire to overcome this particular failure constitutes the leading motivation for international migration today (Massey et al. 1998). Contrary to popular belief, most immigrants from the developing world do not move to developed nations intending to settle permanently. Rather, they seek to work abroad *temporarily* to amass savings that will enable them to construct or purchase a home. In the absence of well-functioning mortgage markets, households are forced to migrate internationally in order to self-finance the acquisition of housing and to overcome other market failures.

Creating Infrastructure

In order for transactions to occur, buyers and sellers must come together within a mutually accepted arena. Sometimes the arena is delimited physically (such as the trading pit in the New York Stock Exchange) and at other times it is geographically diffuse (as with NASDAQ, where trades are effected over the Internet); but always the competitive arena is defined socially by rules that have been adopted to govern the transactions. As markets have evolved, the rules have increasingly shifted from the informal to the formal, but even today most markets still function as a mixture of formal and informal mechanisms.

Formal rules are laws and regulations written down by public authorities to define the rights of buyers and sellers, create a legal tender, establish a basis for the execution and enforcement of contracts, and define acceptable behaviors within a competitive arena. Informal rules are unwritten codes of conduct that are implicitly understood by market participants and reinforced through mechanisms of enforceable trust such as ridicule, gossip, shaming, exclusion, and ostracism (Portes and Sensenbrenner 1993). Whereas some markets are predominantly formalized (e.g., mortgage markets), others remain highly informal (e.g., the diamond trade).

In addition to being supported by a social infrastructure of laws, regulations, expectations, and conventions, many competitive arenas also require a physical infrastructure. The necessary structure may be erected by public or private efforts, but as with social infrastructures, the construction of most arenas involves a mixture of the two. Whereas private interests finance the construction of factories to produce steel, for example, the public builds highways and ports to bring steel products to market. A core responsibility of the state is to make sure, by some combination of public and private means, that the physical and social infrastructure necessary for markets is created and maintained.

Ensuring Equal Access

Once a democratic government has brought a market into existence and created the infrastructure necessary for its operation, its next responsibility is to ensure that all citizens who wish to participate in the market have an equal chance to do so. If a society uses markets to distribute goods and services, generate wealth, and allocate income, then it is incumbent on the government to guarantee that all citizens have the right to compete in all markets. In a market society, lack of access to markets translates directly into a lack of access to social and economic well-being and ultimately into socioeconomic stratification.

The minimum of access that a government must guarantee citizens is their right to participate in markets regardless of ascriptive characteristics such as race, ethnicity, religion, gender, and disability. U.S. history is replete with examples where societal access has been denied to people on the basis of inborn characteristics (Smith 1997). Examples range from covenants that prohibited the rental or sale of property to members of the "Hebrew Race" (legal until 1948) to laws specifying separate (and inferior) services for black people in stores, hotels, and restaurants (allowed under federal law until 1964) to prohibitions on female participation in certain professions (common into the 1970s). In addition to securing a place for minorities in the political arena, the goal of civil rights in the United States is also one of assuring equal access to markets.

Guaranteeing Fair Competition

Of course, simple access to markets, in the sense of being admitted as a participant, does not guarantee equality of opportunity, for in addition to being allowed merely to compete the competition must be seen by citizens as "fair." Unlike access, where a person is either admitted or not, fairness has no objective definition and has been the subject of lengthy debates in the philosophical literature (see Rawls 1999; Carr 2000). When it comes to markets, especially, the concept is inevitably subjective. What seems fair to one market participant may seem quite unfair to another, depending on his or her relative position and power in the marketplace (Hochschild 1981).

At the very least a doctrine of fairness requires ensuring that people who enter a market with equal inputs should achieve, on average and in the long run, equal outcomes. Whites and blacks with equal qualifications should not be paid less for the same work; Latinos and Anglos with the same income should not be charged different prices for the same goods; the quality of services provided to customers should not vary by gender, and so on. Americans evince remarkable consensus on the principle of equal treatment for equal qualifications, though as recently as 1960 this was not the case (Kluegel and Smith 1986; Schuman et al. 1997).

More controversial have been efforts to take the doctrine of "fairness" a step further and grant a special status in markets to those who, through no fault of their own, cannot muster equal inputs. As President Lyndon Johnson argued in a celebrated speech at Howard University in 1965, "you do not take a person who, for years, has been hobbled by chains and liberate him, bring him up to the starting line of a race and then say, 'you are free to compete with all the others,' and still justly believe that you have been completely fair" (Johnson 1966). The view that fairness demands "affirmative" steps to redress past inequities has been extremely controversial (Glazer 1978; Skrentny 1996).

Because the notion of fairness in markets will always be subject to considerable debate, perhaps the most important function of a democratic government is to provide accurate and unbiased information about how markets are performing. Public data on prices, wages, salaries, wealth, income, education, and health are essential inputs for policy debate in a democratic society. When such data are broken down by gender, age, race, and ethnicity, they provide a good indication of who the winners and losers are in any market. If one group is consistently observed to win while others regularly lose it provides prima facie evidence that something is amiss in the way that markets are performing, and that tough questions about fairness need to be asked and publicly debated.

Protection from Market Failures

Markets can never achieve all the goals that citizens would like to see accomplished, nor are they foolproof mechanisms for the production, distribution, and consumption of resources. The history of capitalism is replete with examples of failed and missing markets. As we have seen, mortgage markets were effectively absent in the United States before 1945 and do not exist in most developing nations today. Likewise, from 1929 to 1939 markets failed on a variety of fronts around the world, yielding insufficient employment for workers, goods for consumers, profit for producers, and income for farmers. The widespread market failures of the 1930s were instrumental in creating a new consensus in the United States that it was the responsibility of government to protect citizens from capitalism's failures.

Although improvements in governance and technology have reduced the depth and frequency of market failure, the hazard of failed markets can never be eliminated entirely from a capitalist economy. Citizens of developed countries by substantial majorities agree that law-abiding citizens should somehow be protected from the vicissitudes of the market (Inglehart 1977; Hochschild 1995), and bowing to this sentiment, democratic governments have erected a variety of "social safety nets" to prevent citizens from falling too far down the economic ladder, creating aid programs such as unemployment insurance, welfare payments, medical insurance, old-age benefits, and food subsidies.

The principal problem with any safety net is the "moral hazard" it creates, for in protecting people from the failures of the market it also shields them from the consequences of their own reckless behavior. In so doing, safety nets end up encouraging irresponsible decision making and behavior. For this reason, democratic societies have long debated where, exactly, to place the social safety net: high enough to keep people from misery yet low enough to discourage reckless judgment and indolence. In the United States, this debate has been expressed over time in cycles of social experimentation (Katz 1986), as the welfare system has shifted from one of selective entitlement (widows and veterans) to universal entitlement (all those below a certain income threshold) and then to contingent entitlement (those below an income threshold who demonstrate a willingness to work—see Skocpol 1992 and Katz 2001).

Public attention to the moral hazard has focused mostly on the poor (Murray 1984; Gilens 1999); but the rich also face their own moral hazard arising from government protection. Perhaps the best example is the federal bailout of the savings and loan industry during the late 1980s. In this case, the existence of deposit insurance encouraged bankers to make high-risk loans. Banks profited immensely from origination fees and interest payments, but when the loans went bad they did not suffer the consequences, as the federal government covered the deposits. Despite the independent, swashbuckling self-image of American entrepreneurs, they are as fond as anyone else of using government to privatize profits while socializing risks (Phillips 1990).

Citizens demand state action not only when markets fail but also when they fail to materialize. Missing markets are a problem that all governments must face. A good example is education. Modern democratic societies have concluded that all citizens should be educated up to a certain minimal level (around 12 years of schooling) regardless of ability to pay. Although private schools exist and market their services to paying customers, if the distribution of education was left entirely to the market, children from poor families would not receive the minimum necessary education. For both moral and practical reasons, democratic societies cannot allow this to happen and therefore support the public provision of education outside of the market.

CLASS AND MARKETS

In an ideal world, markets are constituted by society and managed effectively by the state, which works on behalf of citizens to identify and create those markets that are needed, erect the necessary infrastructure, ensure fair competition and open access, and protect citizens from market failures. These responsibilities require the state to produce reliable and timely public data about the performance of markets in different areas of social and economic life. Engaged citizens then use this information to monitor outcomes and through their elected officials make sure that market performance matches democratic preferences.

The foregoing is the ideal, of course, and in the real world the supervision of markets for the public good is threatened by the intrusive realities of class: the unequal distribution of resources generated by the market itself and the use of those resources to create infrastructures and write rules that benefit the wealthy rather than the interests of society as a whole. Although the self-interested abuse of markets by the wealthy is not inevitable, it nonetheless constitutes a serious threat that requires constant vigilance.

Throughout U.S. history wealthy interests have periodically gained the upper hand and used their economic and political power to skew the rules of the market in their favor (Phillips 2002). Such was the case in the 1920s, when the rich in this period gained control of government and rewrote the rules of the political economy in their favor while coopting the state to generate private wealth. Their excesses ultimately brought the market economy crashing down in 1929 and in the political realignment of the 1930s U.S. citizens elected a government committed to managing markets for the public good.

In a very real way, Franklin D. Roosevelt saved capitalism from the capitalists, and under new rules introduced by the New Deal, productivity steadily rose in the four decades after 1932, incomes tripled, the middle class ballooned, and inequality with respect to income and wealth fell to record lows (Levy 1998). After 1972, however, the political coalition that had supported the political economy of the New Deal came undone and a realignment under the Republican Party brought the proponents of the wealthy back into power during the 1980s and 1990s (Phillips 2002). Marginal tax rates were lowered, social spending was cut, military spending (which creates private wealth) was increased, industries were deregulated, unions were busted, and government stewardship of markets was curtailed.

From 1974 to 2004 incomes stagnated, the middle class shrank, the social health of the nation deteriorated, and inequalities of wealth and income
rose to unprecedented levels (Levy 1998; Phillips 2002). As in the 1920s,
however, excesses ultimately led to a market bubble that burst in 2000. At
about the same time, years of corporate fraud and mismanagement came to
a head and brought a wave of bankruptcies and business failures. Whether
or not these disasters bring about another realignment and the reassertion of
citizen control over the political economy remains a central question of the
day, despite the results of the 2004 elections.

RACE AND MARKETS

In the course of U.S. history, a variety of racial and ethnic groups have been
systematically denied access to markets and subjected to blatant wage and
price discrimination. In their turn, the Irish, Asians, Jews, Italians, Poles, and
Latinos all felt the sting of exclusion and discrimination; but no group experienced the kind of systematic, sustained, and pervasive disenfranchise-
ment from markets as African Americans. Although black access to markets
was *theoretically* guaranteed by the 13th and 14th amendments to the U.S.
Constitution and by the 1866 Civil Rights Act, *in practice* racial exclusion
and discrimination were not prohibited from most markets in the United
States until the 1960s.

Racial discrimination in markets for goods, services, and employment
was only banned in 1964; in real estate and insurance markets in 1968; and
in lending markets in 1974. Since the close of the Civil Rights Era, access and
treatment has improved for African Americans in many markets, with especially large gains in those for goods and services but with significant improvement also in markets for labor, credit, and finance. But in one market
racial progress has been exceedingly slow, almost glacial: that for housing.
High levels of discrimination in real estate and high levels of housing segregation are ongoing realities.

Evidence for the persistence of housing discrimination comes from quasi-
experimental studies known as audits. In an audit study, teams of equally
qualified black and white home seekers query rental or sales agents about the
availability, price, and terms under which housing might be acquired. Without knowing what happened to other-race auditors, members of each team
fill out a questionnaire describing their experiences with the agent, and these

data are compiled and analyzed by researchers to see whether blacks and whites experience systematic differences in treatment or access (Fix, Galster, and Struyk 1993).

Results from audit studies conducted over the past two decades indicate that whites are systematically preferred over blacks at every stage in the marketing of housing (Galster 1990; Yinger 1995). Compared with whites, blacks are significantly less likely to have their phone calls answered, less likely to be shown advertised units, less likely to be invited to inspect other units, and less likely to be taken to see units in white neighborhoods. Once any neighborhood comes to contain a significant number of black residents, moreover, it is systematically avoided by white agents and home seekers (Farley et al. 1993; Charles 2000). This avoidance is very clearly on the basis of race rather than "objective" criteria such as crime rates, school quality, or property values (Farley et al. 1994; Emerson, Yancey, and Chai 2001).

In their audit of the Philadelphia rental market, for example, Massey and Lundy (2000) found that 81 percent of whites were able to get through to a rental agent and 83 percent of those who did were told that a unit was available. In contrast, only 72 percent of blacks reached an agent and just 70 percent were told that a unit was available, yielding an overall accessibility rate of 50 percent for blacks compared with 68 percent for whites. For black females, the rate of access was only 38 percent. Among those who gained access, moreover, application fees were requested of 36 percent of blacks but only 15 percent of whites. According to statistical estimates developed by Yinger (1995) on the basis of a national housing audit, whenever an opportunity to discriminate presents itself, whites are quite likely to take it.

Consistent with the observed high levels of housing discrimination, black-white residential segregation is also very high (Weinberg, Iceland, and Steinmetz 2002; Charles 2003). Indeed, within a subset of large metropolitan areas that contain nearly 40 percent of all African Americans, levels of segregation are so extreme and so persistent across multiple geographic dimensions that they have been labeled as "hypersegregated" (Massey and Denton 1993; Denton 1994; Wilkes and Iceland 2004). Such high levels of segregation are comparable only to those achieved in the Union of South Africa under apartheid and characterized no other multiracial society (Massey 1999).

As long as racial discrimination and residential segregation persist so blatantly in U.S. housing markets, African Americans cannot access the full range of resources available in U.S. society. Housing markets are particularly crucial in stratification because they not only distribute places to live, they also distribute anything that is *correlated* with where one lives (Massey and Denton 1993). Thus, housing markets distribute education, insurance rates, wealth, safety, peer groups, and employment. In each case, African Americans are denied access to an important socioeconomic resource because they are denied access to the housing market. For this reason alone they are condemned to a self-perpetuating cycle of racial disadvantage.

Within market societies, economic and residential mobility are necessarily interconnected. Historically, poor immigrant minorities have settled within disadvantaged urban enclaves; but as they moved up the economic ladder they were able to translate their socioeconomic gains into improved residential circumstances by moving to a "better" neighborhood characterized by higher home values, safer streets, higher-quality schools, lower insurance rates, more salubrious peer groups, and more efficient services. In doing so, they put themselves, and most importantly their children, in a better position to move farther up the economic ladder in the future.

Thus, for most racial and ethnic groups in the United States, economic mobility has translated into residential mobility, which has been converted into economic mobility, and so on over time. Through this interplay between economic and spatial mobility, groups such as Italians and Poles in the past and Latinos and Asians today ratchet themselves up the social ladder, eventually to achieve parity with whites of native parentage. Because of ongoing segregation and discrimination in the U.S. housing market, however, this ladder of mobility has not worked for African Americans. Segregation thus represents the "linchpin" of the American system of racial stratification (Pettigrew 1979; Bobo 1989; Massey and Denton 1993).

THE WAY FORWARD

During the 1980s and 1990s, social scientists, policy makers, and citizens engaged in a prolonged debate about the origins of "the urban underclass," a journalistic term that came to stand for a large and disproportionately black population of urban poor who were removed socially, economically, and culturally from the rest of American society. One of the more specious threads in this debate was the false opposition posed by some between race and class as causes of urban poverty. Within sociology, the conflict was often posed as a theoretical "debate" between William Julius Wilson (whose writings emphasized the structural transformation of the urban economy) and Douglas Massey (who emphasized racial segregation).

In reality, however, Wilson and I agree that the core issue is not whether urban poverty is caused by factors associated with class *or* race, but how race *and* class factors *interact* to render urban poverty such an intractable social problem. The political economy *has* been transformed by the wealthy in ways that have increased inequality and deepened poverty; but racism also remains a potent and corrosive force in U.S. society, especially in its housing markets. It is the imposition of structural economic change on a racially segregated society that accounts for the intractability of urban poverty and its correlation with race.

Research shows that when income inequality rises sharply in urban areas that are highly segregated by race, poverty inevitably becomes more concentrated geographically (Massey 1996), and this concentration is especially acute for the segregated group (Massey and Fischer 2000). As poverty becomes more spatially concentrated, moreover, so does any trait or behavior that is associated with poverty. Thus, the concentration of poverty also brings about a geographic intensification of crime, delinquency, drug abuse, joblessness, and fragmented families, creating a uniquely disadvantaged social environment that is disproportionately inflicted on the black poor. A large research literature has established that growing up and living in neighborhoods of concentrated poverty systematically undermine individual life chances net of other social and economic conditions, raising the odds of educational failure, joblessness, death, injury, single parenthood, criminality, and dependence (for a review see Sampson, Morenoff, and Gannon-Rowley 2002).

If policies are to be successful in breaking the cycle of poverty, therefore, the geographic concentration of poverty must be reduced. Achieving this goal requires citizens and policy makers to attend to issues of race as well as class. With respect to the latter, citizens must return to the active management of markets for the public good. They must recognize that markets are not naturally occurring phenomenon but artifacts created by human actions that must be watched closely and managed wisely if they are to operate in the broad interests of society. Markets can assume different forms and produce a variety of outcomes depending on how they are structured. Citizens must reassert themselves and wrest control of markets away from the wealthy, who have, over the past few decades, managed them for the benefit of the few rather than the many.

The restoration of citizen control requires that we face up to the realities of race and racism. The most important single reason that the wealthy were able to gain control of the political economy in the first place was their use of race as a "wedge issue" to pry apart the New Deal coalition (Phillips 1969). By rallying poor southern whites and northern blue-collar workers against civil rights, Republicans were successful in putting together a political coalition that systematically stripped away the protections and reforms of the New Deal (Edsall and Edsall 1991). Behind the smokescreen of race, privileged elites successfully conned the white middle and working classes into supporting regressive policies that were against their economic interests. As a result, since 1973 the rich have gotten richer, the poor have gotten poorer, and a shrunken middle class has been forced to work harder just to stay in place.

The time has come for the 80 percent of the citizenry that has not benefited from the political-economic arrangements of the past thirty years to move forward on a vigorous agenda of racial equality, and in so doing they will be able to reassert their authority in managing markets for the benefit of the many rather than the few. The crucial arena for improvement is in housing. As long as the United States remains a racially segregated society, it will remain a stratified and polarized society (Massey 2004).

Polls indicate that the vast majority of Americans believe in the principle of open markets, and in particular that 90 percent of whites agree that people should be able to live wherever they want regardless of race (Schuman et al. 1997). The moment has come to translate this ideal into reality by amending the Fair Housing Act, finally empowering the federal government to identify and root out discrimination from U.S. housing markets. Since the act's passage in 1968, federal authorities have been largely prohibited from enforcing the law. The onus of enforcement has fallen on individual victims, who must go to the courts one by one to assert their rights. If racial segregation is to be reduced, then federal agents must enforce the law, using audits to identify, prosecute, and convict those who discriminate, and to impose penalties sufficient to deter agents from racially biased actions in the future.

Such a program should be seen as a bipartisan action in the national interest. For liberals, housing segregation remains America's dirty little secret and the principal unfinished business of the Civil Rights Era, when a devil's

bargain was brokered by Republican Congressman Everett Dirksen to secure passage of the Fair Housing Act. In return for conservative assent in de-
claring racial discrimination in housing to be illegal, liberals agreed to strip
from the legislation virtually all enforcement mechanisms (Metcalf 1988).

For conservatives, the core issue is one of market access. If competition
and participation in markets are the means by which societies and peoples
maximize achievement, how can conservatives stand idly by and tolerate
clear and irrefutable evidence that one group of people is systematically denied full access to a crucial market on the basis of skin color? If we are truly
to move toward a "race blind" society, and if markets are to lead the way to
a world where debates about the need for affirmative action will be moot,
then persons of African origin must be given free and unhindered access to
U.S. housing markets, something that is manifestly not presently the case.

The only way to reduce inequality, lessen racial stratification, and make
progress in eliminating the urban underclass is to move forcefully to attack
race- and class-related problems simultaneously. If citizens can once again
come to view markets as their responsibility and to reassert their authority
in managing them for the public good, and if they can take steps to ensure
that all racial and ethnic groups have full and equal access to all markets,
then the United States will take a significant step toward building a more just
and stable society.

CHAPTER SEVEN

Dependency and Social Debt

Martha Albertson Fineman

INTRODUCTION

Sociologists, philosophers, and economists approach poverty and inequality from slightly different perspectives. To some extent the interdisciplinary debates seem to be about how to measure the well-being of individuals within a society. We are told that sociologists focus on the conditions of poverty, describing how it is embedded in social and cultural organizations or contexts. Traditional economists, by contrast, seem more interested in identifying and measuring factors that they argue produce (or predict) poverty/wealth and inequality/autonomy. They quantify human actions under terms such as "preference" and "efficiency." Philosophers grapple with universalized notions of rights and entitlement, building theories of justice on endless regressions into nuance.

What these approaches tend to share, however, is an inattention to gender as a major organizing category in their work. In part, this inattention results from the fact that such mainstream treatments of law and justice persistently fail to seriously consider the institution of the family and its ideological and structural relationship to the larger society. This is not an argument that the family is ignored. Quite the contrary. What I assert is that some version of the family is assumed in the work of most economists, sociologists, and philosophers.

Because they assume not only its existence, but also its functioning in a certain way, the family remains relatively unexamined and its assigned societal role does not become an independent focus of theory centered on the individual. A relevant example is the recent treatment of the family by

John Rawls. He had been criticized for previously omitting a sense of what would constitute justice within the family (Kittay 1999:76). Perhaps in response to such criticism, Rawls' latest book (2001:10–11) explicitly addresses the family, but in limited terms. He mentions the family in Part IV, "Institutions of a Just Basic Structure," in a section entitled "The Family as a Basic Institution." He opens with the caveat, however, that his aims are "modest"—he intends to indicate why the principles of justice apply to the family but will not indicate what reorganization is required by these principles. He suggests that the family performs a socially necessary function— the care and education of children, who must develop a "sense of justice" so they can be effective citizens.

According to Rawls, the principles of justice and fairness apply to the family, but not within the family. Principles of justice can promote equality by guaranteeing the "the basic claims [to rights and liberties] of equal citizens who are members of families." Rawls (2001:164) does not seem to believe that the unequal distribution of labor between women and men is a pervasive problem, as he asserts that: "[s]ince wives are equally citizens with their husbands, they have all the same basic rights and liberties and fair opportunities as their husbands; and this, together with the correct application of the other principles of justice, should suffice to secure their equality and independence."

In failing to confront family position (or status) as conferring advantage or disadvantage, Rawls leaves an empirically significant source of actual social and economic injustice beyond his consideration. This is important not only because it obscures injustice within the family. It seems to me that it is important to focus on the relationships within the family not only because they themselves are a source of inequality in need of correction but also because these relationships are essential to understanding arrangements outside of the family.

If family were a central part of a justice analysis and family roles were also assessed behind the "veil of ignorance," the structural position of the family in society and the attendant appropriation of domestic labor by the state and the market would become apparent. Thus, the injustice that would be revealed would not only be that between the genders, but also what results through the ordering of our social institutions. The family interacts with, shapes, and is shaped by those institutions, and its structure and functioning affect abilities and capabilities in those other arenas. Therefore, an appreciation of inequities in the family is essential to understanding the justice of other institutional arrangements.

What follows is an example of how engaging the family as a societal institution might alter the way in which we think about poverty and inequality in the United States today—an analysis in which the "private" marital family serves on an ideological level as the repository for the theoretically troublesome issue of dependency.

THE CONCEPT OF DEPENDENCY

One of the most important tasks for those concerned with the welfare of vulnerable members of society, particularly poor mothers and their children, is the articulation of a compelling and complex theory of dependency. I do not underestimate the difficulty of this task. Dependency is a particularly unappealing and stigmatized term in American political and popular consciousness. The specter of dependency is incompatible with our beliefs and myths. We venerate the autonomous, independent, and self-sufficient individual as our ideal. We assume that anyone can cultivate these characteristics, consistent with our belief in the inherent equality of all members of our society, and we stigmatize those who do not. Ideals of independence and self-sufficiency historically have been complementary themes in our political discourse about the poor. Both of these core concepts seem subsumed within the contemporary manifestation of the ideal of autonomy, giving it its current content. Invoking autonomy, we create and perpetuate cultural and political practices that stigmatize and punish the dependent among us. However, only some interrelationships among individuals and institutions are seen as constituting dependency. In recent years, much of the content of dependency has been provided by debates in the welfare context.

Specifically, we stigmatize with the label "dependent" the welfare mother, who, unemployed and trapped within poverty, needs subsidies from the government in order to undertake her caretaking responsibilities. Her circumstances are considered of her own making; she is unworthy of a bailout and must become self-sufficient—that is, assume responsibility for herself by leaving her children behind and taking up low-waged work.

The illusion that independence is attainable for some leads to increased resistance to responding to the obvious dependency of others, as the better off taxpayer detaches himself from the poor and struggling in society. Economist

Frank Levy, of the Massachusetts Institute of Technology, says that prosperous Americans "have caught on to the fact that they can do better if there is no redistribution of income, and since power correlates with income, they are in a position to push the argument"(Uchitelle 1997).

This point of view may not be considered selfish and greedy if those same Americans can convince themselves that we are all capable of becoming economically "self-sufficient" and "independent," regardless of the socio-economic circumstances of our lives. Those who need the government subsidy of welfare payments or other programs simply are not "taking responsibility" for themselves, a premise exemplified by the current political rhetoric about the poor.

However, American politicians apply differing standards of self-sufficiency across different situations. At the same time that we stigmatize mothers on welfare, we commiserate with industries that experience other forms of "disaster" that we define as outside of individual control. Hence we "bail out" some who run amok economically, such as farmers, airlines, saving and loan associations, and highway construction firms. Sometimes the cash transfers such entities receive are justified as being in the national interest—an investment to secure jobs, ensure national defense, or otherwise promote the "American way."

At other times, the government is seen as playing the role of an insurer, such as when it responds to disasters that occur when houses built on flood plains or over fault lines are destroyed through predictable natural occurrences. We rationalize disaster assistance for "acts of nature," but bristle at providing relief for the disasters that have resulted from decades of neglect and discrimination. Governmental response in the former cases is seen as a matter of investment or preservation, an entitlement, not a grudging response to dependency, as it would be if the subsidy were going to impoverished urban ghetto mothers and children.

In an ultimately disastrous manner for our families, we valorize activities associated with work for wages and the accumulation of wealth, while we take for granted dependency work and the production of human beings. Yet raising the future generation is certainly of at least equal value and significance to society as the economic activities we subsidize and facilitate. I argue both that dependency is inevitable and also that reliance on governmental largess and subsidy is universal. We delude ourselves when we think that many (perhaps any) endeavors in our complex modern society can be undertaken in an autonomous and independent manner. And we are unjust and unfair when we blame the poor because they too are dependent and in need of subsidy.

THE RHETORIC OF INDEPENDENCE

Politicians, social conservatives, and advocates of small government use the labels of "dependency," which signifies the condition of being dependent, and "subsidy," which denotes a governmental handout, in an accusatory, simplistic, and divisive manner. The mere invocation of the term "dependency" prompts and justifies mean-spirited and ill-conceived political responses, such as the 1996 welfare "reform" designed to "wean" women and their children from the "cycle of dependency" and "free them" for the world of work. These "reforms" were compounded in the reauthorization process begun in 2002.

Even women on welfare themselves perpetuate a feeling of shame and stigmatize their condition in these terms. The response to a widely publicized statement by a woman who worked her way off welfare illustrates the point. The woman asserted the benefits to her family of leaving welfare: "the success of it is my children see me go to work every day. And that makes them go to school every day, because they see mama isn't staying at home." President Bush applauded this particular mother by stating that: "The ability for somebody to realize kind of an independent life, less dependent upon government not only affects that person but also affects a lot of other people, starting with the children—starting with the children." [1]

The force of the rhetorical assault has served to derail, or limit, contemporary policy discussions about important issues of public welfare. Condemnation or pity is considered the appropriate responses for those unable to live up to ideals of autonomy by acting in an independent and self-sufficient manner. However, the very idea of an independent individual is fashioned on unrealistic and unattainable (dare I even say, "undesirable") premises.

"Inevitable" Dependency

It is puzzling, as well as paradoxical, that the term "dependency" should have such negative connotations. Far from being pathological, avoidable, and the result of individual failings, a state of dependency is a natural part of the human condition, and biological and developmental in nature.

Understood from this perspective, biological dependency should at least be regarded as both universal and "inevitable" and, for these reasons, certainly not deserving of generalized stigma.[2] All of us were dependent as children and many of us will be dependent as we age, become ill, or suffer disabilities. Surely this form of unavoidable and inescapable dependency cannot be condemned. Historically, such dependants were referred to as the category of the "deserving poor" and, thus, deemed worthy of society's largess.

Of course we recognize that the label "dependency" is applied beyond those conditions and relations that are biological or physical in nature. Other forms of reliance on or attachments to others are also characterized as "dependency." Examples include economic, psychological, or emotional reliance or dependence. In fact, these other categories of dependence may accompany the physical or biological form that I am labeling "inevitable." One lesson, therefore, is that dependency is a term that encompasses more than one set of relationships or circumstances. It cannot be reduced to simplistic and pejorative phrases—it must be understood to be a complex and multifaceted concept, potentially taking many different forms.

Therefore, in considering how to shape our social policy in a more focused and sophisticated manner, we must begin to distinguish among various forms of dependency. For example, unlike biological dependency, economic, psychological, and emotional dependencies are not generally understood to be universally experienced. This distinction suggests that these forms of dependency may appropriately be treated differently than forms that are considered inevitable or developmental. The characteristic of universality, which indisputably accompanies inevitable dependence, forms a theoretical basis on which to construct a claim that society as a whole must respond to the situation of the inevitable dependent.

The universal nature of inevitable dependency is central to the argument for the imposition of societal or collective responsibility (Schultz 2000:62n). The realization that this form of dependency is inherent in the human condition is the conceptual foundation on which can be built a claim to societal resources on the part of the caretakers of inevitable dependents in order to facilitate their care. This claim is for an un-stigmatized form of social subsidy for caretakers. Justice demands that society recognize that the dependency labor caretakers perform produces a good for the larger society. Equality demands that the labor must not only be counted, but also must be valued, compensated, and accommodated by society and its institutions.

Society has not, however, responded to the caretaker by counting, valuing, compensating, or accommodating her caretaking. Instead of a societal response, inevitable dependency has been assigned to the quintessentially private institution—the traditional, marital family. This family has been considered as separate from other societal institutions, occupying a "separate sphere." It is conceptualized as placed beyond and protected from intervention by the state. Dependency, through its assignment to the private, marital family, is hidden—privatized within that family, its public and inevitable nature concealed.

Our attitude toward family follows scripts rooted in historic and, therefore, contingent ideologies, particularly those of patriarchy and capitalism. It is naturally assumed that the family is the repository for dependency and that collective societal responsibility is therefore unwarranted and inappropriate. The family assigned this essential societal task is also believed to have a "natural" form. It is organized as though the reproductive imperative necessarily determines the social organization of the family unit around the sexual affiliation necessary for biological reproduction. The core of the family is the heterosexual couple, formally united in marriage.

The poor are caught within and stigmatized by this current understanding of dependency as a private matter. The market can act "irresponsibly"—without considering the demands dependency might place on its workers, freed from any notion that demands for flexibility and other "family-friendly" policies to accommodate those workers are legitimate. The state escapes a primary role in regard to dependency. It is cast as a default institution providing minimal, grudging assistance should families fail. Each individual family is ideally responsible for its own members' dependency, and resorting to collective resources is considered a failure, deserving of condemnation and stigma. In fact, the failure to adequately provide for its members can move a family from the private to the public sphere, where it may be regulated and disciplined (Fineman 1995:177).

In addition to and consistent with the policy of privatizing dependency, provisions of the economic resources necessary for undertaking caretaking tasks are to come from the family. Historically, the breadwinner (the spousal complement to the caretaker) provided these resources. Through such complementary gendered arrangements, each individual private family was ideally and ideologically perceived as able to assume responsibility for its own members and their dependency. A need to call on collective resources, such as welfare assistance, therefore, has been considered a familial as well as an individual failure.[3]

"Derivative" Dependency—Social Assignment and Individual Choice

One result of this privatization of inevitable dependency within the family has been the frustration of our aspirations toward gender equality. It has proven difficult, if not impossible, to break unequal historic patterns of gendered division of labor within the family when the family is also saddled with almost exclusive responsibility for dependency. Combined with the fact that other institutions fail to accommodate the demands of dependency are the cultural and economic forces, which dictate that dependency work is appropriately performed by women. In the pattern of long-standing tradition, caretaking continues to be delegated to women—assigned as the responsibility of the person occupying the gendered role of wife, or mother, or grandmother, or daughter, or daughter-in-law, or sister (Waite and Gallagher 2000: 107).

The assignment of responsibility for dependency to the family in the first instance, and within the family (ultimately to women) in the second, operates in an unjust manner. Meeting the needs of dependents has significant material implications for the caretaker. Paradoxically, undertaking dependency—caring for an inevitable dependant—generates a different form of dependency in the caretaker. I label this form of dependency, often overlooked in policy discussions or collapsed into stigma, "derivative dependency." Derivative dependency arises when a person assumes (or is assigned) responsibility for the care of an inevitably dependent person. I refer to this form of dependency as "derivative" to capture the very simple point that those who care for others are themselves dependent on resources in order to undertake that care. Derivative dependents, as a result of the dependency work they are doing, have a need for monetary or material resources. This explains phenomena such as the "feminization of poverty" noted in recent years. Dependency work is demanding. The norms of sacrifice and selflessness are clear—and costly.

It is important to emphasize that, unlike inevitable dependency, derivative dependency is *not* a universal experience. Derivative dependency is inherent in the status of caretaker, but not all of us perform that role. In fact, many people in our society totally escape the burdens and costs that arise from assuming the role of a caretaker, perhaps are even freed for other pursuits by the caretaking labor of others. We assume that people who are derivative dependents (caretakers or mothers) voluntarily assume that status—they "consent." But why and how is it that only some in our society are asked to undertake the sacrifices that caretaking entails?

Dependency and Choice

People operate in society, expressing preferences as structured by and through existing societal institutions. Choices are made in social relations that reflect long-standing cultural and social arrangements and dominant ideologies about gender and gender roles. The beliefs about the appropriateness of arrangements function at an unconscious (and therefore, unexamined) level. Our notions of what are "natural" behaviors channel our beliefs and feelings about what are considered appropriate institutional arrangements. We know what constitutes the good mother, the ideal husband, and the perfect marriage. When individuals act according to the scripts culturally crafted for these roles, consistent with prevailing ideology and institutional arrangements, we may say that they have chosen their own path. Choice is problematic in this regard. Ideology and beliefs limit and shape what are perceived as available and viable options for all individuals in a society.

The notion that it is an individual choice to assume responsibility for dependency work and the burdens it entails allows us to ignore arguments about our general responsibilities. Choice trumps any perceived inequity and justifies maintenance of the status quo. We ignore the fact that choice occurs within the constraints of social conditions, including history and tradition. Such conditions funnel individual decision making into prescribed channels, often operating along practical and symbolic lines to limit and close down options.

Women have been historically identified with the role of mothering, and presumed to have the responsibility for children (Franke 2001:183–187). Women who choose not to have children are seen as having made a nontraditional, even unnatural choice (185). Even when women choose to have children, they are assumed to care for their children at home.[4] Negative media attention to alternative modes of childcare, such as placement with nannies or day care facilities, has instilled a fear in many people that only parents can properly, safely, and conscientiously raise a child. The cultural context that places responsibility for caretaking primarily on mothers creates further pressure for women to stay at home and raise their children (Porrazzo 1999:12).[5] Even the public school system is structured in a way that is not consistent with families in which women work. The structures remain even though the historic assumption that most mothers remain at home to take care of their children after school and during holidays is no longer valid.[6]

Whenever we use individual choice as a justification for ignoring the inequities in existing social conditions concerning dependency, we also fail to recognize that, quite often, choice of one status or position carries with it consequences not anticipated or imagined at the time of the initial decision. For example, we may say that a woman "chose" to become a mother (societal and family pressures aside), but does this choice mean she also has consented to the societal conditions accompanying that role and the many ways in which that status will negatively affect her and her children's economic prospects?

Further, individual choice should not be the end of the matter if what we are seeking is social justice or fairness. Even if someone does "consent" in that she knew she was taking risks or foregoing opportunities to rise to the challenges dependency work provides, should that let society off the hook? Should society tolerate the situation of dependency within the family and the mandated personal sacrifices a caretaker typically encounters under current societal arrangements? In other words, are some conditions just too oppressive or unfair to be imposed by society even if and when an individual openly agrees to or chooses them?

In response to the argument that caretakers should be compensated for their labor, I have been struck by two contemporary and quasi-economic retorts based on the idea of choice. I refer to one as the "Porsche Preference." This argument states that if someone prefers to have a child, this preference should not be treated differently than any other choice (like the choice to own a Porsche). Society should not be responsible for subsidizing either preference—if you can afford to own a Porsche or have a child, fine, but you can't expect the rest of us to chip in.

I do not accept the basic premise that children are merely another commodity. The nature of children hopefully distinguishes the choice to reproduce from the whims of the auto fan. Further, it seems to me that a decision to have a child sets up a qualitatively different relationship between the decision maker and the collective or state. As I argue in the next section of this chapter, having and caring for dependency is a society-preserving task—care of children in particular is essential to the future of the society and all of its institutions. It is a different sort of "preference," providing a social good as well as individual satisfaction.

Responding to this type of reasoning, some have argued that the consumption of Porsches is also essential to society. Consumption leads to jobs and the creation of stockholder wealth, just like a preference for children (Franke 2001:190–191). Accepting only for arguments' sake the troublesome premises of this kind of argument through analogy, it seems clear that the appropriate comparison is not between the *consumers* of children and of Porsches, but the *producers* of children and those of Porsches. If we make that kind of comparison, my arguments for subsidy for caretakers are supported by the analogy. The producers of Porsches are subsidized (heavily) through regulatory measures such as tariff and tax policy and labor regulations, as well as directly, such as when communities bid for location of plants or lawmakers slash taxes and make investments in services to entice businesses with roaming eyes.

Further, when we think of just who are the consumers and who are the producers for purposes of comparison, it is important to remember that the government and the market are the consumers for the products of caretaking labor. And they are not paying a fair price; in fact, they are paying very little (Belle 1999:12; Helburn and Bergmann 2002:98). Not subsidizing the caretaker in this kind of comparison is the equivalent of the consumer stealing the Porsche its manufacturer so lovingly created and skillfully constructed.

The second argument about choice is also framed in economic terms. I label this the "efficiency as exploitation" model of excuse for not requiring society to pay a fair share for the necessary care work that must occur. This argument is really nothing more than the assertion that if caretakers allow themselves to be exploited—unpaid or underpaid—then this must be the most "efficient" solution. Voluntary assumption of the costs of caretaking and dependency should not be disturbed.

Sometimes this is expressed as simply the result of the fact that women have more of a "preference" for children and, as such, are willing to make other sacrifices—that is simply what the market will bear. Aside from the fact that this type of arrangement creates situations that negatively affect society far beyond the individual caretaker and her charges, a free market in care work is not working. It has resulted in poverty, which generates other social ills. I think the implications of this type of laissez-fare approach to important issues of social policy also demonstrates how little economics has to offer to considerations of justice.

THE DEPENDENCY DEFICIT — A SOCIETY IN DEFAULT

As it now stands in this society, derivative dependents are expected to get both economic and structural resources within the family. The market is unresponsive and uninvolved, and the state is perceived as a last resort for financial resources, the refuge of the failed family. A caretaker who must resort to governmental assistance may do so only if she can demonstrate, through a highly stigmatized process, that she is needy.

Deficit

Unfortunately, in many situations, neither the economic nor the structural supports for caretaking are adequate. Within families, caretaking work is unpaid, expected to be gratuitously and uncomplainingly supplied. Even when nonfamily members, such as nannies or nurses, supply caretaking labor, the family remains primarily responsible for the care. And, furthering the assumption that this type of work is not valuable, the wages are supplied from family funds, not through social subsidies, ensuring that they are low.[7]

In some atypical instances, employers offer a more communal approach to caretaking or the state may assume some responsibility, such as a company-sponsored childcare or home health aids provided by public funds. However, such nonfamily assistance with caretaking is not compelled (and in fact is contradicted) by our understanding of who is responsible for dependency. This sort of assistance is viewed as "generous," an unexpected benefit supplementing the primary responsibility of the family.

If we measure success by poverty statistics, it seems clear that many families are failing in their socially assigned task as the repository for dependency. Many caretakers and their dependents find themselves impoverished or severely economically compromised even if they are operating within the context of a marital family. Helburn and Bergmann (2002) illustrate that, even with both parents working full time at minimum wage, taking into consideration the required poverty line expenditures, they are unable to pay the cost of licensed childcare.[8] As can be expected, single mothers have an even more difficult time making ends meet and providing for childcare as they are also engaged in the workforce.[9]

For others, the death of a primary wage earner or divorce can prompt an economic freefall into poverty. Some women in these situations are in worse positions than women who remain single, because these newly single women have cut back on their career commitments as a result of the partnership in order to raise children or to allow the partner to advance his career (Waite and Gallagher 2000:99).

Even families that "conform," in that they are both intact and economically self-sufficient (are not poor), are often suffering a crisis, either in caretaking or from work demands, or both. Most two-parent households must send both parents into the workforce in order to make ends meet, all at the cost of quality time spent with their children.[10] In some two-parent households the childcare or after-school care is designated to one parent, and the other parent spends less time with the child(ren) (Belle 1999:7).

Assessing the Costs of Care

Direct costs associated with caretaking burden the person doing the dependency work. Caretaking labor interferes with the pursuit and development of wage labor options. Caretaking labor saps energy and efforts from investment in career or market activities, those things that produce economic rewards. There are foregone opportunities and costs associated with caretaking. Even caretakers who work in the paid labor force typically have more tenuous ties to the public sphere because they must also accommodate caretaking demands in the private sphere (Waite and Gallagher 2000:99).

Also, psychological or spiritual costs result from the attenuated and compromised relationships a caretaker is forced to have with both the market and family (if she works in both), or from the need to choose, thus sacrificing one to gain the other.[11] The caretaker is caught within social configurations and institutional arrangements that are unjust.

Further, most institutions in society remain relatively unresponsive to innovations that would lessen the costs of caretaking. Caretaking occurs in a larger context, and caretakers often need accommodation in order to fulfill multiple responsibilities. For example, many caretakers also engage in market work (Novkov 1992:165–166; discussing the role of working mothers). Far from structurally accommodating or facilitating caretaking, however, workplaces operate in modes incompatible with the idea that workers also have obligations for dependency. Workplace expectations displace the demands of caretaking—we assume that workers are those that are free to work long and regimented hours.

These costs are not distributed among all beneficiaries of caretaking (be they institutional or individual). Unjustly, the major economic and career costs associated with caretaking are typically borne by the caretaker alone (Belle 1999:75–78). If she is lucky, the caretaker is able to persuade her partner in the private family to share the costs with her, spreading them out a bit. But the costs remain confined to the family in a world where market institutions assume workers are unencumbered by family and dependency and the government assumes that (functioning) families provide for basic needs.

Dually responsible workers currently suffer penalties while market institutions are relieved of responsibility for dependency. It is important to note here that, although caretaking remains gendered in practice, it is the caretaking itself, not the gender of the caretaker, that is inherently disadvantageous in our system. When men do care work, they also suffer costs. It is the caretaking itself that institutions are free to punish. These penalties must be removed and there must be a more equitable distribution of responsibility for dependency among the primary societal institutions of family, market, and state.

Default—Accruing a Social Debt for Social Goods

I argue that caretaking work creates a collective or social debt and that each and every member of society is obligated by this debt. Furthermore, this debt transcends individual circumstances. In other words, we need not be elderly, ill, or children any longer to be held individually responsible. Nor can we satisfy or discharge our collective responsibility within our individual, private families. Merely being financially generous with our own mothers or duly supporting our own wives will not suffice to satisfy the share of the societal debt we generally owe to all caretakers (Fineman 2000:18).

My argument that the caretaking debt is necessarily a collective one is based on the fact that biological dependency is a universal and inevitable phase in the human condition, and therefore, of necessity, a collective or societal concern. Individual dependency needs must be met if we, as individuals, are to survive, and our aggregate or collective dependency needs must be met if our society is to survive and perpetuate itself. The mandate that the state (collective society) respond to dependency, therefore, is not a matter of altruism or empathy (which are individual responses often resulting in charity), but one that is primary and essential because such a response is fundamentally society preserving.

If infants or ill persons are not cared for, nurtured, nourished, and perhaps loved, they will perish. We can say, therefore, that they owe an individual debt to their individual caretakers. But the obligation is not theirs alone—nor is their obligation confined only to their own caretakers. Social justice demands a broader sense of obligation. Without aggregate caretaking, there could be no society, so we might say that it is caretaking labor that produces and reproduces society. Caretaking labor provides the citizens, the workers, the voters, the consumers, the students, and others who populate society and its institutions. There are essential tasks to be performed in every society that are legitimate state concerns. One of these is the response to dependency (Fineman 2000:13, 21, 15n). The fact that biological dependency is inherent in the human condition means that it is of collective or societal concern.

Society-preserving tasks, like dependency work, are commonly delegated. The delegation is accomplished through the establishment and maintenance of social institutions. For example, the armed services are established to attend to the collective need for national defense. But delegation is not the same thing as abandonment. The armed services are structured simultaneously as both the responsibility of only some designated members (volunteers or draftees) and of all members of society (taxpayers and voters) (Fineman 2000:19).

This dual and complementary responsibility is consistent with our deeply held beliefs about how rights and obligations are accrued and imposed in a just society: societal obligations have both an individual and a collective dimension. Certain members of society may volunteer, be recruited, or even drafted for service, but they have a right to be compensated for their services from collective resources. They also have a right to the necessary tools to perform their assigned tasks and to guarantees that they will be protected by rules and policies that facilitate their performance. Caretakers should have the same right to have their society-preserving labor supported and facilitated. Provision of the means for their task should be considered the responsibility of the collective society.

THE RHETORIC OF SUBSIDY AND SELF-SUFFICIENCY

In popular and political discourse, the idea of "subsidy" is the equally stigmatized companion to dependence, the opposite of the ideal of self-sufficiency. In fact, dependency is assumed if an individual is the recipient of certain governmental subsidies, such as welfare. The specter of dependency serves as an argument against subsidies in the form of governmental social welfare transfers. Policy makers, who argue for the goal of independence, favor the termination of subsidy so the individual can learn to be self-sufficient.

But a subsidy is nothing more than a process of allocating collective resources to some persons or endeavors, rather than other persons or endeavors, because a social judgment is made that they are in some way "entitled" or that the subsidy is justified (Cimini 2002). Entitlement to subsidy is asserted through a variety of considerations, such as the status of the person receiving the subsidy, their past contribution to the social good, or their need. Often, a subsidy is justified because of the position the subsidized group holds, or the potential value their endeavors have, for the larger society. Sometimes the benefits we receive are public and financial, such as direct governmental transfer programs to certain individuals or business entities, such as farmers or sugar growers (Fineman 2000:17n). Public subsidies can also be indirect, such as the benefits given in tax policy (18n; see also McCluskey 2000). Private economic subsidy systems work in the forms of foundations, religions, and charities.

Types of Subsidy

Typically, a subsidy is thought of as the provision of monetary or economic assistance. However, a subsidy can also be delivered through the organization of social structures and norms that create and enforce expectations. A subsidy can also be nonmonetary, such as the subsidy provided by the uncompensated labor of others in caring for us and our dependency needs as individuals, as well as members of a larger dependent society. Taking this observation into account, along with the ideas of inevitable and derivative dependency, it seems obvious that we must conclude that subsidy is also universal. We all exist in contexts and relationships, in social and cultural institutions, such as families, which facilitate, support, and subsidize us and our endeavors.

In complex modern societies no one is self-sufficient, either economically or socially. Whether the subsidies we receive are financial (such as in governmental transfer programs or favorable tax policy) or nonmonetary (such as those provided by the uncompensated labor of others in caring for us and our needs), we all live subsidized lives. In fact, all of us receive both forms of subsidy during our lives. In particular, for those who adhere to the myths of autonomy and independence, it is important to confront the fact that the uncompensated labor of caretakers is an unrecognized subsidy, not only to the individuals who directly receive it, but more significantly, to the entire society.

The interesting question is why some subsidies are differentiated and stigmatized while others are hidden. Subsidies to market institutions and middle-class families are called "investments," "incentives," or "earned," when government supplies them, but deemed "gifts," "charity," or the product of "familial love" when they are contributions of caretaking labor. The actions of our government thus far reflect the inconsistent and hypocritical stance taken with regard to subsidy. The family is to be self-sufficient, but the situation of others is viewed sympathetically.

Subsidy and Politics—A Contemporary Comparison

The same politicians who seem to be out of touch with the actual situation of welfare recipients, by insisting on their self-sufficiency,[12] choose to disregard these myths when it comes to matters such as the farm subsidy.[13] These conflicting concepts of autonomy and subsidy were highlighted recently, when, on the very same day that certain Democratic senators joined with Republicans in proposing stricter requirements for welfare recipients, the House of Representatives passed a bill that would provide large subsidies to America's farms.[14]

The language used in each case is revealing: the agricultural bill is named the Farm Security and Rural Investment Act, and was described by President Bush (Bush 2002),[15] ironically, as establishing a "reliable *safety net* for our Nations' Farmers and ranchers." The President emphasized that the act would provide the "support" that "[h]ardworking . . . farm and ranch families" deserve. Obscenely, because the House voted down a motion that would cap payments at $275,000 a year per farmer, the result is that three-quarters of the subsidy payments will go to the largest and richest 10 percent of farmers—in other words, to agribusinesses, not to the "hardworking farm and ranch families" who deserve support (Tyson 2002).

On the same day, a dozen Democratic Senators "declared that Congress must adopt 'tougher work requirements'" so that by 2007, 70 percent of welfare recipients must be engaged in work and other supervised activities, an increase from the current requirement of 50 percent.[16] Unlike the Farm Bill, earlier undertaken welfare reform *does* allow states to cap their payments, so that if a child is born to a mother already receiving welfare payments, she will not receive any additional funds to support and feed that child.[17] For example, New Jersey has implemented a system whereby a woman on welfare receives a basic $488 per month with an additional $64 for each child. But if a woman on welfare gets pregnant and has a child while receiving assistance, she receives no additional cash allotment for the new baby.[18] It was argued that to provide the funds would create an incentive for reproduction.

CONCLUSION

The societal arrangement whereby dependency was the responsibility of the private family may have made some sense when marriage was cast as a lifelong commitment and assumed a certain gendered role-playing pairing. If we have both a caretaker and a wage earner who make differentiated but complementary contributions—one providing the caretaking and emotional resources, the other the material necessities—then perhaps dependency can be handled within this family. But what about the situation of millions of families that do not conform to that (some would say antiquated) ideal? And what about the costs to individuals within families that do conform—the losses of opportunity and access because of the burdens of caretaking? Further, what about the responsibility of the rest of us—society and its institutions? How is it just that we appropriate the labor of caretakers and refuse to contribute a fair share of the burdens associated with that care?

The myths about autonomy, independence, and self-sufficiency both for individuals and for families have only been able to flourish and perpetuate themselves because dependency has been hidden within the family. When certain families reveal the fallacy of the assumption that they can adequately manage their members' needs, we do not reexamine the premises, but demonize those families as failures. Therefore, those in need of economic assistance are viewed as deviating from the stated norm of independence and self-sufficiency. It is time to rethink "subsidy" as well as "autonomy" and "dependency."

If caretaking is society-preserving (therefore productive) work, the political and policy questions should focus on an optimal reallocation of responsibility for dependency across societal institutions. Reallocation in this scheme may be provided through economic transfers to caretaking units, as well as by the provision of structural supports that accommodate caretaking responsibilities within workplaces so that those who both work for wages and work for love or duty do not have to compromise one to do the other.

Chapter One

1. The history of class analysis is in large part a series of disputes over which of these various structural conditions should be treated as fundamental. Indeed, one conventional approach among class analysts is to define classes in terms of some single dimension that is deemed especially crucial (e.g., authority, property ownership), a dimension that is typically understood as defining the main axis of exploitation, interests, or life chances. Although one might therefore conclude that class analysts are just as unidimensional as "income paradigm" economists (and differ merely by virtue of elevating some nonincome dimension to the privileged standing that economists reserve for income), such a conclusion would ignore another, competing theme within the class analytic literature that treats classes as organic wholes signaling a package of structural conditions. We emphasize the latter tradition here because of its obvious and productive connection to multidimensionalist approaches within economics.

2. As we before noted, most class analysts assume that classes convey more information than can be captured in any simple hierarchical dimension, thus implying that conventional scales (e.g., socioeconomic scales) are unacceptable substitutes for class-based measurement (e.g., Goldthorpe and Erikson 1992).

3. The claim that classes have distinctive cultures has a complicated Marxian and non-Marxian provenance that long predates the work of Wilson (1987) and Bourdieu (1984). Although this long line of scholarship was well regarded (esp. Thompson 1966; Kohn 1969; Lukács 1972), the contributions of Wilson (1987) and Bourdieu (1984) were truly transformative and thus merit a special place in the history of class analysis.

4. Indeed, whereas economists typically wish to assess whether a particular society or time period is more or less unequal than another (with inequality measured multidimensionally), sociologists have shown little interest in making ordinal comparisons of this sort, nor does a class-based approach lend itself to such comparisons. That is, a class-based approach allows analysts to represent multidimensional

distributions parsimoniously, but it does not allow them to compare two such distributions and assess in any straightforward way which is the more unequal.

Chapter Two

Based on a presentation at the Cornell University Conference on Conceptual Challenges in Poverty and Inequality, April 16–17, 2002. I have drawn also on my Yan Fu Memorial Lecture at the International Symposium on Equity and Social Justice in Transitional China at the China Center for Economic Research, Peking University, Beijing, July 11–12, 2002.

1. These estimates are taken from Khan and Riskin (2001). The quoted figures, in particular, occur in Table 3.5 on p. 41.

2. The numbers are taken from Table 2.

3. See also Anand and Segal (2002), and Crafts (2002). Important methodological issues are also addressed in Anand (1993).

4. Foster et al. (1984).

5. The relevance of the perspective of entitlement deprivation in famine analysis is discussed in Sen (1981). In the studies presented there, although famines in the Sahel countries in the 1970s were linked, if only indirectly, with declines in food supply (Chapter 8), other famines studied, namely the Bengal famine of 1943, the famine in Wollo in Ethiopia in 1973, the Bangladesh famine of 1974 (Chs. 6, 7, and 9) occurred with little or no fall in food supply.

6. On this see Sen (1981, Ch. 10), and also Drèze and Sen (1989), and Osmani (1995).

7. Lin and Yang (2000) illuminatingly investigate, among other causal factors, the influence of state-related entitlements on entitlements and real incomes in a centrally planned system.

8. These issues were discussed in Sen (1985a; 1985b), and Nussbaum and Sen (1993).

9. Aristotle (1980, book I, section 5, p. 7).

10. The "human development" perspective, championed by Mahbub ul Haq and reflected in the *Human Development Reports*, and even the "human development index," with its focus on longevity and education (in addition to basic income), can, in this broad sense, be directly linked to Buddha's famous quest, more than 2,500 years ago.

11. See particularly Volume 2, Book V, Chapter II (section on "Taxes upon Consumable Commodities"); in Smith (1776, 469–71).

12. The "social exclusion" approach, now widely used, was pioneered by Renê Lenior (1974).

13. I have discussed these issues in Sen (1983), reprinted in Sen (1984), and also in Sen (1992, Ch. 7).

14. Another area in which China's post-reform performance could make good use of its pre-reform achievements is that of land reform. When the "responsibility

system" was introduced in China as a part of the reform package, China had the benefit of not having to deal with great inequalities in land ownership that bedevil the prospects of economic development in many poor countries.

15. China remains, of course, well ahead of India as a whole, in terms of a low infant mortality rate. These comparisons are discussed more fully in Drèze and Sen (2002).

16. I have discussed these issues extensively, jointly with James Foster, in the "substantial annexe" in the expanded edition (published in 1997) of Sen (1973).

17. See A. F. Shorrocks (1988).

18. On this see Sen (1973; revised edition, Sen 1997b).

19. In particular, being "Lorenz-consistent, normalized, continuous."

20. Sen (1976), reprinted in Sen (1982).

21. As was mentioned earlier, this measure, along with a wider class of decomposable poverty indicators, was proposed by J. E. Foster, J. Greer, and E. Thorbecke (1984).

22. See also Martin Ravallion (1994) who has been a leading contributor to the World Bank's estimates of poverty.

23. See for example Khan and Riskin (2001), as was mentioned earlier.

24. For references to the large number of different variants, see the Annexe by James Foster and myself in the 1997 edition of *On Economic Inequality*. The variants include Hamada and Takayama (1977); Blackorby and Donaldson (1980); and Shorrocks (1995) among a number of other proposed indicators.

25. I have tried to defend that rough wisdom in a different context in Sen (1973, Ch. 3).

Chapter Three

An earlier version of this paper appears in *Feminist Economics*, as "Capabilities as Fundamental Entitlements: Sen and Social Justice," in a special issue devoted to the work of Amartya Sen. I develop related arguments, with a focus on constitutional and legal issues, in Nussbaum (forthcoming).

1. I make this case at greater length in Nussbaum (2000a); see also Nussbaum (forthcoming).

2. See especially Kittay (1999), Folbre (1999, 2001); Williams (2000); Harrington (1999). Earlier influential work in this area includes Fineman (1991, 1995); Ruddick (1989); Tronto (1993); Held (1993); West (1997). For an excellent collection of articles from diverse feminist perspectives, see Held (1995). See also Nussbaum (2000b). And, finally, see *Human Development Report 1999*.

3. See Sen (1980, 1982, 1985a, 1992, 1999), representative examples of the many publications in which Sen has advanced this position.

4. See for example Sen (1990, 1995, 1999).

5. See Nussbaum (2001a). See also Nussbaum (2004a), where I point out that all societies cater to the disabilities of the average person. Thus, we do not have

staircases with steps so high that only giants can climb them, or orchestras tuned to play at pitches inaudible to human ears and audible only to dogs.

A further problem not mentioned by Sen, but relevant to his critique of Rawls: even if the person in the wheelchair were equally well off with regard to economic well-being, there is a separate issue of dignity and self-respect. By measuring relative social positions by income and wealth alone, Rawls ignores the possibility that a group may be reasonably well-off economically, but suffer grave disabilities with regard to the social bases of self-respect. One might argue that gays and lesbians in our society are in precisely that position. Certainly the physically and mentally handicapped will be in that position, as their economic fortunes rise—unless society makes a major and fundamental commitment to inclusion and respect.

6. Obviously the case for this depends very much both on what capability we are considering and on how we describe it. Thus, equality of capability seems to be important when we consider the right to vote, the freedom of religion, and so on; but if we consider the capability to play basketball, it seems ludicrous to suppose that society should be very much concerned about even a minimum threshold level of it, much less complete equality. With something like health, much hangs on whether we define the relevant capability as "access to the social bases of health" or "the ability to be healthy." The former seems like something that a just society should distribute on a basis of equality; the latter contains an element of chance that no just society could, or should, altogether eliminate. So the question of whether equality of capability is a good social goal cannot be well answered without specifying a list of the relevant capabilities, another point in favor of the argument I advance in the section "Capabilities and the Social Contract Tradition."

7. See his reply to letters concerning Sen (2001).

8. Not invariably: Art. 14, closely modeled on the equal protection clause of the U.S. 14th amendment, reads: "The State shall not deny to any person equality before the law or the equal protection of the laws within the territory of India."

9. Of course this account of both is in many ways too simple; I refer primarily to the wording of the documents here, not to the complicated jurisprudential traditions stemming from them.

10. I am thinking of the suspension of civil liberties during the Emergency, in the former case, and of the new proposal for military tribunals to try foreign nationals suspected of terrorism, in the latter.

11. See further discussion in Nussbaum (2002).

12. For the relation of this idea to objectivity, see Nussbaum (2001c).

13. See my discussion of this issue in Nussbaum (2000a, Ch. 1), and for a rejoinder to perfectionist critics, see Nussbaum (2000c).

14. I am very skeptical of attempts to add group cultural rights to the list because every group contains hierarchy. Thus, to give a group rights *qua* group is often to give the powerful members a license to continue subordinating the less powerful. Moreover, ethnic and cultural groups are likely in this way to be promoted above other groups around which many people define the meaning of their

lives: the women's movement, for example, or groups formed around occupation or sexual orientation.

15. This is what Sen said in response to an earlier version of the present chapter when it was first presented at the conference in Bielefeld.

16. Sen stated at the Bielefeld conference that this is not his concern.

17. The argument of this section is a somewhat shorter version of the argument of Nussbaum (2000b). I develop these lines of thought in a different and fuller way in my Tanner Lectures in Human Values, *Beyond the Social Contract: Toward Global Justice*, given at the Australian National University in November 2002, and in the Tanner Lectures series, University of Utah Press (Nussbaum 2004b).

18. Although Rawls's list also includes some capability-like items, such as opportunities and liberties, only wealth and income are used to define who is "least well off" in the society, a key notion for the application of Rawls's difference principle.

19. The list is actually heterogeneous, including liberties, opportunities, and powers alongside income and wealth; recently Rawls has added still other capability-like items to the list, such as access to health care and the availability of leisure time.

20. Locke, *Second Treatise on Government*, Ch. 8.

21. Gauthier (1986:18) is speaking of all "persons who decrease th[e] average level" of well-being in a society.

22. For one particularly valuable treatment of this theme, see Rachels (1990). Two wonderful pictures of the animal sort of dignity: Smuts (1999) and Pitcher (1995). I discuss the implications of recognizing the dignity of nonhuman animals in Nussbaum (2000d). See also MacIntyre (1999).

23. I do not mean to deny that Kant gives need an important role in his theory: for just one good treatment of this aspect of Kant's thought, see Wood (1999). What I mean is that whereas for Kant personality and animality are conceptually independent, and personality is not itself understood in terms of need, for Rawls these two elements are more thoroughly integrated, and the person is understood from the first as in need of material and other goods.

24. As Eva Kittay has argued in an excellent discussion in Kittay (1999), there are five places in Rawls's theory where he fails to confront facts of asymmetrical neediness that might naturally have been confronted. (1) His account of the "circumstances of justice" assumes a rough equality between persons, such that none could dominate all the others; thus, we are not invited to consider relations of justice that might be obtained between an adult and her infants, or her senile demented parents. (2) Rawls's idealization of citizens as "fully cooperating" puts to one side the large facts about extreme neediness I have just mentioned. (3) His conception of social cooperation, again, is based on the idea of reciprocity between equals, and has no explicit place for relations of extreme dependency. (4) His account of the primary goods, introduced, as it is, as an account of the needs of citizens who are characterized by the two moral powers and by the capacity to be "fully cooperating,"

has no place for the need of many real people for the kind of care we give to people who are not independent. And (5) his account of citizens' freedom as involving the concept of being a self-authenticating source of valid claims (e.g. Rawls [1996:32]) fails to make a place for any freedom that might be enjoyed by someone who is not independent in that sense.

25. "Dependency must be faced from the beginning of any project in egalitarian theory that hopes to include all persons within its scope" (Kittay 1999:77). For a remarkable narrative of a particular life that shows exactly how many social structures play a part in the life of a mentally handicapped child from the very beginning, see Bérubé (1996).

26. In Rawls (1971), primary goods were characterized as all-purpose means to the pursuit of one's own conception of the good, whatever it is; in Rawls (1980; 1996) the interpretation shifts, and Rawls (1996:187–190) acknowledges that they are means with regard to the Kantian political conception of the person.

27. As the late Peter Cicchino eloquently put this point, Aristotle's conception is not deductive or a priori: it respects widely held views about human reality, but takes experience as its source and guide. Second, it takes seriously the materiality of human beings—their need for food, shelter, friendship, care, what might be called their basic dependency. Third, it is epistemologically modest—it does not claim to have the exactitude of mathematics, but rather is content to look for "such precision as accords with the subject-matter" (Cicchino 1999).

28. In that way my view is close to the type of liberalism defended (against Lockean contractarianism) by T. H. Green, though my form is not perfectionistic, but is, rather, a form of political liberalism. I have found very illuminating the discussion of the liberal tradition in Deigh (2001).

Chapter Four

1. See Atkinson (1998) and Atkinson et al. (2002).
2. See Dollar and Kraay (2002).
3. For recent extensive presentations, see for instance Seidl (1988), Ravallion (1992), and Jantti and Danzinger (2000).
4. For a theoretical discussion of the definitions of the poverty line, see Ravallion (2002). For a critique of common international poverty measures such as the US$1 a day, see Srinivasan (2001).
5. These results were established independently by Atkinson (1987) and Foster and Shorrocks (1988).
6. See Bourguignon and Fields (1990).
7. On imperfect targeting, see Kanbur (1987). For an interesting application of this principle to the allocation of foreign aid see Collier and Dollar (2000).
8. A summary of Sen's views and the development of that literature over the last twenty years may be found in the last annexe in Sen (1997b).
9. Referred to as "functionings" by Sen.

10. See Roemer (1998).

11. See Atkinson (1998, sections 2.3 and 2.4). Note also that some authors prefer to define social exclusion in the space of outcome, Q, rather than the space of capabilities or opportunities *(A, Z)*. See for instance Atkinson et al. (2002).

12. For a good illustration of these techniques and concepts see Sahn and Younger (1999) and Bourguignon and Pereira da Silva (2003). Note that the evidence in support of this theory is problematic (see Persson and Tabellini 1994).

13. See Bourguignon (1999).

14. This argument is similar to the "veil of ignorance" reasoning in social justice theory.

15. When discussing that issue, Sen (1997b, Appendix A-7) refers to using a specific point on the frontier of K and the whole frontier as the "choice application" and the "options application" respectively.

16. Note that the weighing considered here differs from the weighing assigned in Sen (1997b, pp. 203–209). Weights in the latter case are associated with the outcome vector, instead of the endowment variables. The problem here is that the knowledge of the frontier $F°(A, Z, .)$ is still necessary to compare two distributions on the vector X. As stated above, the knowledge of that function is essentially imperfect. Tsui (1999) considers a more general case.

17. Assuming of course that a meaningful quantitative concept may be used to measure poverty in education. See the section "Handling Human Capital Endowment."

18. Bourguignon and Chakravarty (2003); see also Atkinson (2003).

19. A complication that arises when dealing with multiple outcomes is that they may be linked with each other through the production function $F( )$ in equation (1). The treatment of multidimensionality would thus require distinguishing carefully between trade-offs arising on the production side and those arising on the welfare side. This problem does not exist in the space of opportunities or capabilities.

20. The Human Development Index, which is sometimes cited as an illustration of the multidimensional concepts discussed here, is not such a good example after all because it is concerned with population averages rather than individual observations. (See the definition of this index in the various annual issues of UNDP's annual Human Development Report.)

21. EITC stands for the Earned Income Tax Credit. It is a subsidy given to low wage earners. Equivalent systems in European countries are the Working Family Tax Credit in the UK and the Prime pour l'emploi in France.

22. Unemployment is both voluntary and involuntary if $w = w^* = w°$.

23. Note that this issue differs from the problem of stochastic income and "vulnerability" in poverty analysis. Here, the problem is about the uncertainty surrounding the value of a constant parameter not about the properties of a stochastic process that may lie behind income or consumption expenditures.

24. Bourguignon et al. (2003) estimate such an equation for various successive cohorts in Brazil and evaluate the role of the inequality of opportunities in

overall earning inequality by simulating the effect of equalizing schooling and parents' characteristics across all individuals.

25. For a general discussion of the concept of mobility with relevance to the
following arguments, see Fields (2001).

26. Note that the measure of inequality of opportunities proposed by Roemer
(1998) has the same problem because it is based on inequalities related to some observed innate or inherited characteristics. The rank of blacks' and whites' earnings in
their respective distribution may reflect identical levels of efforts, as assumed by that
author, but also other unobserved differences, which may be innate or inherited.

27. See, for instance, Deininger (1999) and World Bank (2003).

28. See Harberger (1998) for a compelling defense of this policy.

29. For a general discussion of vulnerability, see Fields (2001). For evidence
of the school desertion effect in periods of crisis see the analysis of the distributional effects of the Indonesian crisis by Frankenberg et al. (2002). Note, however,
that Schady (2002) presents opposite evidence in the case of Peru. Lowering the
cost of opportunity of schooling crises would in fact increase school attendance.

30. Jacoby (2000) gives a measure of these propensities to consume by studying differences in consumption behavior of households whose children may or may
not benefit from school lunches. See also the analysis by Duflo (2003) of the effect
of pension income transfers on the anthropometric characteristics of children in
South African households entitled to such transfers.

31. For a general survey on child labor, see Basu (1999).

32. For the education effect of Progresa, see Behrman et al (2001); for the
health effect, see Gertler (2000).

33. See, for instance, World Bank (2000).

Chapter Five

1. Several empirical assessments of the size and growth of the underclass by
social scientists did appear in the late 1980s, but rather than help to draw attention
to the underlying causes of chronic poverty, these studies tended to contribute to
the perception that as a group the underclass was synonymous with deviant behavior. (See, for example, Ricketts and Sawhill, 1988, and Nathan, 1986.)

2. Social scientists tend to use census tracts as proxies for neighborhoods.
And census tracts with poverty rates of at least 40 percent are defined as ghetto or
high-poverty neighborhoods. For example, in Chicago we found that 82 percent of
the residents who live in high-poverty census tracts inhabit the South and West
sides of the city in areas that have been overwhelmingly black for half a century
and more. These tracts make up the historic core of Chicago's black ghetto. An additional 13 percent live in immediately adjacent tracts.

Thus, when we contrast high-poverty areas with other areas in the inner city,
we are in effect comparing ghetto neighborhoods with other black areas, most of
which are moderately poor, that are not part of Chicago's traditional black belt
(Wacquant and Wilson, 1990). Using the same rationale on a national level, Jar-

gowsky and Bane (1991) state: "Based on visits to several cities, we found that the 40 percent criterion came very close to identifying areas that looked like ghettos in terms of their housing conditions. Moreover, the areas selected by the 40 percent criterion corresponded rather closely with the judgments of city officials and local census bureau officials about which neighborhoods were ghettos" (pp. 8–9).

3. In the ensuing discussion in this section, I benefited from Zelditch's formal explication of *The Truly Disadvantaged* (1989).

4. The point here is that the elimination of racial barriers creates the greater opportunities for the talented, more educated, and better-trained minority group members because, as James Fiskin (1983) has pointed out, they possess the resources to compete most effectively. These resources derive from a variety of advantages made possible or provided by their families including financial means, schooling, and peer groups. However, if the more advantaged members of minority groups profit disproportionately from policies that enhance individual opportunity, they also benefit disproportionately from policies of affirmative action based solely on their racial group membership. Minority individuals from the most advantaged families tend to be more heavily represented among those of their racial group most qualified for college admissions, higher paying jobs, and promotions.

5. See above note 2.

6. Of the large cities in the United States, Boston is unique in that it includes a significant number of whites who live in high-poverty census tracts. Thus, the use of the term "white underclass" would be more applicable to Boston than to other metropolises in this country.

7. Alejandro Portes and Ruben G. Rumbaut (2001) use the term "underclass" to refer to those second generation Latino immigrants who have experienced the downward assimilation path, including residence in barrios, not the more stable and socially organized immigrant enclaves, and whose experiences are similar to those African Americans who reside in ghettos.

Chapter Seven

The ideas and concepts explored in this chapter are more fully developed in my most recent book (Fineman 2004). See also (Fineman 1995).

1. George W. Bush, "Remarks by President Bush to the North Carolina Chamber of Commerce," *Federal News Service* (Feb. 27, 2002). http://www.lexis-nexis.com/.

2. Peter Edelman, Professor of Law, Georgetown University Law Center, speaking to the Senate Health, Education, Labor and Pensions Committee, on Feb. 14, 2002. *Federal News Service.* http://www.lexis-nexis.com/.

3. One set of resulting relations that are typically ignored concern the racial and class implications of this system. In thinking about the privatization of dependency and the role of the family, our history of racism is also relevant. This is apparent when we consider caretaking situations in the paid labor force where women of color are substituted for the unpaid family laborer at low wages with few, if any,

benefits. Because the resources for childcare come from the family, wages are depressed, as family resources are needed for provision of other basic goods and services. Ironically, a good deal of the training for work that is occurring in the wake of welfare reform is for positions in childcare.

4. See Lamorey and Robinson (1999:19) arguing that the major myth that expects mothers to stay at home and be the primary caretaker of children arises from society's negative attitude towards maternal employment, divorce, day care, single parenting, and latchkey children.

5. Approximately 60–70 percent of those who videotape their nannies end up firing them. One parent found their nanny to be taking wonderful care of the child, but was also overheard saying: "I take much better care of you than your mother."

6. "The U.S. public school day is substantially shorter than the full-time work day and shorter than the school day in many other nations of the world. The school year is also interrupted by frequent holidays, early release days, and closings for inclement weather, and then concluded with a lengthy summer vacation, all of which vastly exceeds the vacation allotments of most employed parents. Nor are extended day or after-school programs available in many communities or to many children who need them" (Belle 1999:7).

7. See Helburn and Bergmann (2002:28), when a family at or near the poverty level is looking for child care, they will obviously look for the cheapest available, which is most likely to be unlicensed care; furthermore, if there are any questions as to the quality, many families in this situation would resolve them in favor of cheapness.

8. See Helburn and Bergmann (2002:98): two parents working at minimum wage, for 52 forty-hour weeks, with two preschool children earn $27,962 in disposable income-after taxes. With the official U.S. poverty line living expenses set at $17,493 the family only has $10,496 to spend on childcare estimated to cost between $9,980 and $11,870.

9. Ibid. One parent, with two preschool children, working at minimum wage for 52 forty-hour weeks, with government benefits earns $15,736 in disposable income. With the official U.S. poverty line living expenses set at $13,898, the mother has only $1,838 to spend on care estimated to cost between $9,980 and $11,870.

10. See Edelman, above note 3.

11. *See* Fuchs (1988:60–64) discussing the hidden costs of children for women in the workplace. Compare Schultz (2000:1894) arguing that women do not choose lower-paying, lower-status jobs because of their heavier family obligations, but rather that the segregation of women into these jobs forces women into household labor.

12. See Douglas MacKinnon, "The Welfare Washington Doesn't Know," *New York Times*, May 21, 2002, at A21 (discussing how most congressmen cannot comprehend the amount of shame and pain that comes with the experience of being in poverty, the frustration of trying to help yourself out of it).

13. See "Making Hay," *New Republic*, May 20, 2002, p. 9 (pointing out that President Bush is not keeping with his market-driven approach to agriculture). Yes.

14. See Dick Lugar, "The Farm Bill Charade," *New York Times*, Jan. 21, 2002, p. A15. (The majority of payments in most states go to the top tenth of farmers. Farms in just six states will take almost half of the federal payments. "Ineffective agricultural policy has, over the years, led to a ritual of overproduction in many crops and most certainly in the heavily supported crops of corn, wheat, cotton, rice and soybeans and the protected specialty products like milk, sugar and peanuts.") Elizabeth Becker, "Farmers Market Program Wins Support but Loses Subsidy," *New York Times*, Mar. 17, 2002, p. 32.

15. See *Statement by the President, Office of the Press Secretary*, May 2, 2002 at http://www.whitehouse.gov/news/releases/2002/05/20020502.html (accessed June 2002).

16. See Bush, above note 2 (referring to ideals of hard work and self-sufficiency).

17. See Center for Law and Social Policy at http://www.clasp.org/pubs/TANF/finalregs.html (last visited June 18, 2002). The proposed bill would also require welfare recipients to work forty hours a week, up from the current requirement of thirty hours per week. See Personal Responsibility, Work, and Family Promotion Act of 2002, H.R. 4737, 107th Cong. (2002).

See Sarah Lueck, "House Passes Bill Lengthening Workdays of Welfare Recipients," *Wall Street Journal*, May 17, 2002 (quoting Health and Human Services Secretary Tommy Thompson, who was a key player in the overhaul of the state welfare system when he was governor of Wisconsin).

18. This family cap is being challenged in court. See Leslie Brody, "Welfare Reform in Spotlight as Milestone Nears," *New Jersey News*, Mar. 24, 2002 (one of five of the families no longer on welfare in New Jersey is living in poverty).

REFERENCES

Agarwal, Bina. 1994. *A Field of One's Own: Gender and Land Rights in South Asia*. Cambridge: Cambridge University Press.

———. 1997. "Bargaining" and Gender Relations: Within and Beyond the Household. *Feminist Economics* 3(1): 1–51.

Aghion, Philippe, Eve Caroli, and Cecilia Garcia-Penalosa. 1999. Inequality and Economic Growth: The Perspective of the New Growth Theories. *Journal of Economic Literature* 37(4):1615–1660.

Akerlof, George. 1970. The Market for "Lemons": Quality Uncertainty and the Market Mechanism. *Quarterly Journal of Economics* 90: 475–498.

Alderman, Harold, Pierre-Andre Chiappori, Lawrence Haddad, John Hoddinott, and Ravi Kanbur. 1995. Unitary versus Collective Models of the Household: Is It Time to Shift the Burden of Proof? *World Bank Research Observer* 10(1): 1–19.

Anand, Sudhir. 1993. Inequality Between and Within Nations. Mimeographed, Harvard Center for Population and Development Studies, Cambridge, MA.

Anand, Sudhir, and Paul Segal. 2002. Global Income Inequality. Mimeographed, St. Catherine's College, Oxford.

Anderson, Elizabeth. 1993. *Value in Ethics and Economics*. Cambridge, MA: Harvard University Press.

Aponte, Robert. 1990. Definitions of the Underclass: A Critical Analysis. In *Sociology in America*, ed. Herbert J. Gans. Newbury Park, CA: Sage.

Aristotle. 1980. *The Nicomachean Ethics*. Oxford: Oxford University Press.

Arneson, Richard. 1989. Equality and Equal Opportunity for Welfare. *Philosophical Studies* 56: 77–93.

Arrow, Kenneth. 1973. Some Ordinalist-Utilitarian Notes on Rawls's Theory of Justice. *Journal of Philosophy* 70: 245–263.

Atkinson, Anthony B. 1970. On the Measurement of Inequality. *Journal of Economic Theory* 2: 244–263.

———. 1987. On the Measurement of Poverty. *Econometrica* 55: 749–764.

———. 1997. Bringing Income Distribution in From the Cold. *The Economic Journal* 107(441): 297–321.

———. 1998. *Poverty in Europe*. Blackwell: Oxford.

———. 2003. Multi-dimensional Deprivation: Confronting Social Welfare and Country Approaches. *Journal of Economic Inequality* 1: 51–65.

Atkinson, Anthony, and François Bourguignon. 1982. The Comparison of Multi-Dimensioned Distributions of Economic Status. *Review of Economic Studies* 49(2): 183–201.

———. 2000. *Handbook of Income Distribution*, Vol. I. Amsterdam: Elsevier.

Atkinson, Anthony, Bea Cantillon, Eric Marlier, and Brian Nolan, eds. 2002. *Social Indicators: The EU and Social Inclusion*. Oxford: Oxford University Press

Auletta, Ken. 1982. *The Underclass*. New York: Random.

Austen-Smith, David, and Roland Fryer. 2003. The Economics of "Acting White." Processed. Harvard University.
http://post.economics.harvard.edu/faculty/fryer/papers/as_fryer_revision.pdf. Accessed August 3, 2004.

Bandura, Albert. 1982. Self-Efficacy Mechanism in Human Agency. *American Psychologist* 37(February): 122–147.

Bardhan, Pranab, Samuel Bowles, and Herbert Gintis. 2000. Wealth Inequality, Wealth Constraints and Economic Performance. In *Handbook of Income Distribution*, eds. A. Atkinson and F. Bourguignon. Amsterdam: North Holland-Elsevier.

Basu, Kaushik. 1997. *Analytical Development Economics*. Cambridge, MA: MIT Press.

———. 1999. Child Labor: Cause, Consequence and Cure, with Remarks on International Labor Standards. *Journal of Economic Literature* 37(3): 1083–1119.

Behrman, Jere, Pilali Sengupta, and Petra Todd. 2001. Progressing through PROGRESA: An Impact Assessment of a School Subsidy Experiment. April. University of Pennsylvania and Washington, DC: International Food Policy Research Institute.

Belle, Deborah. 1999. *The After-School Lives of Children: Alone and With Others While Parents Work*. Mahwah, NJ; London: Lawrence Erlbaum.

Berry, Brian J. L. 1973. *The Human Consequences of Urbanization*. New York: St. Martin's.

Bertola, Giuseppe. 2000. Macroeconomics of Distribution and Growth. In *Handbook of Income Distribution*, eds. A. Atkinson and F. Bourguignon. Amsterdam: North Holland-Elsevier.

Bérubé, Michael. 1996. *Life As We Know It: A Father, a Family, and an Exceptional Child*. New York: Vintage.

Bettinger, Robert L. 1991. *Hunter-Gatherers: Archaeological and Evolutionary Theory*. New York: Plenum.

Birkelund, Gunn Elisabeth, Leo A. Goodman, and David Rose. 1996. The Latent Structure of Job Characteristics of Men and Women. *American Journal of Sociology* 102: 80–113.

Blackorby, Charles, and David Donaldson. 1980. Ethical Indices for the Measurement of Poverty. *Econometrica* 48.

Bobo, Lawrence. 1989. Keeping the Linchpin in Place: Testing the Multiple Sources of Opposition to Residential Integration. *International Review of Social Psychology* 2:305–323.

Bourdieu, Pierre. 1984. *Distinction: A Social Critique of the Judgement of Taste.* Trans. Richard Nice. New York: Cambridge University Press.

Bourguignon, François. 1999. The Cost of Children: May the Collective Approach Help? *Journal of Population Economics* 12: 503–521.

Bourguignon, François, and Gary Fields. 1990. Poverty Measures and Anti-Poverty Policy. *Recherches Economiques de Louvain* 56: 409–427.

Bourguignon, François, and Satya Chakravarty. 2003. The Measurement of Multidimensional Poverty. *Journal of Economic Inequality* 1: 25–49.

Bourguignon, F. and L. Pereira da Silva, eds. 2003. *The Impact of Economic Policies on Poverty and Income Distribution: Evaluation Techniques and Tools.* Oxford University Press and the World Bank.

Bowles, Samuel. 1972. Schooling and Inequality from Generation to Generation. *Journal of Political Economy* 80(3): S219–251.

Braudel, Fernand. 1979. *The Wheels of Commerce: Civilization and Capitalism in the 15th–18th Century.* New York: Harper and Row.

Brockerhoff, Martin P. 2000. *An Urbanizing World.* Washington, DC: Population Reference.

Camerer, Colin, George Loewenstein, and Matthew Rabin. 2003. *Advances in Behavioral Economics.* Princeton, NJ: Princeton University Press.

Carr, Craig L. 2000. *On Fairness.* Burlington, UK: Ashgate.

Carruthers, Bruce. 1996. *City of Capital: Politics and Markets in the English Financial Revolution.* Princeton, NJ: Princeton University Press.

Carruthers, Bruce G., and Sarah L. Babb. 2000. *Economy/Society: Markets, Meanings and Social Structure.* New York: Pine Forge.

Castells, Manuel. 1996. *The Rise of the Network Society.* Cambridge: Blackwell.

Charles, Camille Z. 2000. Neighborhood Racial Composition Preferences: Evidence from a Multiethnic Metropolis. *Social Problems* 47: 379–407.

———. 2003. The Dynamics of Racial Residential Segregation. *Annual Review of Sociology* 29: 67–207.

Chen, Martha A. 1983. *A Quiet Revolution: Women in Transition in Rural Bangladesh.* Cambridge, MA: Schenkman.

Cicchino, Peter. 1999. Building on Foundational Myths: Feminism and the Recovery of "Human Nature." A Response to Martha Fineman. *American University Law Review* 50.

Cimini, Christine N. 2002. Welfare Entitlements in the Era of Devolution. *Georgetown Journal on Poverty Law & Policy* 9: 89–134.

Clark, Kenneth B. 1965. *Dark Ghetto: Dilemmas of Social Power.* New York: Harper and Row.

Clark, Terry N., and Seymour M. Lipset, eds. 2001. *The Breakdown of Class Politics.* Washington, DC and Baltimore: Woodrow Wilson Center Press and The Johns Hopkins University Press.

Collier, Paul, and David Dollar. 2002. Aid Allocation and Poverty Reduction. *European Economic Review* 46(8): 1475–1500.

Crafts, Nicholas. 2002. Text of address at the Centenary Celebrations of the British Academy, London, 3 July 2002. Mimeographed, London School of Economics.

Danziger, Sheldon, and Peter Gottschalk. 1995. *America Unequal.* Cambridge: Harvard University Press.

Davies, Glyn. 2002. *A History of Money: From Ancient Times to the Present Day.* Cardiff: University of Wales Press.

Deigh, John. 2001. Liberalism and Freedom. In *Social and Political Philosophy: Contemporary Perspectives*, ed. James P. Sterba. London: Routledge.

Deininger, Klaus. 1999. Making Negotiated Land Reform Work: Initial Experience from Colombia, Brazil and South Africa. *World Development* 27(4): 651–672.

Denton, Nancy A. 1994. "Are African Americans Still Hypersegregated?" In Robert D. Bullard, J. Eugene Grigsby III, and Charles Lee, eds., *Residential Apartheid: The American Legacy*, 49–81. Los Angeles: CAAS, University of California.

Dollar, David, and Aart Kraay. 2002. Growth Is Good for the Poor. *Journal of Economic Growth* 7: 195–225.

Drèze, Jean, and Amartya Sen. 1989. *Hunger and Public Action.* Oxford: Clarendon.

———. 2002. *India: Development and Participation*, 2nd ed. Oxford: Oxford University Press.

Duclos, Jean-Yves, David Sahn, and Stephen Younger. 2001. Robust Multi-Dimensional Poverty Comparisons. Mimeo, Cornell University, Ithaca, NY.

Duclos, Jean-Yves, Joan Esteban, and Debraj Ray. 2004. Polarization: Concepts, Measurement and Estimation. *Econometrica* 72(6): 1737–1772.

Duflo, Esther. 2003. Grandmother and Granddaughters: The Effects of Old Age Pension on Child Health in South Africa. *World Bank Economic Review.* 17: 1–25.

Edsall, Thomas B., and Mary Edsall. 1991. *Chain Reaction: The Impact of Race, Rights, and Taxes on American Politics.* New York: Norton.

Emerson, Michael O., George Yancey, and Karen J. Chai. 2001. Racial Residential Segregation: An Exploration of White Housing Preferences. *American Sociological Review* 66: 922–935.

Engbersen, Godfried. 1990. Modern Poverty in the Netherlands. Paper presented at the Workshop on Social Policy and the Underclass, University of Amsterdam, the Netherlands, August.

Engbersen, Godfried, Kees Schuyt, and Jaap Timmer. 1990. Cultures of Unemployment: Long-Term Unemployment in Dutch Inner Cities. Working Paper 4, Vakgroep Sociologie Rijksuniversiteit, Leiden, the Netherlands.

Esping-Andersen, Gøsta. 1999. *Social Foundations of Postindustrial Economies.* Oxford: Oxford University Press.

Evans, Geoffrey, and Colin Mills. 1998. Identifying Class Structure: A Latent Class Analysis of the Criterion-Related and Construct Validity of the Goldthorpe Class Schema. *European Sociological Review* 14: 87–106.

Evans, William N., Wallace E. Oates, and Robert M. Schwab. 1992. Measuring Peer Group Effects: A Study of Teenage Behavior. *Journal of Political Economy* 100: 966–791.

Farley, Reynolds, Maria Krysan, Tara Jackson, Charlotte Steeh, and Keith Reeves. 1993. Causes of Continued Racial Residential Segregation in Detroit: "Chocolate City, Vanilla Suburbs" Revisited. *Journal of Housing Research* 4: 1–38.

Farley, Reynolds, Charlotte Steeh, Maria Krysan, Tara Jackson, and Keith Reeves. 1994. Stereotypes and Segregation: Neighborhoods in the Detroit Area. *American Journal of Sociology* 100: 750–780.

Fields, Gary. 2001. *Distribution and Development: A New Look at the Developing World.* Cambridge, MA: MIT Press.

Fineman, Martha. 1991. *The Illusion of Equality.* Chicago: University of Chicago Press.

———. 1995. *The Neutered Mother, the Sexual Family, and Other Twentieth Century Tragedies.* New York: Routledge.

———. 2000. Cracking the Foundational Myths: Independence, Autonomy, and Self-Sufficiency. *American University Journal of Gender, Social Policy & the Law* 8(1): 13–29.

———. 2004. *The Autonomy Myth: A Theory of Dependency.* New York: New Press. Distributed by W. W. Norton.

Fiskin, James S. 1983. *Justice, Equal Opportunity, and the Family.* New Haven: Yale University Press.

Fix, Michael, George C. Galster, and Raymond J. Struyk. 1993. An Overview of Auditing for Discrimination. In Michael Fix and Raymond J. Struyk, eds., *Clear and Convincing Evidence: Measurement of Discrimination in America,* 1–68. Washington, DC: Urban Institute Press.

Folbre, Nancy. 1999. Care and the Global Economy. Background paper prepared for *Human Development Report 1999.* New York: United Nations Development Programme, Human Development Report Office.

———. 2001. *The Invisible Heart: Economics and Family Values.* New York: The New Press.

Foster, James, and Anthony Shorrocks. 1988. Poverty Orderings. *Econometrica* 56: 173–177.

Foster, James E., Joel Greer, and Erik Thorbecke. 1984. A Class of Decomposable Poverty Measures. *Econometrica* 52: 761–776.

Franke, Katherine M. 2001. Theorizing Yes: An Essay on Feminism, Law, and Desire. *Columbia Law Review* 101(1): 181.

Frankenberg, Elizabeth, James P. Smith, John Strauss, and Duncan Thomas. 2002.

Economic Shocks, Wealth and Welfare. Paper presented at the IMF conference on Macroeconomics and Poverty Reduction, March 14–15, Washington DC.

Fuchs, Victor R. 1988. *Women's Quest for Economic Equality*. Cambridge, MA: Harvard University Press.

Galster, George C. 1990. Racial Discrimination in Housing Markets During the 1980s: A Review of the Audit Evidence. *Journal of Planning Education and Research* 9: 165–175.

Gans, Herbert J. 1995. *The War Against the Poor: The Underclass and Antipoverty Policy*. New York: Basic Books.

Gauthier, David. 1986. *Morals By Agreement*. New York: Oxford University Press.

Gertler, Paul. 2000. Final Report: The Impact of PROGRESA on Health (November). Washington, DC: International Food Policy Research Institute.

Gilder, George. 1981. *Wealth and Poverty*. New York: Basic Books.

Gilens, Martin. 1999. *Why Americans Hate Welfare: Race, Media, and the Politics of Antipoverty Policy*. Chicago: University of Chicago Press.

Glazer, Nathan. 1978. *Affirmative Discrimination: Ethnic Inequality and Public Policy*. New York: Basic Books.

Goldthorpe, John H. 1982. On the Service Class, Its Formation and Future. In *Social Class and the Division of Labor*, ed. A. Giddens and G. MacKenzie, 162–185. Cambridge: Cambridge University Press.

———. 2000. *On Sociology: Numbers, Narratives, and the Integration of Research and Theory*. Oxford: Oxford University Press.

Goldthorpe, John H. and Robert Erikson. 1992. *The Constant Flux: A Study of Class Mobility in Industrial Societies*. New York: Clarendon.

Gorz, Andre. 1982. *Farewell to the Working Class*. London: Pluto.

Granovetter, Mark. 1985. Economic Action and Social Structure: The Problem of Embeddedness. *American Journal of Sociology* 91: 481–510.

Griliches, Zvi, and William Mason. 1972. Education, Income and Ability. *Journal of Political Economy* 80(3): S74–103.

Grusky, David B., and Jesper B. Sørensen. 1998. Can Class Analysis Be Salvaged? *American Journal of Sociology* 103: 1187–1234.

Grusky, David B., and Kim A. Weeden. 2001. Class Analysis and the Heavy Weight of Convention. *Acta Sociologica* 45: 229–236.

Hamada, Koichi, and N. Takayama. 1977. Censored Income Distributions and the Measurement of Poverty. *Bulletin of the International Statistical Institute* Book I, 47.

Hamill, Pete. 1988. Breaking the Silence. *Esquire*, March, 91–102.

Hannerz, Ulf. 1969. *Soulside: Inquiries into Ghetto Culture and Community*. New York: Columbia University Press.

Harberger, Arnold. 1998. Monetary and Fiscal Policy for Equitable Economic Growth. In *Income Distribution and High-Quality Growth*, ed. Vito Tanzi and Ke-young Chu, 203–41. Cambridge, MA: MIT Press.

Harrington, Mona. 1999. *Care and Equality*. New York: Knopf.

Hauser, Robert M., and John Robert Warren. 1997. Socioeconomic Indexes for Occupations: A Review, Update, and Critique. *Sociological Methodology* 27: 177–298.

Heilbroner, Robert L. 1962. *The Making of Economic Society*. Englewood Cliffs, NJ: Prentice-Hall.

Helburn, Suzanne W., and Barbara R. Bergmann. 2002. *America's Child Care Problem: The Way Out*. 1st Palgrave ed. New York: Palgrave for St. Martin's Press.

Held, Virginia. 1993. *Feminist Morality: Transforming Culture, Society, and Politics*. Chicago: University of Chicago Press.

———, ed. 1995. *Justice and Care: Essential Readings in Feminist Ethics*. Boulder, CO: Westview.

Hochschild, Jennifer L. 1981. *What's Fair?: American Beliefs about Distributive Justice*. Cambridge: Harvard University Press.

———. 1995. *Facing up to the American Dream: Race, Class, and the Soul of the Nation*. Princeton, NJ: Princeton University Press.

Hughes, Mark A. 1989. Concentrated Deviance and the "Underclass" Hypothesis. *Journal of Policy Analysis and Management* 8(2): 274–282.

Inglehart, Ronald. 1977. *The Silent Revolution: Changing Values and Political Styles among Western Publics*. Princeton: Princeton University Press.

Jackson, Kenneth T. 1985. *Crabgrass Frontier: The Suburbanization of the United States*. New York: Oxford University Press.

Jacoby, H. 2000. *Evaluating Decentralized Social Sectors Programs: Evidence from Morocco's BAJ*. The World Bank.

Jantti, Markus, and Sheldon Danziger. 2000. Income Poverty in Advanced Countries. In *Handbook of Income Distribution*, eds. A. Atkinson and F. Bourguignon. Amsterdam: North Holland-Elsevier.

Jargowsky, Paul. 1997. *Poverty and Place: Ghettos, Barrios, and the American City*. New York: Russell Sage Foundation.

Jargowsky, Paul, and Mary Jo Bane. 1991. Ghetto Poverty in the United States, 1970–1980. In *The Urban Underclass*, ed. Christopher Jencks and Paul E. Peterson, 235–273. Washington DC: Brookings Institution.

Jencks, Christopher. 1992. *Rethinking Social Policy: Race, Poverty and the Underclass*. New York: Harper Perennial.

Jencks, Christopher, Lauri Perman, and Lee Rainwater. 1988. What Is a Good Job? A New Measure of Labor-Market Success. *American Journal of Sociology* 93: 1322–1357.

Johnson, Lyndon B. 1966. To Fulfill These Rights: Commencement Address at Howard University. *Public Papers of the Presidents of the United States: Lyndon B. Johnson, 1965*. Vol. II: 635–640. Washington, DC: Government Printing Office.

Kakwani, Nanak. 2004. New Global Poverty Counts. *In Focus* (September): 9–11.

Kanbur, Ravi. 1987. Measurement and Alleviation of Poverty. *IMF Staff Papers* 34: 60–85.

———. 2001. Economic Policy, Distribution and Poverty: The Nature of Disagreements. *World Development* 29(6): 1083–1094.

Kanbur, Ravi, Michael Keen, and Matti Tuomala. 1994. Optimal Non-Linear for the Alleviation of Poverty. *European Economic Review* 38(8): 1613–1632.

Kanbur, Ravi, and Xiaobo Zhang. 2005. Fifty Years of Regional Inequality in China: A Journey through Revolution, Reform and Openness. *Review of Development Economics* 9: 87–106.

Katz, Lawrence. 1996. Wage Subsidies for the Disadvantaged. Working Paper 5679. Cambridge, MA: National Bureau of Economic Research.

Katz, Michael B. 1986. *In the Shadow of the Poorhouse: A Social History of Welfare in America*. New York: Basic Books.

———. 1989. *The Undeserving Poor: From the War on Poverty to the World on Welfare*. New York: Pantheon.

———. 1993. Reframing the "Underclass Debate." In *The "Underclass" Debate: Views from History*, ed. Michael B. Katz, 440–478. Princeton, NJ: Princeton University Press.

———. 2001. *The Price of Citizenship: Redefining America's Welfare State*. New York: Metropolitan.

Khan, Azizur Rahman, and Carl Riskin. 2001. *Inequality and Poverty in China in the Age of Globalization*. New York: Oxford University Press.

Kingston, Paul W. 2000. *The Classless Society*. Stanford, CA: Stanford University Press.

Kittay, Eva Feder. 1999. *Love's Labor: Essays on Women, Equality, and Dependency*. New York: Routledge.

Kloosterman, Robert C. 1990. The Making of the Dutch Underclass? A Labour Market View. Paper presented at the Workshop on Social Policy and the Underclass, University of Amsterdam, the Netherlands, August.

Kluegel, James R., and Eliot R. Smith. 1986. *Beliefs about Inequality: Americans' Views of What Is and What Ought to Be*. New York: Aldine de Gruyter.

Kohn, Melvin. 1969. *Class and Conformity: A Study in Values*. Chicago: University of Chicago Press.

Krueger, Alan B., and Jitka Malecková. 2003. Education, Poverty, Political Violence, and Terrorism: Is There a Causal Connection? *Journal of Economic Perspectives* 17(4): 119–144.

Lamorey, Suzanne, and Bryan E. Robinson. 1999. *Latchkey Kids: Unlocking Doors For Children and Their Families*, 2nd ed. Thousand Oaks, CA: Sage.

Lee, David J., and Bryan S. Turner, eds. 1996. *Conflicts about Class: Debating Inequality in Late Industrialism*. London: Longman.

Lenior, René. 1974. *Les Exclus: Un Francais sur Dix*. Paris: Editions du Seuil, republished 1989.

Levy, Frank. 1998. *The New Dollars and Dreams: American Incomes and Economic Change*. New York: Russell Sage.

Liebow, Elliot. 1967. *Tally's Corner: A Study of Streetcorner Men*. Boston: Little, Brown.

Lin, Justin Yifu, and Dennis Tao Yang. 2000. Food Availability, Entitlements and the Chinese Famine of 1959–61. *The Economic Journal* 110: 136–158.

Livi-Bacci, Massimo. 1992. *A Concise History of World Population*. Oxford: Blackwell.

Lukács, Georg. 1972. *History and Class Consciousness*. Cambridge: MIT Press.

MacIntyre, Alasdair. 1999. *Dependent Rational Animals: Why Human Beings Need the Virtues*. Peru, IL: Open Court Publishing.

Magnet, Myron. 1987. America's Underclass: What to Do? *Fortune*, 115(10): 130–150.

Marx, Karl. 1959. *Economic and Philosophical Manuscripts of 1844*. Moscow: Progress.

Massey, Douglas S. 1996. The Age of Extremes: Concentrated Affluence and Poverty in the 21st Century. *Demography* 33: 395–412.

———. 1999. American Apartheid. *Perspectives*, Primis Online Publishing, McGraw-Hill. www.mhhe.com/primis/online.

———. 2002. A Brief History of Human Society: The Origin and Role of Emotion in Social Life. *American Sociological Review* 67: 1–29.

———. 2004. Segregation and Stratification: A Biosocial Perspective. *DuBois Review: Social Science Research on Race* 1: 1–19.

———. 2005. *Strangers in a Strange Land: Humans in an Urbanizing World*. New York: W. W. Norton.

Massey, Douglas S., and Nancy A. Denton. 1993. *American Apartheid: Segregation and the Making of the Underclass*. Cambridge: Harvard University Press.

Massey, Douglas S., and Mary J. Fischer. 2000. How Segregation Concentrates Poverty. *Ethnic and Racial Studies* 23: 670–691.

Massey, Douglas S., and Garvey F. Lundy. 2000. Use of Black English and Racial Discrimination in Urban Housing Markets: New Methods and Findings. *Urban Affairs Review* 36: 470–496.

Massey, Douglas S., Joaquín Arango, Graeme Hugo, Ali Kouaouci, Adela Pellegrino, and J. Edward Taylor. 1998. *Worlds in Motion: International Migration at the End of the Millennium*. Oxford: Oxford University Press.

McCluskey, Martha T. 2000. Subsidized Lives and the Ideology of Efficiency. *American University Journal of Gender, Social Policy & the Law* 8(1): 115–152.

Mead, Lawrence. 1986. *Beyond Entitlement: The Social Obligations of Citizenship*. New York: Free Press.

Metcalf, George R. 1988. *Fair Housing Comes of Age*. New York: Greenwood.

Milanovic, Branko. 2002. True World Income Distribution, 1988 and 1993: First

Calculation Based on Household Surveys Alone. *The Economic Journal* 112: 51–92.

Mill, John Stuart. 1859. *On Liberty*. London: Parker and Son.

Mirrlees, James. 1971. An Exploration in the Theory of Optimal Income Taxation. *Review of Economic Studies* 38: 175–208.

Morris, Martina, Annette D. Bernhardt, Mark S. Handcock, and Marc A. Scott. 2001. *Divergent Paths: Economic Mobility in the New American Labor Market*. New York: Russell Sage Foundation.

Moynihan, Daniel Patrick. 1965. *The Negro Family: The Case for National Action*. Washington, DC: Office of Planning and Research, U.S. Department of Labor.

Murray, Charles A. 1984. *Losing Ground: American Social Policy, 1950–1980*. New York: Basic Books.

Myrdal, Gunnar. 1962. *Challenge to Affluence*. New York: Pantheon.

Nathan, Richard. 1986. November. The Underclass—Will It Always Be with Us? Paper presented at the New School for Social Research, New York.

Nisbet, Robert A. 1959. The Decline and Fall of Social Class. *Pacific Sociological Review* 2: 11–17.

Novkov, Julie. 1992. A Deconstruction of (M)otherhood and a Reconstruction of Parenthood. *Review of Law and Social Change* XIX (1): 155.

Nozick, Robert. 1974. *Anarchy, State and Utopia*. Oxford: Basil Blackwell.

Nussbaum, Martha. 1997. Capabilities and Human Rights. *Fordham Law Review* 66: 273–300.

———. 2000a. *Women and Human Development: The Capabilities Approach*. Cambridge: Cambridge University Press.

———. 2000b. The Future of Feminist Liberalism. Presidential Address delivered to the Central Division of the American Philosophical Association. *Proceedings and Addresses of the American Philosophical Association* 74: 47–79.

———. 2000c. Aristotle, Politics, and Human Capabilities: A Response to Antony, Arneson, Charlesworth, and Mulgan. *Ethics* 111: 102–140.

———. 2000d. Animal Rights: The Need for a Theoretical Basis. *Harvard Law Review* 114(5): 1506–1549.

———. 2001a. Disabled Lives: Who Cares? *The New York Review of Books* 48: 34–37.

———. 2001b. The Costs of Tragedy: Some Moral Limits of Cost-Benefit Analysis. In *Cost-Benefit Analysis: Legal, Economic, and Philosophical Perspectives*, ed. Matthew D. Adler and Eric A. Posner, 169–200. Chicago: University of Chicago Press.

———. 2001c. Political Objectivity. *New Literary History* 32: 883–906.

———. 2002. Women and the Law of Peoples. *Politics, Philosophy, and Economics* 1: 282–306.

———. 2003. The Complexity of Groups. *Philosophy & Social Criticism* 29: 57–69.

———. 2004a. *Hiding From Humanity: Disgust, Shame, and the Law*. Princeton: Princeton University Press.

———. 2004b. Beyond the Social Contract: Toward Global Justice. In *The Tanner Lectures on Human Values 24*, eds. Grethe B. Peterson, 413–508. Salt Lake City: University of Utah Press.

———. Forthcoming. Constitutions and Capabilities. In a volume edited by M. Krausz and D. Chatterjee (title not yet firm). Oxford: Oxford University Press.

Nussbaum, Martha, and Amartya Sen. 1993. *The Quality of Life*. Oxford: Clarendon Press.

O'Connor, Alice. 2001. *Poverty Knowledge: Social Science, Social Policy, and the Poor in Twentieth-Century U.S. History*. Princeton, NJ: Princeton University Press.

Offe, Claus. 1985. *Disorganized Capitalism*. Cambridge: Polity.

Olson, Mancur. 1982. *The Rise and Decline of Nations: Economic Growth, Stagflation, and Social Rigidities*. New Haven, CT: Yale University Press.

Olzak, Susan. Forthcoming. *The Global Dynamics of Race and Ethnic Mobilization*. Stanford, CA: Stanford University Press.

Osmani, Siddiq R. 1995. The Entitlement Approach to Famine: An Assessment. In *Choice, Welfare and Development*, eds., Kaushik Basu, Prasanta K. Pattanaik, and K. Suzumura. Oxford: Clarendon.

Pakulski, Jan, and Malcolm Waters. 1996. *Death of Class*. Thousand Oaks, CA: Sage.

Persson, T. and G. Tabellini. 1994. Is Inequality Harmful for Growth? *American Economic Review* 84: 600–621.

Pettigrew, Thomas F. 1979. Racial Change and Social Policy. *Annals of the American Academy of Political and Social Science* 441: 114–131.

Phillips, Kevin P. 1969. *The Emerging Republican Majority*. New Rochelle, NY: Arlington House.

———. 1990. *The Politics of Rich and Poor: Wealth and the American Electorate in the Reagan Aftermath*. New York: Random House.

———. 2002. *Wealth and Democracy: A Political History of the American Rich*. New York: Broadway.

Pitcher, George. 1995. *The Dogs Who Came to Stay*. New York: G. Putnam.

Plotnick, Robert, and Saul Hoffman. 1993. Using Sister Pairs to Estimate How Neighborhoods Affect Young Adult Outcomes. Working Papers in Public Policy Analysis and Management, No. 93–8, Graduate School of Public Affairs, University of Washington, Seattle.

Porrazzo, Kimberly A. 1999. *The Nanny Kit: Everything You Need to Hire the Right Nanny*. New York: Penguin.

Portes, Alejandro, and Julia Sensenbrenner. 1993. Embeddedness and Immigration: Notes on the Social Determinants of Economic Action. *American Journal of Sociology* 98: 1320–1350.

Portes, Alejandro, and Ruben G. Rumbaut. 2001. *Legacies: The Story of the Immigrant Second Generation*. Berkeley: University of California Press.

Rabin, Matthew. 1998. Psychology and Economics. *Journal of Economic Literature* 36: 11–46.

Rachels, James. 1990. *Created From Animals: The Moral Implications of Darwinism*. New York: Oxford University Press.

Rainwater, Lee. 1966. Crucible of Identity: The Negro Lower-Class Family. *Daedalus* 95 (Winter): 176–216.

Ravallion, Martin. 1992. On Hunger and Public Action: A Review Article. *World Bank Research Observer* 7: 1–16.

———. 1994. *Poverty Comparisons*. Switzerland: Harwood Academic.

———. 2002. Poverty Lines: Economic Foundations of Current Practices. Mimeo, The World Bank, Washington DC.

Rawls, John. 1971. *A Theory of Justice*. Cambridge, MA: Harvard University Press.

———. 1980. Kantian Constructivism in Moral Theory: The Dewey Lectures. *The Journal of Philosophy* 77: 515–571.

———. 1996. *Political Liberalism*. Expanded Paperback Edition. New York: Columbia University Press.

———. 1999. *A Theory of Justice*. Cambridge: Harvard University Press.

———. 2001. *Justice as Fairness: A Restatement*, ed. E. Kelly. Cambridge, London: Belknap Press of Harvard University Press.

Reddy, Sanjay. 2004. A Capability-Based Approach to Estimating Global Poverty. *In Focus* (September): 6–8.

Ricketts, Earl R., and Isabell Sawhill. 1988. Defining and Measuring the Underclass. *Journal of Policy Analysis and Management* 7: 316–325.

Robbins, Lionel. 1932. *The Nature and Significance of Economic Science*. London: Macmillan.

Roemer, John E. 1998. *Equality of Opportunity*. Cambridge, MA: Harvard University Press.

Ruddick, Sarah. 1989. *Maternal Thinking*. New York: Beacon.

Sahn, David, and Stephen Younger. 1999. Dominance Testing of Social Sector Expenditures and Taxes in Africa. Working Paper, WP/99/172, International Monetary Fund, Washington DC.

Sampson, Robert J., Jeffrey D. Morenoff, and Thomas Gannon-Rowley. 2002. Assessing "Neighborhood Effects": Social Processes and New Directions in Research. *Annual Review of Sociology* 28: 443–478.

Schady, Norbert. 2002. The (Positive) Effect of Macroeconomic Crises on the Schooling and Employment Decisions Taken by Children in a Middle-Income Country. Mimeo. Washington, DC: The World Bank.

Schultz, Vicki. 2000. Life's Work. *Columbia Law Review* 100 (7): 1881.

Schuman, Howard, Charlotte Steeh, Lawrence Bobo, and Maria Krysan. 1997. *Racial Attitudes in America: Trends and Interpretations*. Cambridge: Harvard University Press.

Schuyt, Kees. 1990. The New Emerging Underclass in Europe: The Experience of Long-Term Unemployment in Dutch Inner Cities. Paper presented at the Workshop on Social Policy and the Underclass, University of Amsterdam, the Netherlands, August.

Schwartzman, David. 1997. *Black Unemployment: Part of Unskilled Unemployment*. Westport, CT: Greenwood.

Seidl, Christian. 1988. Poverty Measurement: A Survey. In *Welfare and Efficiency in Public Economics*, eds. Dieter Bös, Manfred Rose, and Christian Seidl. Berlin: Springer-Verlag.

Sen, Amartya. 1973. *On Economic Inequality*. Oxford: Clarendon; enlarged edition, 1997.

———. 1976. Poverty: An Ordinal Approach to Measurement. *Econometrica* 44: 219–231.

———.1980. Equality of What? In *Tanner Lectures on Human Values*, ed. S. M. McMurrin. I. Salt Lake City: University of Utah Press. Reprinted in Sen (1982, 353–369).

———. 1981. *Poverty and Famines: An Essay on Entitlement and Deprivation*. Oxford: Clarendon.

———. 1982. *Choice, Welfare, and Measurement*. Oxford: Blackwell, and Cambridge, MA: Harvard University Press, 1997.

———. 1983. Poor, Relatively Speaking. *Oxford Economic Papers* 35. Repr. Sen, Amartya. 1984. *Resources, Values, and Development*. Cambridge, MA: Harvard University Press.

———. 1984. *Resources, Values, and Development*. Cambridge, MA: Harvard University Press.

———. 1985a. *Commodities and Capabilities, Professor Dr. P. Hennipman Lectures in Economics, Theory, Institutions, Policy; v. 7*. Amsterdam: North-Holland.

———. 1985b. Well-being, Agency and Freedom. *Journal of Philosophy* 82.

———. 1987. *The Standard of Living*. Cambridge: Cambridge University Press.

———. 1990. Gender and Cooperative Conflicts. In *Persistent Inequalities*, ed. Irene Tinker, 123–149. New York: Oxford University Press.

———. 1992. *Inequality Reexamined*. Oxford: Clarendon and Cambridge, MA: Harvard University Press.

———. 1995. Gender Inequality and Theories of Justice. In *Women, Culture, and Development*, eds. M. Nussbaum and J. Glover, 259–273. Oxford: Clarendon.

———. 1997a. Human Rights and Asian Values. *The New Republic*. July 14/21: 33–40.

———. 1997b. *On Economic Inequality*. Expanded version with a substantial annexe by James Foster and Amartya Sen. Oxford: Clarendon.

———. 1999. *Development As Freedom*. New York: Knopf.

———. 2001. The Many Faces of Misogyny. *The New Republic*. September 17: 35–40.

Sen, Amartya, and James E. Foster. 1997. *On Economic Inequality.* Enl., ed. Oxford: Clarendon and New York: Oxford University Press.

Shorrocks, Anthony F. 1980. The Class of Additively Decomposable Inequality Measures. *Econometrica* 48.

———. 1984. Inequality Decomposition by Population Subgroups. *Econometrica* 52.

———. 1988. Aggregation Issues in Inequality Measurement. In *Measurement in Economics: Theory and Applications of Economic Indices*, eds. W. Eichhorn and W. E. Diewert. Heidelberg: Physica-Verlag.

———. 1995. Revisiting the Sen Poverty Index. *Econometrica* 63.

Skocpol, Theda. 1992. *Protecting Soldiers and Mothers: The Political Origins of Social Policy in the United States.* Cambridge: Harvard University Press.

Skrentny, John D. 1996. *The Ironies of Affirmative Action: Politics, Culture, and Justice in America.* Chicago: University of Chicago Press.

Smelser, Neil J., William Julius Wilson, and Faith Mitchell. 2001. Introduction. In *America Becoming: Racial Trends and Their Consequences*, Vol. 1, eds. Neil J. Smelser, William Julius Wilson, and Faith Mitchell. Washington DC: National Academy Press.

Smith, Adam. 1776. *An Inquiry into the Nature and Causes of the Wealth of Nations*, eds. R. H. Campbell and A. S. Skinner. Oxford: Clarendon, 1976.

Smith, Rogers M. 1997. *Civic Ideals: Conflicting Visions of Citizenship in U.S. History.* New Haven: Yale University Press.

Smuts, Barbara. 1999. Untitled reply to J. M. Coetzee. In *The Lives of Animals*, ed. Amy Gutmann, 107–120. Princeton, NJ: Princeton University Press.

Srinivasan, T. N. 2001. Comment on Angus Deaton, "Counting the World's Poor." *The World Bank Research Observer*, Washington DC.

———. 2004. The Unsatisfactory State of Global Poverty Estimation. *In Focus* (September): 3–5.

Stiglitz, Joseph. 1973. Approaches to the Economics of Discrimination. *American Economic Review* 62: 287–295.

Swidler, Ann. 1986. Culture in Action: Symbols and Strategies. *American Sociological Review* 51 (January).

Thaler, Richard. 1991. *Quasi-Rational Economics.* New York: Russell Sage Foundation.

The American Underclass. 1977. *Time*, August 29, 14–27.

Theil, Henri. 1967. *Economics and Information Theory.* Amsterdam: North-Holland.

Thomas, Vinod, Yanling Wang, and Xibo Fan. 2001. Measuring Education Inequality: Gini Coefficient for 140 Countries, 1960–2000. Mimeo, The World Bank, Washington DC.

Thompson, E. P. 1966. *The Making of the English Working Class.* New York: Vintage.

Tienda, Marta. 1991. Poor People and Poor Places: Deciphering Neighborhood Effects on Poverty Outcomes. In *Macro-Micro Linkages in Sociology*, ed. Joan Huber. Newbury Park, CA: Sage.

Tilly, Charles S. 1998. *Durable Inequality*. Berkeley: University of California Press.

Tronto, Joan. 1993. *Moral Boundaries: A Political Argument for an Ethic of Care*. New York: Routledge.

Tsui Kai-yuen. 1999. Multidimensional Poverty Indices. Repr. 2002. *Social Choice and Welfare* 19(1): 69–93.

Tyson, Laura D' Andrea. 2002. The Farm Bill Is a $200 Billion Disaster. *Business Week*, June 3: 26.

Uchitelle, Louis. 1997. A Shift to Self-Reliance: Proposals to Revamp Social Security Reflect the Larger National Trend. *New York Times*, Jan. 13.

UNDP. 1990. *Human Development Report*. New York: Oxford University Press.

UNDP. 2001. *Human Development Report*. New York: Oxford University Press.

Van Haitsma, Martha. 1989. A Contextual Definition of the Underclass. *Focus* (Newsletter of the Institute for Research on Poverty) 12 (Spring–Summer): 27–31.

Wacquant, Loic, and William Julius Wilson. 1990. The Cost of Racial and Class Exclusion in the Inner City. *Annals of the American Academy of Political and Social Science* 501 (January): 8–25.

Waite, Linda J., and Maggie Gallagher. 2000. *The Case For Marriage: Why Married People Are Happier, Healthier, and Better Off Financially*. New York: Doubleday.

Weber, Adna F. 1899. *The Growth of Cities in the Nineteenth Century*. New York: Macmillan.

Weber, Max. 1946 [2001]. Class, Status, and Party. In *Social Stratification: Class, Race, and Gender in Sociological Perspective*, ed. David B. Grusky, 132–142. Boulder, CO: Westview.

———. 1947. *Max Weber: The Theory of Social and Economic Organization*. Trans. A. M. Henderson and Talcott Parsons. New York: Free Press.

Weeden, Kim, and David B. Grusky 2004. Are There Big Social Classes? Working paper, Dept. of Sociology, Cornell University, Ithaca, NY.

Weinberg, Daniel H., John Iceland, and Erika Steinmetz. 2002. *Ethnic and Racial Segregation in the United States: 1980–2000*. Washington, DC: U.S. Bureau of the Census.

West, Robin. 1997. *Caring For Justice*. New York: New York University Press.

White, Harrison C. 1981. Where Do Markets Come From? *American Journal of Sociology* 87: 517–547.

Wilkes, Rima, and John Iceland. 2004. Hypersegregation in the Twenty-First Century. *Demography* 41: 23–36.

Williams, Joan. 2000. *Unbending Gender: Why Family and Work Conflict and What to Do About It*. New York: Oxford University Press.

Wilson, William Julius. 1987. *The Truly Disadvantaged: The Inner City, The Underclass, and Public Policy*. Chicago: University of Chicago Press.

———. 1996. *When Work Disappears: The World of the New Urban Poor*. New York: Knopf.

Wood, Allen. 1999. *Kant's Ethical Theory*. Cambridge: Cambridge University Press.

World Bank. 1999. *Economics of Tobacco Control*. Washington, DC: World Bank. http://www1.worldbank.org/tobacco/reports.htm. Accessed August 3, 2004.

World Bank. 2000. Attacking Poverty. *World Development Report 2000/2001*. Washington, DC: World Bank.

World Bank. 2001. Income Poverty: Recent Regional Trends. http://www.worldbank.org/poverty/data/trends/regional.htm. Accessed August 3, 2004.

World Bank. 2003. Land Policies for Growth and Poverty Reduction. *Policy Research Report*. Washington DC.

Wright, Erik O. 1979. *Class Structure and Income Determination*. New York: Academic Press.

———. 1997. *Class Counts: Comparative Studies in Class Analysis*. Cambridge: Cambridge University Press.

Yinger, John. 1995. *Closed Doors, Opportunities Lost: The Continuing Costs of Housing Discrimination*. New York: Russell Sage.

Zelditch, Morris, Jr. 1989. Levels in the Logic of Macro-Historical Explanation. Paper presented at the annual meeting of the American Sociological Association.

Zelizer, Viviana A. 1979. *Morals and Markets: The Development of Life Insurance in the United States*. New York: Columbia University Press.

———. 1994. *The Social Meaning of Money*. New York: Basic Books.

Zhang, Xiaobo, and Ravi Kanbur. 2001. What Difference Do Polarization Measures Make? *Journal of Development Studies* 37: 85–98.

Social relations: poverty measures based on, 45–46; underclass and, 109–16, 130
Social safety nets, 124–25
Socioeconomic scales, 13–14
Sociology, theories based on, 13–26
South Africa, 128
The Standard of Living (Sen), 6
Stiglitz, Joseph, 6
Structural adjustment programs, 8
Structuralism, and class models, 15–19
Subgroup consistency, 42
Subsidy, 147–50

Thirteenth Amendment, 127
Thomas, Vinod, 96
Thorbecke, Erik, 5, 12, 32
Two-earner families, 144–45

Underclass: challenges to concept of, 24, 111; culture and, 104–6, 114–16, 130; definition of, 14, 103–6, 112, 129–30; historical use of concept, 103–6; labeling of, 103–4; labor force attachment and, 109–16; lower class versus, 111; marginal status of, 18–19; as poverty indicator, 14; residential segregation and, 19, 130; self-commodification and, 18–19; social transformation of inner city and, 106–8. *See also* Maladaptive cultures

Unemployment, inner city, 109–16
"Unitary versus Collective Models of the Household" (Alderman, et al.), 7
United Nations Development Programme (UNDP), 47
United States: Constitution of, 54; housing discrimination in, 127–29, 131–32; hunger in, 37; ideology of autonomous individual in, 135–36; market access in, 123; markets and class interests in, 126–27, 131; markets and race in, 127–29; the poor as categorized in, 104; social safety nets in, 125
Utilitarianism: criticism of, 48, 50; policy and, 5–6

Van Haitsma, Martha, 109
Veteran's Administration, 121

Washington Consensus, 8
Weber, Max, 26
Welfare, 125, 135–37, 149–50
Welfare cost of poverty, 81
Well-being, *see* Quality of life
Wilson, William Julius, 19, 22, 130
Workplace segregation, 20
World Bank, 43

Yang, Dennis, 34

Zhang, Xiaobo, 31